Yale Language Series

Readings

in

Biblical Hebrew

An

Intermediate

Textbook

Ehud Ben Zvi

Maxine Hancock

Richard Beinert

Yale University Press

New Haven and London

Set in Trump Medieval type by The Composing Room of
Michigan, Inc., Grand Rapids, Michigan. Printed in the
United States of America.

Library of Congress Cataloging-in-Publication Data

Readings in biblical Hebrew : an intermediate textbook /
[prepared by] Ehud Ben Zvi, Maxine Hancock, and
Richard Beinert.
    p.   cm. — (Yale language series)
Includes bibliographical references and index.
ISBN 978-0-300-05573-3
1. Hebrew language—Self-instruction. 2. Bible. O.T.
Pentateuch—Language, style.   I. Ben Zvi, Ehud, 1951–
II. Hancock, Maxine, 1942–   . III. Beinert, Richard,
1968–   .   IV. Series.
PJ4567.3.R35   1993
492.4'86421—dc20   93-18751 CIP

A catalogue record for this book is available from the
British Library.

The paper in this book meets the guidelines for
permanence and durability of the Committee on
Production Guidelines for Book Longevity of the Council
on Library Resources.

10   9   8   7   6   5

Contents

Introduction

After finishing an introductory Hebrew course, the intermediate reader often finds that there is still a gap between his or her reading ability and the demands of the biblical texts. This book has been designed to help bridge this gap between reader and text. By helping the reader continue to develop an ability to read Hebrew biblical texts, this book leads the student beyond a rudimentary knowledge of biblical Hebrew through direct interaction with the text. As the student gains confidence and experience in dealing with progressively more difficult Hebrew biblical texts, she or he is enabled to move toward competent reading of a wider range of Old Testament/ Hebrew Bible (OT/HB) texts.

This book is intended for use by the individual student, whether as part of a university or seminary class or on her or his own. It therefore has been developed in a text-plus-workbook format, with space in the textbook for student responses. Since the intention is to help the student towards competent reading of the OT/HB, the student will grapple with text by translating directly from the Bible. But his or her own efforts will be conducted in dialogue with the notes and supported by references to familiar textbooks. This book presupposes that the student has completed an entry-level biblical Hebrew course. It will be most comfortable for the student who has used as an introductory textbook B. P. Kittel, V. Hoffer, and R. A. Wright, *Biblical Hebrew: A Text and Workbook* (New Haven: Yale University Press, 1989), since it follows its terminology and pedagogical approach. Other introductory textbooks and grammars to which the book is cross-referenced throughout are (in alphabetical order): Moshe Greenberg, *Introduction to Hebrew* (Englewood Cliffs, N.J.: Prentice-Hall, 1965); Page H. Kelley, *Biblical Hebrew: An Introductory Grammar* (Grand Rapids, Mich.: Eerdmans, 1992); Thomas O. Lambdin, *Introduction to Biblical Hebrew* (New York: Scribner, 1971); C. L. Seow, *A Grammar for Biblical Hebrew* (Nashville: Abingdon Press, 1987); Jacob Weingreen, *A Practical Grammar for Classical Hebrew* (2d ed.; Oxford: Clarendon Press, 1959). Students who have been introduced to biblical Hebrew through some textbook other than these will be able to make use of this book, but may wish to provide themselves with one of these texts for reference purposes. Translation work will require constant use of *The New Brown-Driver-Briggs-Gesenius Hebrew-English Lexicon* (Peabody: Hendrickson, 1979), still the most commonly used biblical Hebrew-English dictionary. Students will be directed for more detailed analysis of grammatical points to Willhelm Gesenius-Emil Kautzch, *Gesenius' Hebrew Grammar* (trans. A. E. Cowley; Oxford: Clarendon Press, 1910); Paul Joüon-Takamitsu Muraoka, *A Grammar of Biblical Hebrew* (2 vols., Subsidia Biblica 14/1, 14/2; Rome: Editrice Pontificio Istituto Biblico, 1991); and Bruce K. Waltke and M. O'Connor, *Biblical Hebrew Syntax* (Winona Lake, Ind.: Eisenbrauns, 1990).

Throughout the textbook, the focus is on reading selected biblical texts, with references offered to the grammars and textbooks listed to review matters of grammar which the student will have learned at the elementary level but may have forgotten. These references are marked with the symbol **?** throughout the book. Other references to the grammars and textbooks, as well as to other books and articles, which are designed to carry the reader's knowledge forward are marked with the symbol → and include references which expand the topic, offer more detailed analysis, or supply a source for ideas in the discussion.

This book is designed to offer a number of different levels of use to the intermediate reader. The reader may focus entirely on the main text, and will be led by it into translation and understanding of the biblical Hebrew text under discussion. Or, the reader may go beyond the main text to read the "Notes" as well. These notes offer further information, most often concerning structure, genre, literary devices, and accents. In addition, the reader is invited to consider the discussions "For Further Thought," which are placed at strategic points in the text to open avenues of thought concerning reading and interpreting biblical texts. Moreover, from time to time, the reader is encouraged to expand her or his knowledge of biblical Hebrew and of biblical Hebrew texts, and to be introduced to the ongoing critical discussion of these texts, by the suggestions under "For Further Reading." The student is also invited to follow the references marked by the → symbol for detailed information on specific issues. Often, these references point to several sources. In such cases, the reader may choose to follow one of these sources, a combination of them, or all of them. The reader may also decide that, for the time being, it would be better to concentrate on the main text and skip all these references. In sum, this textbook can be used at any of the mentioned levels or, at various times or for various readings, in any combination of these levels.

There is no attempt in this book to provide a full or systematic treatment of grammar. Furthermore, since this is primarily a textbook, there has been no attempt whatsoever made to present an exhaustive bibliography on any topic. Our listings are intended only to provide a selection of entry points for the student.

Because the book is organized by readings of passages of widely varying lengths and difficulty, the discussions are also of varying length. We have not artificially divided these discussions into "lessons," but the student or instructor will find it easy to divide the work into relatively even sections if that is desirable.

In order to create a truly dialogic book, the process of authorship has been collaborative, involving an ongoing interaction between Dr. Ehud Ben Zvi, who teaches Hebrew at the University of Alberta, and two intermediate Hebrew readers and former students of his, Richard Beinert, an undergraduate linguistics and Semitic languages student, and Dr. Maxine Hancock, a doctoral fellow in English during the composition of the book. By working as a team, the authors have endeavored to capture and re-create for the user of this book the experience of a warm and vigorous interaction with the text and with other readers of the text. In this regard, we are of course indebted to every work mentioned either by the cross-referencing system or in other parts of the discussion. The work of these other scholars is embedded in ours. Because of the nature of this work, comprehensive documentation by way of footnotes has not been supplied. We have, however, identified seminal works which have influenced the discussion as we present it, and we suggest that our readers follow our steps into other readings.

If, through the use of this textbook, the intermediate biblical Hebrew reader begins to feel a part of the long conversation about the OT/HB text, drawn into discussion and debate, our work will have been well done.

Note on the Text

1. Symbols and Sub-headings in Text

? For Help, see . . .

References marked with this symbol are designed to help you refresh your memory of grammatical points learned in introductory biblical Hebrew courses.

→ For Additional Information, You May Consult . . .

References marked with this symbol are designed to help you expand your knowledge of biblical Hebrew and biblical Hebrew texts. These references encompass what, in a different kind of book, might be included in footnote documentation. They expand a topic under discussion, offer a more detailed analysis, or document sources referred to within the discussion or embedded in it.

Note

These sub-sections offer notes additional to the main discussion of the biblical text, including insights on various matters of literary or contextual interest.

For Further Thought

These sub-sections are designed to open avenues of thought concerning reading and interpreting biblical texts and to prompt consideration of aspects of interpretation and offer additional readings.

For Further Reading

At the end of some sections, references for further reading are offered to provide entrance points for more advanced studies of the text discussed in the section, as well as related matters.

Works Cited in This Section

All works other than those used regularly for cross-reference will be given full bibliographic reference at the end of each section in which mention is made of them.

2. Cross-references

Cross-references are supplied from this textbook to several others, one or more of which the student is expected to consult as a reference on a regular basis. The abbreviations of the books which are cross-referenced are listed below in alphabetical order. As a rule, references to these books that follow the **?** symbol will be in parentheses throughout the textbook. The reference to Kittel (K.) will be given first mention, followed by the other works according to the alphabetical order of their abbreviations. References following the → symbol will also be arranged in alphabetical order by abbreviation. (See List of Abbreviations.)

All scriptural references follow the system accepted by the Society of Biblical Literature and published in *JBL* 107 (1988): 579–96 and in *SBL Membership Directory and Handbook* (Decatur, Ga.: Society of Biblical Literature, 1991), 193–210.

Please also note that 'ה, the short form for the divine name YHWH (the Tetragrammaton), will be used throughout this text (e.g., כִּי־סָנַר ה' בְּעַד רַחְמָה in 1 Sam 1:6).

3. Alternative Terms

In the first unit (1.1), where two grammatical terms are offered, they will be shown with Kittel's term followed by an alternative term written inside parentheses. Alternative terms are offered only if they differ very significantly from Kittel's terms.

4. Verb Analysis Grid

We will ask you to "analyze the verb" frequently, since the verb holds so much of the grammatical information you need for translating the sentence and keeps you on your toes, grammatically speaking. We invite you to do your analysis by means of a grid that looks like this:

Root	Stem	Form	PGN	SF	OS	BRM

This verb analysis chart is adapted from the one used in Kittel et al., *Biblical Hebrew*. **Stem** here is equivalent to "binyan," and **form** to "inflection" in other textbooks. **PGN** stands for "person, gender, and number" of the subject of the verb; **SF** stands for "Special Features." The SF column will be useful to students who have learned Hebrew grammar through Kittel. **OS** stands for (pronominal) object suffixes attached to the verb (**?** K. 215, 385; Gr. 71–72; Ke. 153–59; S. 131–36, 179–81; W. 123–33; → GKC §57–61; JM §61–66). **BRM** stands for the basic range of meaning(s) of the root in this stem.

5. A Practical Suggestion

Many new and intermediate readers of Hebrew find the fine print with so many vowel and accent markers quite difficult to follow or to locate their place in. You may find that study and translation of a passage is easier if you make an enlarged photocopy of the passage you are studying and work from that.

Abbreviations

1. Grammars and Lexicons

BDB = Francis Brown, S. R. Driver, and Charles A. Briggs, *The New Brown-Driver-Briggs-Gesenius Hebrew-English Lexicon* (Peabody, Massachusetts: Hendrikson, 1979; original edition of Francis Brown, S. R. Driver, and Charles A. Briggs, *A Hebrew and English Lexicon of the Old Testament*, Oxford: Clarendon, 1907).

GKC = Willhelm Gesenius-Emil Kautzch, *Gesenius' Hebrew Grammar* (trans. A. E. Cowley; Oxford: Clarendon Press, 1910).

Gr. = Moshe Greenberg, *Introduction to Hebrew* (Englewood Cliffs, N.J.: Prentice-Hall, 1965).

JM = Paul Joüon-Takamitsu Muraoka, *A Grammar of Biblical Hebrew* (2 vols., Subsidia Biblica 14/1, 14/2; Rome: Editrice Pontificio Istituto Biblico, 1991).

K. = Bonnie P. Kittel, Vicki Hoffer, and Rebecca A. Wright, *Biblical Hebrew: A Text and Workbook* (New Haven: Yale University Press, 1989).

Ke. = Page H. Kelley, *Biblical Hebrew: An Introductory Grammar* (Grand Rapids, Mich.: Eerdmans, 1992).

L. = Thomas O. Lambdin, *Introduction to Biblical Hebrew* (New York: Scribner, 1971).

S. = C. L. Seow, *A Grammar for Biblical Hebrew* (Nashville: Abingdon, 1987).

W. = Jacob Weingreen, *A Practical Grammar for Classical Hebrew* (2d ed.; Oxford: Clarendon Press, 1959).

W.O'C. = Bruce K. Waltke and M. O'Connor, *Biblical Hebrew Syntax* (Winona Lake, Ind.: Eisenbrauns, 1990).

2. Bibles and Periodicals

AB	Anchor Bible
ABRL	Anchor Bible Reference Library
ANET	J. B. Pritchard, ed., *Ancient Near Eastern Texts*
BA	Biblical Archaeologist
Bib	Biblica
BibOr	Biblica et orientalia
BSO(A)S	Bulletin of the School of Oriental (and African) Studies
BZAW	Beihefte zur ZAW
CBQ	Catholic Biblical Quarterly

ExpT	Expository Times
FOTL	Forms of the Old Testament Literature
HSS	Harvard Semitic Studies
HUCA	Hebrew Union College Annual
ICC	International Critical Commentary
Int	Interpretation
JBL	Journal of Biblical Literature
JSOT	Journal for the Study of the Old Testament
JSOTSup	Journal for the Study of the Old Testament—Supplement Series
JSS	Journal of Semitic Studies
JThS	Journal of Theological Studies
KJV	King James Version
NCB	New Century Bible
NEB	New English Bible
NJPSV	New Jewish Publication Society Version
NRSV	New Revised Standard Version
OTL	Old Testament Library
OTS	Oudtestamentische Studiën
REB	Revised English Bible
RSV	Revised Standard Version
SBLDS	Society of Biblical Literature—Dissertation Series
SBLSCS	Society of Biblical Literature—Septuagint and Cognate Studies
VT	Vetus Testamentum
WBC	Word Biblical Commentary
ZAW	Zeitschrift für die altestamentische Wissenschaft

1.   Readings in the Historical Books

1.1 1 Samuel 1:1–28

In this reading from the Book of Samuel you will encounter some distinctive characteristics of Hebrew biblical narrative. A brief prologue sets the story in time and place; be on the alert for geographic place names and a genealogy in this first segment. After the prologue, the narrator swiftly focuses on the main character and main action of the story. In this story, we find a woman taking a strong personal initiative to change her life and her status—and thereby to affect the course of the history of Israel.

This story and the prayer of praise that follows in 1 Sam 2 are used in the Jewish liturgy for Rosh Hashanah, the Jewish New Year. As absorbed into the Magnificat (Luke 2:46–53), the prayer of praise has an important place in Christian liturgy as well.

Verse 1.

וַיְהִי

This formula introduces a past tense narrative by pointing to a particular time in the past; it opens the books of Joshua, Judges, 1 and 2 Samuel (cf. 2 Sam 1:1), Ezekiel, Ruth, Esther, and Nehemiah. (**?** [Need help?] see K. 232; L. 123; S. 159, 162, 191; W. 91–92.)

(→ WO'C 33.2.4.b, pp. 553–54; GKC §111 f; JM §118 b–c; L. 279–82; see List of Abbreviations.)

אִישׁ אֶחָד

אֶחָד ("one") is used here and on many other occasions (e.g., Judg 13:2; 2 Kgs 4:1) in the sense of "a certain one." אִישׁ אֶחָד is translated as "a certain man." אֶחָד serves as a marker of an indefinite noun. (→ WO'C 13.8.a., p. 251.)

מִן־הָרָמָתַיִם צוֹפִים מֵהַר אֶפְרָיִם

The expression מִן־הָרָמָתַיִם צוֹפִים may be translated as "from HaRamathaim (literally, The Two Hills) at Zophim" (cf. יַרְדֵּן יְרֵחוֹ e.g., Num 26:3; 31:12), or "from Ramathaim of the Zophites," or "from Ramathaim-Zophim." It shows, however, some grammatical peculiarities that have led a number of scholars to propose that the original text read מִן־הָרָמָתַיִם צוּפִי ("from Ramathaim, a Zuphite," → McCarter, *1 Samuel*, 51). Also note that according to v 19, Elkanah is living in Ramah ("the hill").

Note

Whether we translate this phrase as "from Ramathaim of the Zophites" or "from Ramathaim, a Zuphite," the geographical references move from a narrow circle to a larger one—that is, from the city/village of The Two Hills to Zuph, an area within the territory of Ephraim, and finally to Ephraim, the largest territorial unit. (This is similar to modern addresses, such as "Atlanta, Georgia.") Significantly, the genealogy of Elkanah ends with a reference to Zuph, the Ephraimite (i.e., from the children of Ephraim), linking the genealogy with the geographical location. Genealogies in the Old Testament/Hebrew Bible (OT/HB) often reflect geography.

וּשְׁמוֹ

Why וּ instead of וְ? (**?** K. 111; Gr. 28; Ke. 209–10; L. 40; S. 34–35; W. 40–41; → GKC §104 e; JM §104 c–d.) ....

To whom does the pronominal suffix וֹ refer? How do you translate it? ....

....

Note

This form of clarifying the identity of a person just introduced in the narrative is quite common in the OT/HB. (See, for instance, Gen 24:29; 1 Sam 9:1; Ruth 1:2; 2:1; cf. Num 11:26.)

For Further Thought

The genealogical list serves the purpose of presenting Elkanah. Long genealogical lists are rare in the historical narratives in Joshua through Kings. Why might the text contain such a long genealogy? Comparing it with another passage containing a long genealogy, 1 Sam 9:1, may suggest an answer.

Verse 2.

To whom does לוֹ refer? ....

This is the possessive לוֹ, equivalent to the English "have," in the sense of possessing (K. 32). (→ on the wide range of meanings of the preposition, see WO'C 11.2.10, pp. 205–12.) The question, therefore, is "who had what?"

וְלוֹ שְׁתֵּי נָשִׁים שֵׁם אַחַת חַנָּה וְשֵׁם הַשֵּׁנִית פְּנִנָּה

When two persons are introduced together, the clause opening with וְשֵׁם needs some clarifying expression to specify which name belongs to which person. The expression אַחַת . . . שֵׁנִית in v 2 does exactly that. It occurs elsewhere in several similar situations (e.g., Exod 1:15; Ruth 1:2,4; cf. Gen 2:11–13).

After the atnaḥ (**?** K. 44, 53, 344; Gr. 132–33; Ke. 16–17; L. 201–02; S. 290), the chain of vav conversive + prefix (wyqtl; hereafter וַיִקְטֹל) continues. In this case, the chain does not refer to a sequence of events but to the thread of the discourse. It provides an introduction to the narrative proper, which begins with the temporal clause in v 4. (→ WO'C 33.2.1.c, pp. 549–50.)

Should the ו in וּלְחַנָּה be translated as "and" or as "but"? *Explain.* ....

....

Translate vv 1–2.

```
┌─────────────────────────────────────────────┐
│                                             │
│                                             │
│                                             │
│                                             │
│                                             │
│                                             │
└─────────────────────────────────────────────┘
```

Note

The contrast between the two women is stressed by a repetitive parallel structure, and the pattern is inverted: Hannah—Peninnah, Peninnah—Hannah. Hannah not only is mentioned first but also is at the center of the climactic contrast at the end of the verse. An inverted pattern of two syntactic elements or sounds in parallel phrases, called **chiasm,** is a common stylistic device in the OT/HB. (❓ K. 269, 345; → GKC §114 r n1, 456 §142f n1.) Note, too, the emphasis on Hannah's condition brought about by the particle of nonexistence, אֵין.

For Further Thought

Stories about two wives, one beloved but barren and the other less well loved but blessed with children, are common in the OT/HB (e.g., Sarah and Hagar, Leah and Rachel). Moreover, several biblical heroes (e.g., Isaac, Joseph, and Samson) were born either to mothers who considered themselves barren or under such circumstances that the infant's premature death seemed unavoidable (e.g., Moses). These stories suggest something beyond the ordinary concerning these persons, from the moment of birth. How does this contribute to the shaping of the hero's image?

Verse 3.

וְעָלָה

This vav is not conversive (consecutive before imperfect). How do you know that? (❓ K. 7; Gr. 74–77; Ke. 211; L. 107–09; W. 90–92; → GKC §49; JM §118 a.) ....

....

For those who studied using Seow, *Grammar,* the vav (waw) opening the verse does not belong to a ויקטל form. How do you know that? (❓ S. 159–63.) ....

....

Analyze the verb וְעָלָה. (For an explanation of the grid, see "Note on the Text." You can check the accuracy of your analysis against BDB.)

Root	Stem	Form	PGN	SF	OS	BRM

The verb is in affix (perfect) form. The contrast between the vav conversive + prefix (hereafter vav conversive–prefix; וַיקטל) chain and the affix form וְעָלָה stresses the continuous or repetitive character of the actions of Elkanah. The expression מִיָּמִים יָמִימָה (❓ BDB) makes clear that the affix (perfect) form וְעָלָה is not used here simply to express one action completed in the past, in the sense of the English simple past (→ WO'C 30.2.2, pp. 482–83).

Who is the subject of the verb? ....

הָאִישׁ הַהוּא

Remember that הוּא is not always equivalent to the English "he." Moreover, in this instance הוּא is preceded by the definite article, and therefore it cannot be the independent pronoun "he." The הוּא in הָאִישׁ הַהוּא is a demonstrative pronoun. It indicates that he is not any man but *that* man. One set of demonstratives is identical with the third-person independent pronouns: הֵם, הִיא, הוּא, and הֵנָּה. Demonstratives may function in a sentence as attributive adjectives, that is, adjectives that not only describe and usually follow the noun but also agree with it in number, gender, and definiteness. (❓ about demonstratives, see K. 65, 102, 162–63, 352; Gr. 39; Ke. 52–54; L. 34–35; S. 60–61; W. 62; ❓ about attributive adjectives in general, see K. 232; Gr. 31; Ke. 45–46; L. 13–14; S. 40; W. 32–33.)

מֵעִירוֹ

Identify the preposition and **explain** its vocalization (❓ K. 238; Gr. 23, 84, 203; Ke. 30; L. 23; S. 34; W. 29). ....
....

With the verb construction וְעָלָה, the introduction to the narrative moves from the general background to a specific customary action of Elkanah's which is central to the narrative that follows.

Analyze לְהִשְׁתַּחֲוֺת (❓ K. 182, 361–62; Gr. 141; L. 254–55; S. 230–32; → WO'C 21.2.3.d, pp. 360–61; JM §59 b,g; cf. GKC §75 kk.)

Root	Stem	Form	PGN	SF	OS	BRM

How do you translate this infinitive construct? (**?** K. 47, 153; Ke. 179; S. 190–91; → WO'C 36.2.3, pp. 605–10.) ....

Does "to bow" or "to worship" make more sense than "by bowing" or "by worshiping"?

For Further Thought

The clause providing the names of the sons of Eli does not follow the formula שֵׁם הָאֶחָד . . . הַשֵּׁנִי which we have just encountered in verse 2. In Ruth 1:2, the names of the two sons, Mahlon and Chilion, are given together, almost as a unit. This שֵׁם clause stands in contrast to the clauses referring to Naomi and Elimelech, and to Orpah and Ruth (in v 4). Do you think that the difference in the construction of these double שֵׁם clauses is meaningless? If not, what is the difference between these two forms of double שֵׁם clauses?

Is the final ה of Shiloh a marker of a vowel (*mater lectionis*) or a consonant? (**?** K. 3; Gr. 17–18; Ke. 18; L. xxiii–xxiv; S. 8–10; W. 6–7; please note that ה was used as a marker of any long final vowel other than a long *i*, or a long *u*, and not only of *a*; → GKC §7 b–c; Andersen and Forbes, *Spelling in the Hebrew Bible*, 31–36.) If it is a marker of a vowel, can you think of a different spelling for Shiloh? Check your proposal against 1 Sam 1:24.

Translate v 3.

```


```

For Further Thought

Following the atnaḥ, there is a reference to the sons of Eli, Hophni, and Phinehas. The reader is thus prepared for a confrontation between them and Elkanah's family. As you will see, however, such a confrontation does not seem to occur. Has the reader been offered a false clue? Does reading the first seven chapters of 1 Samuel confirm your answer?

Verse 4.

וַיְהִי הַיּוֹם וַיִּזְבַּח אֶלְקָנָה

הַיּוֹם provides the temporal data, i.e., "the/this day" (**?** BDB).

Analyze וַיִּזְבַּח

Root	Stem	Form	PGN	SF	OS	BRM

Translate the whole phrase.

```
┌──────────────────────────────────────────────────────────────┐
│                                                                │
│                                                                │
│                                                                │
│                                                                │
│                                                                │
│                                                                │
└──────────────────────────────────────────────────────────────┘
```

You may have written: "On that day Elkanah offered a sacrifice"; "And the day came, when Elkanah offered a sacrifice" (cf. BDB). "One day he offered a sacrifice" (WO'C 33.2.1.c, p. 550) is also possible and may be the best translation, for it refers to a day on which a particular action happened. (Cf. 1 Sam 14:1; 2 Kgs 4:8,11,18; Job 1:6,13.)

וְנָתַן לִפְנִנָּה אִשְׁתּוֹ וּלְכָל־בָּנֶיהָ וּבְנוֹתֶיהָ מָנוֹת

Analyze the verb.

Root	Stem	Form	PGN	SF	OS	BRM

Who is the subject? . . . .

What is the direct object? . . . .

Who are the indirect objects? . . . .

In this instance, מָנוֹת refers to the portions of meat from the sacrificed animal that can be eaten by the person who brought the animal.

The sequence *verb–subject–indirect object–direct object* is very common in biblical Hebrew (**?** K. 390; Ke. 87; L. 39–40; S. 94; → GKC §142 f; for a comprehensive analysis of word order in verbal clauses, see JM §155 k–t, 156). Why is the subject omitted here? . . . .

. . . .

(For those who studied using Seow: What else is mentioned in S. 94 that does not occur in this sentence? Can you explain why it does not occur here? . . . .

. . . .)

The verbal form וְנָתַן is different from the one in וַיִּזְבַּח. The latter points to a singular event, but here we are concerned with a customary, repeated series of actions. This chain of events is followed in v 9, or perhaps more likely in v 7b (after the atnaḥ). The affix (perfect) form נָתַן points to something that was habitual, usual. וְנָתַן stops the flow of the narrative to give background for the event that is about to be told. You may then translate v 4 as follows: "One day he offered a sacrifice—he would give portions (of the meat) to his wife Peninnah and to all her sons and daughters." (so WO'C 33.2.1.c, p. 550).

For Further Thought

According to the story, Elkanah took his whole family (including sons and daughters) to Shiloh. His daughters, together with his sons, enjoyed eating the meat from the offered animal. Moreover, although the narrator probably means to draw attention to the contrast between Hannah and Peninnah, one cannot but notice that these sons and daughters are called "her (Peninnah's) sons" and "her daughters."

Verse 5.

וּלְחַנָּה יִתֵּן מָנָה אַחַת אַפָּיִם

וְ- may mean "and," but it may also mean "but." In this case it would be better translated as "but," since contrast is implied. Note the change in the word order. The sentence opens with וּלְחַנָּה, that is, with the indirect object instead of the verb. The usual word order is disrupted in order to highlight the contrast between Hannah and Peninnah (→ K. 248, 284; Ke. 87; S. 94–95; GKC §142 f).

Analyze יִתֵּן

Root	Stem	Form	PGN	SF	OS	BRM

If you identified יִתֵּן as a prefix (imperfect) form, you are right. The verb, however, points to a habitual behavior, like the previous וְנָתַן. In this case, the variation of the verbal forms seems to be due to considerations of style.

The meaning of אַפָּיִם is unclear. You may translate אַפָּיִם as "double," but this meaning is not certain. (→ on a different proposal, see Aberbach, "מנה אחת אפים [1 Sam. I 5].")

For Further Thought

If you look for the word אַפָּיִם in BDB (60a), you will find a proposal for textual emendation based on the Septuagint. According to this emendation, the original text read אפס כי (**?** BDB). This reading leads to the English translation, "But to Hannah he used to give one portion, though he loved Hannah; but YHWH had shut up her womb." See, for example, this passage in the Revised English Bible (REB), Revised Standard Version (RSV), Tanakh (NJPSV), and Today's English Version (TEV).

Which do you think is more likely:

(a) that a very clear text containing a relatively common expression, אֶפֶס כִּי, was turned into a very difficult text containing a rare and problematic expression because of a technical mistake made by a copyist; or

(b) that ancient readers of the received text found a very difficult Hebrew expression whose meaning was unclear to them, so they decided to interpret or simplify it, either in "popular" versions of the book or in translations into other languages, such as Greek, or in both?

The possibility that the presence of the word אַפָּיִם in our text is due to a copyist's mistake cannot be ruled out, even if, generally, such mistakes are likely to produce a difficult text. This explanation has, however, a main drawback. It assumes not only that the scribe erred, which is certainly human, but also that both the copyist and the community of readers of the copied text, both of which knew Hebrew, consistently failed to recognize the difficult reading and its origin in a human error. This being the case, it seems to us reasonable to prefer option (b).

Are you expecting אָהַב as the qal (G) affix (perfect) form of the root אהב? אָהֵב is much more common in biblical Hebrew. Forms like אָהֵב tend to be used for verbs expressing emotional states (→ WO'C 22.2.3 b–e, pp. 366–67). אָהֵב occurs especially before atnaḥ or other major disjunctive (i.e., dividing) markers (? K. 374; Gr. 135–36; Ke. 17; L. 201–02; S. 290; W. 21, 137; → GKC §29 i–w).

וַה' סָגַר רַחְמָהּ

Analyze the verb.

Root	Stem	Form	PGN	SF	OS	BRM

When the whole sentence is in the past tense, the affix (perfect) form may convey the sense of the English past perfect "had shut up" (→ K. 56–57; Ke. 85–86; JM §112 c; WO'C 30.3, pp. 483–85), especially when it occurs in a clause at the end of the sentence. Note that ו introduces a clause that provides factual information needed for understanding the narrative. This expression forms an *inclusio* with the similar expression at the end of v 6. Together they delimit and bracket the note concerning Peninnah's attitude.

Note

Here is a brief explanation of the stylistic device called **inclusio:** "When the word is repeated at the beginning and at the end, in the first and last verses, this is an inclusion. It is a frequent technique for marking the limits of the poem, the poem is 'rounded off.' Sometimes it is used to emphasize an important word. A minor inclusion is one which does not extend to the whole poem, but simply to one of its sections. The inclusion is strengthened when more than one word is repeated" (Alonso Schökel, *Manual,* 78). Such inclusions occur frequently in Hebrew prose and poetry. In fact, many features generally associated with poetry (inclusio, chiasm, repetition of sounds and letters) are common in Hebrew prose.

For Further Thought

Neither Elkanah nor the narrator claims that something is wrong with Hannah, although she cannot conceive.

Verse 6.

וְכִעֲסַתָּה

What does תָּה- contribute to the meaning of this word?

    This is one of the suffixes that point to the third-person feminine objective pronoun ("her") when attached to an affix (perfect) verbal form. The other suffixes are הָ, and ָהּ (→ K. 215; Ke. 155–56; L. 266; S. 131–34; W. 123,125; GKC §58 a, 59 g). The ending תָּה- occurs only when the verb is in both the affix (perfect) form and the third-person feminine singular. (If you would like to know why the third-person feminine singular shows this special ending, → Ke. 156; S. 132–33; W. 125; GKC §59 g; JM §42 f, 63 d.)

    To which stem (binyan) does this verbal form belong? Is this pi'el (D)? Note that the verb has an *i* vowel underneath the first letter of the root. (**?** K. 71–73; Gr. 58–59; Ke. 114; L. 195–96; S. 111–15; W. 105–07.) If it is pi'el (D), why is the ע not doubled? (**?** K. 4; Gr. 30; Ke. 23; L. xx–xxi; W. 15; S. 3; → GKC §22 b.) . . . .

    The meaning conveyed by the root כעס is not only "to provoke anger" but "to provoke unwarranted anger." גַם in this sentence is emphatic. Note the strengthening of the message by both the presence of גַם and the repetition of sounds between כַּעַס and וְכִעֲסַתָּה. Note also the similar endings of וְכִעֲסַתָּה and צָרָתָה.

    בַּעֲבוּר is a combination of עֲבוּר and the preposition בְּ-. Check its meaning in BDB. בַּעֲבוּר generally introduces a telic clause, that is, one that explains the goal or endpoint of an action. The English equivalent of these Hebrew clauses is usually introduced by "in order to" or "so that."

    הַרְעִמָה is a hif'il infinitive construct with a third-person feminine singular suffix. Infinitive constructs may act as verbal nouns (→ K. 364–65; Gr. 55; Ke. 179; L. 128; S. 187,190; W. 131–32; → GKC §114 a–c; JM §124 a–j). הַרְעִמָה may be translated as "to irritate her" or "to complain aloud" ("to thunder"). Post-biblical Hebrew and Aramaic point to the second understanding. A known midrash based on this reading claimed that Peninnah irritated Hannah in order to make her pray to the Lord, but this is not the straightforward meaning of the text.

For Further Thought

Note that the ר in הַרְעִמָה takes dagesh forte. There are relatively few cases of double ר in the OT/HB. With this double ר, v 6 contains no less than six רs. The sound of ר recalls the sound of thunder, the basic meaning of the root רעם. This repetition of sounds may enhance the force of the text, provided that רעם is understood as "to complain aloud." If this understanding is preferred, then כִּי־סָגַר ה' בְּעַד רַחְמָהּ can be understood in two ways: (a) Peninnah vexed Hannah because the Lord shut Hannah's womb, and (b) Peninnah vexed Hannah so that Hannah would complain aloud that YHWH has closed her womb (cf. McCarter, *1 Samuel*, 49, 52–53). Do you think that the phrase must convey only one of these meanings? Or may it imply both of them?

Translate vv 4–6.

```



```

Verse 7.

Who is the subject of יַעֲשֶׂה? . . . .
This prefix (imperfect) form, along with תַּכְעִסֶנָּה later in the verse, points to habitual or iterative actions in the past (cf. יִתֵּן in v 5). This meaning of the prefix (imperfect) may be translated in English by "he used to" or "she would." This is one of the potential meanings of a prefix (imperfect) form in biblical Hebrew (→ WO'C 31.2.b, pp. 502–03). You will see many instances of it in your reading of the HB/OT.

The expression שָׁנָה בְשָׁנָה can be translated neither as "year within year" nor as "year against year." What other options are there? (? BDB.) . . . .
What are the words combined in מִדֵּי? . . . .
Since the use of this compound preposition is idiomatic, you should check the reference to מִדֵּי in BDB.

Analyze עָלְתָהּ (? cf. הַרְעִמָהּ in v 6; the context will help you decide to whom the third-person feminine pronouns in this verse refer).

Root	Stem	Form	PGN	SF	OS	BRM

Analyze תַּכְעִסֶנָּה.

Root	Stem	Form	PGN	SF	OS	BRM

Why is the third-person feminine singular pronominal suffix ("her") in תַּכְעִסֶ֫נָּה different from the one in כְּעָסָ֫תָה? (❓ K. 214–15; Gr. 71; Ke. 153–59; L. 266, 271–72; S. 179–81, 131–34; W. 123–27, 130–31; → GKC §59, 60.) To whom does "her" refer? . . . .

Analyze וַתִּבְכֶּה

Root	Stem	Form	PGN	SF	OS	BRM

Who is the subject of this verb? . . . .

Is this the same as the subject of תַּכְעִסֶ֫נָּה? . . . .

Note that the narrative has just moved Hannah from the passive position of direct object to the active position of subject.

Analyze תֹאכַל

Root	Stem	Form	PGN	SF	OS	BRM

This verb belongs to a group of 1st א verbs in which the first vowel is *o* and the א drops out of pronunciation (i.e., is quiescent) in the qal prefix (imperfect). This group includes verbs from the roots אבד, אכל, אמר, and others. (→ K. 395; Gr.; Ke.; L.; S. 148–49; W. 161–63; and esp. GKC §68; cf. JM §73 a–f.)

Before translating v 7, notice

(a) that the ". . . כֵּן . . . וְכֵן" structure is best rendered "as he (Elkanah) would do (this) . . . so she (Peninnah) would do (that) . . .";

(b) that וַתִּבְכֶּה does not seem to belong to the prefix (imperfect) series of יַעֲשֶׂה and תַּכְעִסֶ֫נָּה but to go back to וַיְהִי הַיּוֹם וַיִּזְבַּח אֶלְקָנָה; that is, to what happened on that particular day, and not to what was habitually done (vv 4b–7a) (→ McCarter, *I Samuel*, 49, 59–60; WO'C 33.2.1.c, p. 550).

Translate v 7.

Verse 8.

What are the words combined in לָמֶה? ....

Clue: This form occurs only three times in the OT/HB, all of them in this verse, but a similar form, לָמָה, occurs many times in the OT/HB.

Find the expression ירע לבב in BDB.

Translate the entire unit from vv 4a through 8.

```



```

Note

Verse 8 provides a glimpse into family life at this period. It contains a rare biblical example of a husband speaking directly to his wife. If this way of speaking is representative of the social customs of the period, then husbands, like Elkanah here, may have called their wives by their first names. Unfortunately, there is no similar example of direct speech of a wife to her husband. See, however, "For Further Thought," v 21.

Verse 9.

Analyze וַתָּקָם (❓ K. 400; Gr. 76; L. 149; S. 160–61; W. 197).

Root	Stem	Form	PGN	SF	OS	BRM

Translate וַתָּקָם חַנָּה

```



```

With וַתָּקָם, the narrative turns back to Hannah, and to the precise point in time when she broke with the seemingly ceaseless pattern of events described in vv 4–8.

אַחֲרֵי אָכְלָה בְשִׁלֹה

How do you read אָכְלָה? Is there a qamets or qamets ḥatuf underneath the א? (**?** K. 26; Gr. 19–20; Ke. 19–21; L. xxv–xxvi; S. 12–13; W. 12–13. Seow, *Grammar*, should say "in a closed and unaccented syllable" instead of "in a closed syllable.") How do you read וַתָּקָם?

Many temporal clauses in the OT/HB are formed by a preposition followed by an infinitive construct. The preposition indicates the time relation (as do the English "when," "before," "after," "from the time that," "as soon as," etc.) between the action or situation referred to by the infinitive construct and that of the main sentence (→ WO'C 38.7, pp. 643–44). If the main sentence opens with a vav conversive–prefix (ויקטל) and includes a temporal clause, one may expect the order verb–subject–. . .—temporal clause (cf. Gen 5:4; 14:17).

אָכְלָה may be either a qal (G) infinitive construct with a third-person singular feminine pronominal suffix that lost the mappiq (a phenomenon attested several times in the OT/HB, e.g., עֻזָּה in 2 Kgs 8:6; **?** concerning mappiq, see K. 65, 367–68; Gr. 20 n 3; Ke. 18–19; L. xxiv–xxv; S. 9; W. 17; → GKC §14 a–d; JM §11) or simply an alternative form of the qal (G) infinitive construct of the root אכל, i.e., "eating" instead of "her eating." Note that BDB mentions two forms of the qal (G) infinitive construct of the root אכל.

Write down the second form: . . . .

The OT/HB shows more than one form of infinitive construct from the root אכל in qal (G). In one of the forms the infinitive is patterned according to the feminine pattern of nouns and the other, לֶאֱכֹל (e.g., Gen 28:20), follows the masculine pattern. The same holds true for other verbs. For example, compare לְרָחְצָה in Exod 30:18 with לִרְחֹץ in Gen 24:32 (→ WO'C 36.1.1.d, p. 599; JM §49 d).

For Further Thought

How can you decide between the two possible translations:

(a) "after she had eaten"

(b) "after the eating"

Context may help. וְאַחֲרֵי שָׁתֹה seems to complete the expression, for it brings together "eating" and "drinking" (cf. 1 Kgs 13:23; Exod 24:11). It is natural to expect that if it is "she had eaten," the parallel form would be "she had drunk."

Analyze שָׁתֹה

Root	Stem	Form	PGN	SF	OS	BRM

How can an infinitive absolute like שָׁתֹה follow (i.e., be the object of) a preposition (אַחֲרֵי)? In fact, this is one of the few cases in which this does happen in the OT/HB (→ WO'C 35.3.3.a, p. 591). The only real alternative is to emend the text, which, of course, has been proposed many times.

שָׁתֹה suggests that the translation "after the eating and drinking at Shiloh" is more likely than "after she had eaten and drunk" (as the Targum and Rashi interpret it). See the words of Hannah in v 15: "I have drunk no wine or other strong drink."

Thus, one may translate the entire verse up to the atnaḥ as, "after the eating and drinking at Shiloh, Hannah rose." But one must remember that the possible "after she had eaten" keeps echoing in the mind of the reader, who must wonder to what extent Hannah actually heard Elkanah's words of consolation, to what extent she actually participated in the sacrificial meal with the rest of the family.

For Further Thought

An equivalent to the Hebrew phrase וְאַחֲרֵי שָׁתֹה is not attested in the Septuagint (Vaticanus text). How can we explain this?

וְעֵלִי הַכֹּהֵן יֹשֵׁב

Analyze יֹשֵׁב (**?** K. 39–41, 114; Gr. 55; Ke. 193–94; L. 18–19; S. 46; W. 65–66; → GKC §50.)

Root	Stem	Form	PGN	SF	OS	BRM

-וְ is commonly translated as "and," which suggests some kind of similarity. But vav + noun frequently has a disjunctive value, separating the clause that follows from the one that precedes it. In this case, the vav marks a clear break in the narrative, a point at which a new personage is introduced and at which the story moves from Hannah's specific actions to the general circumstances in which they take place (→ WO'C 8.3.b, p. 129, 39.2.3, pp. 650–52). Taking into account these features, McCarter (1 Samuel, 49) translates v 9b as "(now, Eli, the priest, was sitting . . .)." What justification might he offer for rendering יֹשֵׁב as "was sitting"? (→ WO'C 37.6.c–d, pp. 624–26) . . . .

עַל־הַכִּסֵּא

Note the definite article before כִּסֵּא. What difference would it make if the text had said כִּסֵּא rather than הַכִּסֵּא? . . . .

עַל־מְזוּזַת הֵיכַל ה'

Can this עַל be translated in the same way as the preceding one? . . . .

Note that the construct chain contains three different nouns. Is this a definite construct chain? How do you know? (**?** K. 21–22; Gr. 34–35; Ke. 63; L. 67–70; S. 70–71; W. 46; → GKC §127, esp. 127 a; JM §139, esp. 139 a.) ....

....

Translate v 9b (? BDB).

```



```

Verse 10.

וְהִיא מָרַת נֶפֶשׁ וַתִּתְפַּלֵּל עַל־ה' וּבָכֹה תִבְכֶּה

Who is the "she" in וְהִיא?

Of course, "she" is Hannah. Thus, the narrative goes back to v 9a. Accordingly, one may write all of v 9b within parentheses. Note the use of the vav + (pro-)noun here. Vav + non-verb is a common way of introducing a disjunctive clause. Some of these clauses are circumstantial, that is, they provide information concerning the circumstances in which events take place. Many of them, but not all of them, are verbless (→ WO'C 39.2.3.b, p. 651).

The expected verbal form is התפלל אל but instead one reads התפלל על, which is used elsewhere with the meaning of either "for, on behalf of" (2 Chr 30:18; Job 42:8) or "about, because of" (2 Chr 32:20). This verse is one of several occasions in which על occurs instead of an expected אל (cf. וַיֵּלֶךְ אֶלְקָנָה הָרָמָתָה עַל־בֵּיתוֹ in 1 Sam 2:11).

Since מָרַת נֶפֶשׁ is an expression, you can look for it in BDB. Why does the text say מָרַת נֶפֶשׁ instead of מָרַת נֶפֶשׁ? ....

....

Note

It is likely that the root מרר conveyed not only the meaning of "being bitter" but also the meaning of "being strong." Although in the context of 1 Sam 1:10 the basic meaning of the word is "bitter," it seems reasonable that readers/hearers of the story, who were aware of the second possible meaning, would notice the conveyed connotation: Hannah is bitter, but she is not powerless or passive.

Note

Alonso Schökel proposes that נֶפֶשׁ could mean "neck" in some of its occurrences (e.g., Jonah 2:6, Ps 124:4). He suggests that מַר־נֶפֶשׁ "could mean 'to feel bitterness in the throat'; as long as the expression has not been lexicalised to mean simply any interior bitterness, even metaphorical." (Alonso Schökel, *Manual*, 102–103.)

Analyze both בָּכֹה (❓ K. 171–72, 364; Gr. 54, 90; Ke. 184, 287; L. 158–59, 309 [there the reference to par. 128 is mistaken; the relevant paragraph is 129]; W. 79–80, 217; S. 181–83; → GKC §45 a–b, 113) and תִבְכֶּה (❓ K. 49, 408; Gr. 88–90; Ke. 287–89; L. 143–45; S. 149–50; W. 216–17; → GKC §75).

Root	Stem	Form	PGN	SF	OS	BRM

Root	Stem	Form	PGN	SF	OS	BRM

Unlike וַתָּקָם and וַתִּתְפַּלֵּל עַל, וּבָכֹה תִבְכֶּה is not a part of the chain of vav conversive–prefix (ויקטל) forms. That is, Hannah did not cry once, after praying and before making a vow, but she *began to weep* when she prayed. Waltke and O'Connor correctly translate: "She prayed to YHWH and began weeping bitterly" (WO'C 31.2.c, p. 504; ❓ on the general uses of the infinitive absolute, see K. 171, 364; Gr. 54; Ke. 185; L. 158–59; S. 182–83; W. 79; → GKC §113; JM §123; WO'C 35, pp. 580–97). A prefix (imperfect) form, especially when it stands next to or in the middle of a vav conversive–prefix (ויקטל) chain, may convey the meaning of a nascent action together with the sense of progressive continuance (→ WO'C 31.2.c, pp. 503–04, cf. 31.3.d, pp. 505–6).

Translate v 10.

Verse 11.

Analyze וַתִּדֹּר (❓ K. 77–79, 398; Gr. 103; Ke. 302–03; L. 133; S. 150; W. 141; → GKC §66)

Root	Stem	Form	PGN	SF	OS	BRM

Note

The use of a verbal form and of a noun of the same root (here וַתִּדֹּר נֶדֶר) is a well-attested stylistic device in the OT/HB, e.g., שְׂמֵחִים שִׂמְחָה גְדוֹלָה in 1 Kgs 1:40. The emphatic character of the **alliteration** (repetition of consonant sounds in neighboring words) is self-evident (→ Alonso Schökel, *Manual*, 22–23).

Analyze וַתֹּאמַר

Root	Stem	Form	PGN	SF	OS	BRM

As with וַיֹּאמֶר, the expression introduces direct speech.

Do you remember why the א in וַתֹּאמַר has no vowel marks? (**?** K. 4, 273, 395; Gr. 98, 100; Ke. 18, 237–40; L. 119–20; S. 13, 148; W. 18–19, 161–62.) ....

....

אִם־רָאֹה תִרְאֶה

A conditional sentence in which the condition is real, or realizable, opens in most cases with אִם, followed by a prefix (imperfect) verbal form (→ WO'C 31.6.1.a–b, pp. 510–11).

If you have trouble translating רָאֹה תִרְאֶה, **?** K. 171, 364; Gr. 54; Ke. 185; L. 158–59; S. 182–83; W. 79; → GKC §113.

Now comes a series of vav reversive + affix verbs (hereafter, vav-affix), following the prefix form תִרְאֶה (a yiqtol + weqaṭal sequence). Such a sequence should be translated as if it were a series of prefix (imperfect) forms. (**?** K. 36, 57, 256, 388; Gr. 76–77; Ke. 212–14; L. 108–09; S. 160; W. 90–92; → on vav-affix in general, see WO'C 32, pp. 519–42.)

One verb in this series looks different. Which is it? ....

Should one translate it in a different way? ....

Why doesn't the verb show a vav-affix (weqaṭal) form? ....

....

Note

The word אֲמָתֶךָ ("your servant") occurs three times in Hannah's appeal to YHWH. This word, and the masculine form עַבְדְּךָ, are commonly used in appeals to a higher authority (to God, to a king, or to an important officer). In this case the repetition of "your servant" is a stylistic device to express Hannah's attitude of humility before God. Note, too, the movement from a general plea that notice be taken of her affliction, to the clear and specific request for a child. In many cases, the emotional charge of the biblical verse intensifies from clause to clause, reaching its climax at the end of a series of parallel clauses. (→ Kugel, *Idea of Biblical Poetry*, 13–14, 29, 51–58.)

Note that אֲמָתֶךָ is a pausal form, the ordinary form being אֲמָתְךָ. What is the pausal form of עַבְדְּךָ? (**?** K. 95; Gr. 135–36; Ke. 17, 240–41; L. 201–02; S. 290; W. 137; → GKC §29 h–w; JM §32)

. . . .

Check your proposal against BDB.

The vav after the atnaḥ introduces the **apodosis,** i.e., the "then" clause in an "if . . . then . . . " sentence (→ L. 276–79; S. 259; also JM §176; and WO'C 38.2.b, p. 636, cf. 32.2.1.b, p. 256).

Who is the "him" in וּנְתַתִּיו? . . . .

Translate מוֹרָה (**?** BDB) . . . .

The word מוֹרָה occurs also in Judg 13:5. Do you see some parallels between the story there and the one in 1 Sam 1? . . . .

. . . .

If you wonder why Hannah promised that "no razor will touch his head," see Num 6:2–9 and Judg 13:4–5,7.

For Further Thought

According to the Septuagint, Hannah's vow included "he shall drink no wine nor strong drink." Do you think it more likely

(a) that a scribe forgot to copy one of the main requirements of the Nazirites—and that no one in the community of readers of the book noticed, so that the corrupted text become the accepted one; or

(b) that a scribe well versed in the law of the Nazirites duly recorded the received version of Hannah's vow despite its apparent "defectiveness" in following the Nazirite law?

Translate v 11.

Translate vv 9–11.

Verse 12.

וְהָיָה כִּי הִרְבְּתָה לְהִתְפַּלֵּל לִפְנֵי ה'

Analyze הִרְבְּתָה (**?** K. 409; Gr. 88–91; Ke. 288; L. 227–28; S. 123; W. 219)

Root	Stem	Form	PGN	SF	OS	BRM

Translate הִרְבְּתָה לְהִתְפַּלֵּל (cf. K. 203; see L. 228; BDB) . . . .

וַיְהִי כִּי is a common way of introducing a temporal clause and is translated in English by "when" or "as" (→ K. 232; S. 192). Thus, if one had וַיְהִי כִּי הִרְבְּתָה לְהִתְפַּלֵּל לִפְנֵי ה' one would translate the phrase, "as she continued praying." The problem, of course, is that the text reads וְהָיָה כִּי instead of וַיְהִי כִּי. This seems to be one of only a few cases in which a text reads וְהָיָה where one would expect וַיְהִי. Of the eight proposed instances of such an interchange in the HB/OT, five occur in the Book of Samuel (1 Sam 1:12; 10:9; 17:48; 25:20; 2 Sam 6:16; → GKC §112 uu; JM §119 z).

Here, as on many other occasions, וְהָיָה (or וַיְהִי) marks the beginning of a new segment in the narrative. The next part of the story centers on Eli and Hannah.

וְעֵלִי שֹׁמֵר אֶת־פִּיהָ

For the function of the vav, see the note on v 9. This is the first of two clauses introduced by vav that explain the circumstances of the first action following the וְהָיָה, i.e., וַיַּחְשְׁבֶהָ עֵלִי לְשִׁכֹּרָה.

Analyze שֹׁמֵר

Root	Stem	Form	PGN	SF	OS	BRM

Among the many possible translations of שֹׁמֵר, which one best suits the context? (**?** BDB.)

Translate v 12.

Verse 13a.

וְחַנָּה הִיא מְדַבֶּרֶת עַל־לִבָּהּ

The introduction of the pronoun/copula הִיא between the subject and the verb is a stylistic device to place emphasis on the subject, Hannah (cf. 1 Sam 17:14).

The expression דבר עַל לֵב (in which דבר is in the pi'el, or D) is attested several times in the HB/OT, and can be translated as "comfort" (e.g., Isa 40:2). But this cannot be the meaning of מְדַבֶּרֶת עַל־לִבָּה in our text. Why not? . . . .

. . . .

How, then, shall we translate מְדַבֶּרֶת עַל־לִבָּה? . . . .

Clue: The expression דבר אֶל־לֵב has an attested meaning of "speak to oneself" [e.g., Gen 24:45]; see also our notes concerning וַתִּתְפַּלֵּל עַל in v 10.

שְׂפָתֶיהָ נָּעוֹת וְקוֹלָהּ לֹא יִשָּׁמֵעַ

Analyze נָעוֹת and יִשָּׁמֵעַ

Root	Stem	Form	PGN	SF	OS	BRM

Root	Stem	Form	PGN	SF	OS	BRM

Note the multiple variations within the parallel *verb-noun, verb-noun* structure:

—the form (inflection) of the verb changes;

—the stem (binyan) changes from qal (G) to nif'al (N);

—the "voice" changes from active to passive;

—the noun changes from plural to singular;

—the noun changes from feminine to masculine;

—the first phrase is affirmative, the second negative.

Note

The use of parallel structures is a common stylistic device in Hebrew poetry and prose. In many cases, these parallel structures contain grammatical, semantic, and phonological shifts and contrasts between the first verset and the second. Moreover, in this instance, as in many other cases, the second verset moves the text forward and heightens it. Verse 13a explains the circumstances of Eli's actions. The crucial factor that led to his misunderstanding of Hannah was not that "her lips were moving" (first verset) but that "her voice was not heard" (second verset). (→ Kugel, *Idea of Biblical Poetry*; and Berlin, *Dynamics.*)

Translate vv 12–13a.

```



```

Verse 13b.

וַיַּחְשְׁבֶהָ עֵלִי לְשִׁכֹּרָה

The initial vav has several functions:

—it signals a movement from one subject to another (see note on v 9);

—it belongs to a vav conversive (ויקטל) before prefix form whose chain goes back to v 12 (see note);

—it introduces an apodosis. That is, "Hannah was speaking in her heart, only her lips were moving, but her voice was not heard, *therefore* Eli . . . ".

Analyze the verbal form וַיַּחְשְׁבֶהָ.

Root	Stem	Form	PGN	SF	OS	BRM

To whom does the pronominal suffix refer? Why is there no mappiq in the ה? . . . .
. . . .

Clue: Mappiq tells the reader that the ה is consonantal and not a marker of a vowel (*mater lectionis*). Does the reader actually need the help of a mappiq to know whether the ה in וַיַּחְשְׁבֶהָ is consonantal? (**?** concerning mappiq, K. 65, 367–68; Gr. 20 n 3; Ke. 18–19; L. xxiv–xxv; S. 9; W. 17; → GKC §14 a–d; JM §11.)

Before translating, check חשׁב ל- in BDB.

Compare the word order and the verbal forms in v 13b with those in v 12b. What do you make of the difference? . . . .
. . . .

Translate v 13b.

```
                                                                      
                                                                      
                                                                      
```

Verse 14.

וַיֹּאמֶר אֵלֶיהָ עֵלִי עַד־מָתַי תִּשְׁתַּכָּרִין

עַד־מָתַי is another case of a combination of a preposition (עַד) with an interrogative word (מָתַי). For the meaning of the expression, see BDB.

    Where does the direct speech of Eli begin? . . . .

    Where does it end? . . . .

    How do you know? . . . .

    Before you analyze תִּשְׁתַּכָּרִין, note that

—the final ן is paragogic ן (**?** K. 272; Gr. 189; Ke. 128; L. 99; S. 141; and esp. GKC §47 o; → GKC §47 m, o; 58 1; JM §44 e–f; WO'C 20.2.f, p. 347; 37.7, pp. 514–18). A paragogic ן may occur in the second-person feminine of a verb in its prefix (imperfect) form, though it is much more frequently attested in the third-person masculine plural. It tends to occur before a major disjunctive marker (such as sof-pasuq or atnaḥ; → WO'C p. 516). The second-person feminine singular ending ין occurs in Aramaic (and in Arabic). In the OT/HB, it is attested in Isa 45:10; Jer 31:22; Ruth 2:8,21; 3:4,18, as well as in this reading.

—some letters undergo **metathesis** (that is, they switch places) in the hithpa'el stem (HtD binyan). (**?** K. 370; Gr. 86; Ke. 111; L. 248; S. 229; W. 120; → GKC §54 b–d; JM §17 b.)

After the atnaḥ, in the second part of the verse, Eli's speech moves from reproach to direct command: הָסִירִי אֶת־יֵינֵךְ מֵעָלָיִךְ

Analyze the verb (**?** K. 401; Gr. 81; Ke. 324; L. 231–32; S. 214; W. 201).

Root	Stem	Form	PGN	SF	OS	BRM

Translate v 14 (**?** BDB).

```
                                                                      
                                                                      
                                                                      
```

Note the emphatic repetition of the second-person feminine pronominal suffixes at the end of the verse, which, of course, also provides a repetition of sounds.

For Further Thought

The Jewish sages relate this incident to the ruling that a drunken person is not allowed to pray (b. Ber. 31a). Interestingly, the Septuagint adds a sentence to this verse: "Go out from the presence of the Lord."

Verse 15.

וַתַּעַן חַנָּה וַתֹּאמֶר

Verbal forms from the roots אמר and I ענה (**?** BDB) occur together several times in the OT/HB (e.g., Gen 18:27, Exod 4:1). The name of the person who responds stands between the two verbs.

לֹא אֲדֹנִי

This is a short and sharp reply. Although showing respect to the priest (אֲדֹנִי is the formal address to someone higher than the speaker in rank, status, or authority; cf. Zech 4:5,13), Hannah clearly and unequivocally declares that he is wrong. She lets Eli know the truth in three short versets:

(1) אִשָּׁה קְשַׁת־רוּחַ אָנֹכִי
(2) וְיַיִן וְשֵׁכָר לֹא שָׁתִיתִי
(3) וָאֶשְׁפֹּךְ אֶת־נַפְשִׁי לִפְנֵי ה'

In the OT/HB the expression קְשַׁת־רוּחַ occurs only in this verse. It probably means "firm-spirited," in the sense of a spirit that does not yield to difficulties. If this is the meaning, Hannah portrays herself as a woman who maintains hope, in spite of her seemingly hopeless situation. Some scholars propose the existence of an original text קשת יום instead of קשת רוח, on the basis of the Septuagint and because of the occurrence of קְשֵׁה־יוֹם in Job 30:25, which may be understood as "unfortunate." But as we shall see (v 16), Hannah does not consider herself a passive, powerless woman.

The predicate-subject word order in this sentence gives emphasis to the predicate (e.g., מְרַגְּלִים אַתֶּם in Gen 42:9).

Translate the first verset.

Translate the second verset.

Have you translated שָׁתִיתִי by an English verb in present perfect? If not, why not? . . . .
. . . . Note that whereas the first verset merely implies that Eli's image of Hannah is incorrect, the second verset explicitly contradicts that image.

Remember that a vav conversive–prefix (ויקטל) form that follows an affix (qtl, hereafter, קטל) form translated by a perfect tense (present perfect or past perfect) may also have a perfect meaning (e.g., Gen 39:13; → WO'C 33.1.c, p. 556). For the idiomatic meaning of וָאֶשְׁפֹּךְ אֶת־נַפְשִׁי see BDB.

Translate the third verset.

Verse 16.

אַל־תִּתֵּן אֶת־אֲמָתְךָ לִפְנֵי בַּת־בְּלִיָּעַל

To translate אַל־תִּתֵּן אֶת־אֲמָתְךָ לִפְנֵי (❓ K. 168, 267; Gr. 51; Ke. 173–73; L. 114; S. 144, 173; W. 77) you need to know that לִפְנֵי, which in most cases is translated as "before," used either spatially or temporally, is better rendered by "as" or "like" in this case (as well as in Job 3:24).

בַּת־בְּלִיָּעַל is translated as "worthless woman," with a connotation of antisocial behavior. Hannah and Eli implicitly assume that being drunk is included in this kind of behavior. Hannah claims that she is not בַּת־בְּלִיָּעַל, though Eli (mis)judged her a reprobate. Significantly, the narrator will later explicitly state that it is actually the sons of Eli who are בְּנֵי בְלִיָּעַל (1 Sam 2:12).

Note
The word בְּלִיָּעַל is probably a combination of בְּלִי ("without") and a word from the root יעל (meaning "benefit," "worthy," "of use"), just as בְּלִי־מָה ("nothing") in Job 26:7 is a combination of בְּלִי ("without") and מָה ("anything").

Of course, there is nothing grammatically wrong with the translation "daughter of Belial" (see KJV). Nevertheless, this translation is commonly rejected because it implies that Belial is the proper name of either a human being or a personification of evil, depending upon the context. The first possibility can be immediately ruled out. The text would be meaningless if "Belial" identifies the biological father of Hannah. Furthermore, in the OT/HB the phrase "children of Belial" is applied to various people (e.g., Judg 19:22). The second possibility looks more promising. In fact, Belial (often spelled Beliar) is the personification of evil in Pseudepigrapha (e.g., Martyrdom of Isaiah), in Qumranic literature (e.g., Hodayot), and in the New Testament (2 Cor 6:15). But this literature is later than the OT/HB. In sharp contrast with this later literature, no action or attribute is accorded to Belial in the OT/HB. Thus, there is no evidence that the Israelites in the OT/HB period understood בְּלִיַּעַל as "Evil One."

Translate v 16.

```
┌─────────────────────────────────────────────────────────────┐
│                                                               │
│                                                               │
│                                                               │
│                                                               │
│                                                               │
└─────────────────────────────────────────────────────────────┘
```

Verse 17.

וַיַּעַן עֵלִי וַיֹּאמֶר parallels the opening of v 15. This form introduces Eli's response to Hannah.

Note that Eli's acceptance of Hannah's words, and of his own mistake, is stressed by the language of his response. He turns Hannah's אַל־תִּתֵּן, a negative statement referring to him, into יִתֵּן, a positive statement whose subject is God. That is, Eli's words convey not only that he should not have "taken" Hannah for a worthless woman, but also that he hopes that God will "take" (i.e., fulfill) her request.

For Further Thought

שֵׁלָתֵךְ is another case of a "missing א" (e.g., רֵשִׁית from the root ראש in Deut 11:12). Most of the cases of missing אs concern a final one (e.g., הַמֵּבִי in 2 Sam 5:2). Against this background, how do you analyze the name שְׁלְתִּיאֵל in Hag 2:2? (Cf. Hag 1:1.) Why do you think these אs were dropped?

Translate v 17.

```
┌─────────────────────────────────────────────────────────────┐
│                                                               │
│                                                               │
│                                                               │
│                                                               │
│                                                               │
└─────────────────────────────────────────────────────────────┘
```

Verse 18.

Verse 18a contains Hannah's response to Eli's last words. The form מָצָא חֵן בעיני‎ X (lit. "find favor in the eyes of X") occurs many times in the OT/HB. Here, as in 2 Sam 16:4 and Ruth 2:13, it is the response given by a person of lower rank or status to a superior who has made a promise to, or acted favorably toward, the inferior. This sense of ranking is stressed in this verse by the use of the word שִׁפְחָתְךָ.

The dialogue between Eli and Hannah ends here, and the narrator moves the narrative forward with וַתֵּלֶךְ, which removes Hannah from the scene.

וּפָנֶיהָ refers here to "her (distressed) expression."

Translate v 18.

```



```

Note that the reference to eating in v 18b provides a sharp contrast with v 7. The situation is reversed: Hannah is now able to eat, and she no longer wears her "crying" expression.

Verse 19.

Verse 19 contains a long chain of vav conversive–prefix (ויקטל) forms whose climax is in the last member of the chain.

Analyze וַיִּזְכְּרֶהָ (**?** K. 215; Gr. 71; Ke. 156–59; L. 271; S. 180; W. 130.)

Root	Stem	Form	PGN	SF	OS	BRM

Compare וַיִּזְכְּרֶהָ ה' with וּזְכַרְתַּנִי in v 11. Note the pattern of request and fulfillment.
. . . .
What kind of ה is the final one in הָרָמָתָה? . . . .
(**?** K. 47–48, 246–47; Gr.; Ke.; L.; S. 96; W. 66–67; → GKC §90 c–i, esp. 90 i; JM §93 c–f, esp. 93 c.)

Translate v 19.

```
┌─────────────────────────────────────────────────────┐
│                                                       │
│                                                       │
│                                                       │
│                                                       │
│                                                       │
└─────────────────────────────────────────────────────┘
```

Verse 20.

The events told in vv 20–28 of the narrative are separated from the preceding ones by a new temporal introduction (cf. v 1). Thus, the text is divided into two main narratives, with similar openings. Can you point to the new temporal introduction?

לִתְקֻפוֹת הַיָּמִים may best be translated as "at the turn of the year" (→ Exod 34:22). For הַיָּמִים conveying a sense of "year, yearly," see v 21.

The expression "Y- וַתִּקְרָא אֶת־שְׁמוֹ . . . וַתֵּלֶד בֵּן X- וַתַּהַר" is used in notes concerning the announcements of births (e.g., Gen 29:32–35; 38:3–4; Isa 8:3; 1 Chr 7:23; cf. Isa 7:14; Hos 1:3–8).

Note

It has been proposed that the phrase should be understood as "at the end of the period of gestation." If that were the case, וַתַּהַר should have been before the temporal clause. In fact, this Hebrew sequence is suggested by the Septuagint, but the Septuagint reading may well be the result of interpretation. In the Hebrew text וַתַּהַר follows the temporal clause.

שְׁמוּאֵל כִּי מֵה' שְׁאִלְתִּיו

Observe carefully the vowel markers in the word שְׁאִלְתִּיו. Instead of the expected pataḥ underneath the א one finds hireq. There are some qal affix (G perfect) verbs that show either hireq or tsere instead of the expected pataḥ when an object suffix is attached to them. An *i* class vowel (i.e., segol) also occurs in שְׁאֶלְתֶּם (see 1 Sam 12:13; 25:5; Job 21:29). (→ L. 267–68; S. 135; GKC §44 d.)

Translate v 20.

```
┌─────────────────────────────────────────────────────┐
│                                                       │
│                                                       │
│                                                       │
│                                                       │
│                                                       │
└─────────────────────────────────────────────────────┘
```

Note

The original meaning of the name שְׁמוּאֵל is probably "This name is El." It is by no means self-evident that such a name corresponds to שְׁאִלְתִּיו ("I requested him"). In fact, the word שְׁאִלְתִּיו suggests a name such as שָׁאוּל and not שְׁמוּאֵל. Indeed, there are scholars who think that the birth story of Samuel contains, at the very least, some elements of an original birth story of Saul. In any case, it seems likely that the writer and the community of readers were aware of the suggested reference to Saul. But had this been the only possible communal interpretation, then the message conveyed by the account of Hannah's naming the baby שְׁמוּאֵל would be almost irrelevant. A popular analysis of the name may have led to an interpretation such as "he who is from El" (cf. מוֹאָב, popularly understood as "from my father," see Gen 19:37; → McCarter, *1 Samuel*, 62). If the name שְׁמוּאֵל was understood as "he who is from El/God," the name would certainly underscore the pattern of request and fulfillment in the story (cf. v 19). According to this interpretation, the text states that Hannah has requested an offspring from the Lord, that Hannah bore a child "who is from El/God," and that Hannah is fully aware of that. (→ on biblical Hebrew names containing the name of the deity, see Fowler, *Theophoric Personal Names*.)

Verse 21.

The vav conversive–prefix (ויקטל) chain continues in v 21. The verb וַיַּעַל in v 22 agrees in person, gender, and number with Elkanah, but not with the entire subject of the sentence, that is, "Elkanah and all his house," i.e., his family. When the verb precedes such a compound subject, it often agrees in person, gender, and number with the first and closest noun (e.g., וַיָּבֹא נֹחַ וּבָנָיו in Gen 7:7; → GKC §146 f; JM §150 q).

The expression in this verse, זֶבַח הַיָּמִים, occurs only in the Book of Samuel (see 1 Sam 2:19; 20:6). Though יָמִים is translated as "days" on many occasions, it was understood as "year" in a few of its occurrences in the OT/HB, such as Lev 25:29 (see BDB יוֹם 6.c). Cf. v 20 above.

To whom does the suffix refer in the word נִדְרוֹ? . . . .

Translate v 21.

```



```

Note

The main figure in the compound subject is Elkanah. He opens the sentence, and his vow closes it. In English, you might express the distinction between Elkanah and "all his family" by placing "all his family" in apposition: "Elkanah, and all his family, . . . ". In the Hebrew text, an equivalent to these commas is the ṭifḥa markers (‿), which are one of the main dividers of clauses ending with atnaḥ (ׄ) or silluq + sof pasuq (: ׄ).

For Further Thought

Can you think of a reason for הָאִישׁ אֶלְקָנָה, instead of simply אֶלְקָנָה, following וַיַּעַל? Verse 8 may provide a clue. In addition, read Hos 2:18 (ET Hos 2:16). According to the text in Hosea, what was the common form by which wives addressed their husbands? What alternative mode of address does the text in Hosea suggest? How does Hos 2:18 help us understand 1 Sam 1:21?

Verse 22.

Verse 22 returns to Hannah. The vav introducing the verse is a classical case of adversative vav; it is to be translated as "but." The adversative vav may be seen as a special case of the disjunctive vav discussed in v 9. In both, there is a change or twist in the thread of the text, and the noun attached to the vav serves as the subject of a new clause. However, the adversative vav points to a contrast and should be translated as "but," whereas the disjunctive vav may mean "now" and not necessarily "but" (→ WO'C 8.3.b, p. 129).

Why does the text refer to Hannah's actions by verbs in the affix (perfect) form? . . . . .
. . . .
What kind of dagesh is the one in the ג of יִגָּמֵל? . . . .

Analyze the verb.

Root	Stem	Form	PGN	SF	OS	BRM

Why does the verb occur in prefix (imperfect) form? . . . .
. . . .
What kind of verbal chain do you find in Hannah's speech in v 22? How do you translate this chain? . . . .

Analyze וְנִרְאָה

Root	Stem	Form	PGN	SF	OS	BRM

Translate v 22 (**?** BDB).

For Further Thought

Hannah's words represent her reasons for not coming with the rest of the family to Shiloh. "I will stay" or "I will not go up" is the implied opening of Hannah's speech (before "until the boy be weaned"). **Ellipsis,** the omission of a word or phrase that can be reconstructed from the context, is a common figure of speech in the OT/HB (→ WO'C 11.4.3, pp. 223–25; Alonso Schökel, *Manual*, 166–68).

Note

The words of Hannah in v 22 are enclosed by two similar temporal עַדs. The difference between these two עַד phrases encapsulates the contents of her speech. The first phrase points to a specific time, "until the child be weaned"; the other points to the temporally unlimited "forever." The first sets the time limit for Hannah's being with the child, the second establishes the permanence of Hannah's gift to the Lord.

Verse 23.

The expression עשׂה הטוֹב בְּעֵינֵי-X occurs many times in the HB/OT. What does it mean? . . . . .
. . . .

Nowhere before is it said that Elkanah knows about Hannah's promise. He is described here not only as accepting Hannah's request that she and the lad remain in Ramah when the rest of the family makes its annual pilgrimage to Shiloh, but also as accepting that the child will remain in Shiloh, serving the Lord, for his lifetime.

Analyze גָּמְלֵךְ

Root	Stem	Form	PGN	SF	OS	BRM

How do you pronounce גָּמְלֵךְ? (**?** note on אָכְלָה, v 9.)

The word אַךְ has the restrictive meaning of "only." In English you expect a comma or a semicolon preceding a clause that opens with "only." A similar function is fulfilled by the disjunctive (i.e., separating) marker zaqef qaṭan (˙) above the word אֹתוֹ. Zaqef qaṭan divides atnaḥ clauses. Do you know another marker that divides atnaḥ clauses?

Analyze יָקֵם (**?** K. 400–401; Gr. 81; L. 231–32; S. 212, 287; W. 200; → GKC §72 aa and p. 524).

Root	Stem	Form	PGN	SF	OS	BRM

Translate v 23a.

For Further Thought

Though the translation of this half verse is simple, it seems to cause contextual problems. To which "word" of the Lord does Elkanah refer? None has been mentioned before. Of course, if instead of "his word" the text said "your word," it would read much more easily. This is the reading suggested by the Septuagint and by 4QSamᵃ (manuscript "a" of the Book of Samuel found in Cave 4 at Qumran; another manuscript, called "b," was also found in the same cave). Which reading is the original? To choose between the two alternatives you must ask yourself, Which is more likely?

(a) that questions about which "word of the Lord" Elkanah refers to brought about the reading "your word"; or

(b) that a contextually simple "your word" brought about the MT (masoretic text) reference to an unknown "word of the Lord"?

This "word of the Lord" is not the only "loose end" in the story: Elkanah's vow (v 21) is not explained or developed. In v 21 the Septuagint shows a longer reading: ". . . the yearly sacrifice, and his vows, and all the tithes of his land," which to a certain extent solves the question of the vow by making it a part of a common practice. In any case, if you find yourself unsure as to which alternative to prefer, you may take solace in knowing that many scholars find themselves in a similar situation (→ Tov, *Textual Criticism*, esp. 176).

The vav conversive–prefix (ויקטל) chain is resumed at the beginning of v 23b. From v 23b the narrative turns to describe the fulfillment of the words of Hannah, which have now been endorsed by Elkanah. The first part of this fulfillment is told in v 23b.

Analyze וַתֵּינֶק (**?** K. 397; Gr. 214; Ke. 345–46; S. 214; W. 269).

Root	Stem	Form	PGN	SF	OS	BRM

Translate v 23b.

Verse 24.

וַתַּעֲלֵהוּ עִמָּהּ

Who is the subject of the sentence? . . . .

Who is the only person actively involved in planning the fate of the lad? . . . .

. . . .

Analyze גְּמָלַתּוּ

Root	Stem	Form	PGN	SF	OS	BRM

Why is the object suffix in this verb תּוּ instead of הוּ as in the first verb? . . . .

. . . .

(→ Ke. 156; L. 266–67; S. 133, cf. S. 180–81; W. 123–25.)

Explain why the form of the first verb in this verse is different from the form of the second verb. . . . .

. . . .

When Hannah brings the lad she does not come empty-handed. The text lists the things that Hannah brings with her to the House of the Lord.

Translate v 24 up to the zaqef qatan (ˈ). (**?** BDB.)

For Further Thought

The Septuagint suggests a Hebrew reading בְּפַר מְשֻׁלָּשׁ, "with a three-year-old bull." (**?** BDB; if you do not find the reference to 1 Sam in BDB, analyze the verb מְשֻׁלָּשׁ and check for its meaning in BDB afterward.) This reading is supported by 4QSamᵃ and seems to be supported by הַפָּר in v 25 (but see below). The difference between the two alternative Hebrew texts rests mainly on whether the letter מ begins the word משלש or belongs to the end of the word בפרם. (Remember that the masoretic vocalized text was unknown by the time of the Second Temple, when the Septuagint and the Qumranic material were written, and that the distinction between final and medial mem was probably not made until the third century BCE). There are several occasions on which it seems that letters migrated from the end of one word to the beginning of another or vice versa (→ McCarter, *Textual Criticism*, 49–50).

Although the technical difference between the received Hebrew text and the Septuagint is relatively small, an analysis of these texts shows that it is not by chance that the Septuagint gives the line as saying one bull and the MT gives it as three bulls. It seems reasonable that the described offering was generally interpreted as a thanksgiving offering. Indeed, Hannah's list in both the Septuagint and 4QSamᵃ includes the word "bread," which may well be an attempt to solve possible tensions between this text and the rules in Lev 7:11–13 concerning thanksgiving offerings. If this is the case, the difference between the Septuagint and the Hebrew text concerns the number of the offerings. The Septuagint suggests one bull for all the family, or for Elkanah, who is, according to the Septuagint, the slaughterer of the bull (see below). The MT suggests one bull for each person—Hannah, Elkanah, and Samuel. Of course, both readings could have been the result of exegetical activity on the text. On the one hand, the amount of flour in Hannah's list could have been interpreted as suggesting three bulls (see Num 15:9; 28:12). On the other, the narrative that follows seems to refer to one bull (v 25), and the sacrifice of three-year-old animals was a known custom (Gen 15:9). Thus, a one-bull reading could have been supported.

In any case, the Septuagint's reading is congruent with its tendency to stress the role of Elkanah and diminish that of Hannah (e.g., "his father slew his offering which he offered from year to year to the Lord; and he brought the child near and slew the calf"), while the MT emphasizes Hannah's role (→ Walters, "Hannah and Anna"). In other words, it seems that the main textual differences between these two texts are not the result of random scribal mistakes, but rather of conscious exegesis.

Translate v 24 from the zaqef qaṭan (˙) to the end of the verse.

```



```

Note the "modern" spelling of Shiloh. (See note on v 3.) This spelling occurs several times in the OT/HB (e.g., Judg 21:21; 1 Sam 3:21b; Jer 7:14), and it reflects an advanced stage in the development of a system of markers for vowels in biblical Hebrew. Originally ה was a marker (*mater lectionis*) of any final vowel except *i* and *u*. Later, the final *o* began to be marked by ו. Other examples of final ה/ו spellings include נכו in Jer 46:2 and 2 Chr, and נכה in 2 Kings.

The stress on the word נַעַר in v 24b is self-evident. Although נַעַר as predicate complement does not mean something different from נַעַר as subject of the sentence, the repetition underscores that Hannah is about to give up her son to the Lord, despite his being a very young child who was just weaned. (→ on weaning age, see Meyers, *Discovering Eve*, 151, 206 n30.)

Verse 25.

Who is the subject of the second verb in v 25? . . . .

Do you think that Hannah is included in the subject of the second verb? . . . .
. . . .
Who else besides Hannah might be included in this subject? . . . .
Why? . . . .

Who is the subject of the first verb in v 25? . . . .

If the subject of the first verb in v 25 is the same as the subject of the second verb, then Hannah, a woman, is described as having an active role in the making of the sacrifice. (This position is clearly attested in some traditional Jewish interpretations of the text; moreover, according to one of them, the boy Samuel taught on this occasion that the slaughter of the sacrifice can be done by nonpriests, by women, and even by slaves.) Alternatively, the subject of the first verb may be an impersonal "they" (→ WO'C 4.4.2, p. 71), with the chain of vav conversive–prefix (ויקטל) forms carrying the thread of the narrative but not necessarily referring to the same people in each instance. A third position is that the text is ambiguous. No matter what position you choose, it is worth noting that the verbal plural forms are preceded and followed by a chain of verbal forms whose subject is Hannah. Whether Hannah took part in the sacrifice or not, the thread of the narrative closely follows her actions.

For Further Thought

הַפָּר is commonly translated as "the bull," implying "one bull." This understanding of הַפָּר may be seen as support for the Hebrew reading suggested by the Septuagint (בְּפַר מְשֻׁלָּשׁ, for the other two bulls are not mentioned in v 25) or as its justification (since only one bull is mentioned in v 25, ancient interpreters concluded that v 24 has to refer to one bull instead of three). The translation itself, however, is far from secure. Though it is grammatically correct, it is not the only possible understanding of הַפָּר. Several times in the OT/HB, a definite singular noun that is preceded by the same noun in the plural refers to the group or collective expressed by the plural noun. (For instance, in Num 21:6–7, אֶת הַנְּחָשִׁים . . . אֶת־הַנָּחָשׁ, "the serpents.") Thus, הַפָּר may also be translated as "the bulls," and accordingly the apparent tension between v 24 and v 25 disappears (→ Ratner, "Three Bulls or One? A Reappraisal of 1 Samuel 1,24").

Translate v 25.

```



```

Verse 26.

בִּי אֲדֹנִי (and the similar בִּי אֲדֹנִי) is a phrase that conveys the sense of "pardon me, my Lord." It is used as an opening for direct speech to a person higher in status than the speaker. It has been suggested that it conveys the sense of "on me be any guilt" (❓ BDB; → JM §105 c; WO'C 40.2.3.a, pp. 680–81).

חֵי נַפְשְׁךָ אֲדֹנִי is a specific case of a very common introduction formula to oaths in biblical Hebrew. The general formula is X־חֵי, in which X may be the speaker (חַי־אָנִי), a person of higher status than the speaker, or the Lord (❓ K. 304; Gr. 185; L. 172; S. 233; BDB; → JM §165, esp. 165 e; WO'C 40.2.2, pp. 678–80). But can you find the oath in this verse? . . . .

This formula has also a secondary use as an asseverative. If this is the case in our verse, the phrase may be translated "by your life, my Lord, indeed . . . " Do you think that this translation suits its context? . . . .
. . . .

עִמְכָה is an alternative spelling for עִמְּךָ. It is attested nowhere else in the MT.

For Further Thought

The pronominal suffix ךָ is frequently spelled כה in Qumran scrolls. The MT of the Book of Samuel shows several rare, long, full spellings, such as עִמְכָה, that are well attested in Qumranic material, and that can be considered "modern" spellings. To illustrate, עָשִׂיתָה occurs only eight times in the OT/HB, of which seven occurrences are in Samuel, and this form is common in

Qumran. The Book of Kings, which is the thematic continuation of the Book of Samuel, shows a very conservative spelling. What does this fact suggest to you? (→ Andersen and Forbes, *Spelling in the Hebrew Bible*; on Qumranic orthography, see Qimron, *Hebrew of the Dead Sea Scrolls*.)

The demonstrative זֶה is used idiomatically in the expression בָּזֶה. It is a good idea to check the meaning of idiomatic expressions in BDB.

Translate v 26.

Verses 27–28.

Translate v 27a.

Note the emphatic word order at the beginning of the sentence.

Translate v 27b.

Note that the pattern of supplication, followed by God's fulfillment of the request, characterizes both this verse and the entire story. The related pattern of Hannah's promise and her fulfillment of her promise is central to this part of the narrative and comes to the forefront in v 28. These two patterns are linked not only by a certain symmetry and by the opening וְגַם at the beginning of the next verse, but also by the stressed rhetorical repetition of words from the root שאל. Note the reference back to v 20, in which the reasons for Hannah's naming the boy Samuel are explained, emphasizing her awareness that the boy represents God's fulfillment of her request.

Analyze הִשְׁאִלְתִּהוּ in v 28. (❓ K. 133, 149, 215; Gr. 61–62, 71; Ke. 153, 253; L. 213–14,

266–67; S. 120–22, 133; W. 112–15, 124; → about א instead of the expected אֲ in הִשְׁאִלְתִּהוּ, see GKC §64f.)

Root	Stem	Form	PGN	SF	OS	BRM

Note the use of the affix (perfect) form הָיָה in the clause כָּל־הַיָּמִים אֲשֶׁר הָיָה, which may convey a sense of the future perfect, i.e., "all the days he shall be" (WO'C 30.5.2.b, p. 491), or probably better, this affix (perfect) form points to a situation extending from the present to the future—a persistent future perfective (→ WO'C 30.5.1.e, pp. 489–90).

Note that the temporal clause is demarcated by two zaqef qaṭan (֔) markers.

Analyze וַיִּשְׁתַּחוּ (**?** K. 182, 361–62; Gr. 141; L. 254–55; S. 230–32; → WO'C 21.2.3.d, pp. 360–61, JM §59 b,g; cf. GKC §75 kk.)

Root	Stem	Form	PGN	SF	OS	BRM

Who is the one who is bowing down worshiping the Lord? . . . .

Note

Some MT manuscripts read יִשְׁתַּחוּ instead of וַיִּשְׁתַּחוּ. How does this reading change the meaning of the sentence? . . . .

. . . .

Who now is bowing down and worshiping the Lord? . . . .
4QSamᵃ reads [ו]תשתחו. How would you translate this reading? . . . .

. . . .

Who is the one who is bowing down and worshiping the Lord in this reading? . . . .

. . . .

Translate v 28.

Translate the entire chapter, incorporating your new understandings of the text.

For Further Reading

For an evaluation of the role of 1 Sam 1 in the overall narrative concerning the birth of the monarchy in Israel, see Brueggemann, "I Samuel 1: A Sense of a Beginning."

Several times in this discussion we have touched on textual questions. For an introduction to different scholarly approaches to these issues, see Barthélemy, Hurst, Lohfink, et al., *Preliminary and Interim Report,* ix–xvii; Albrektson, "Difficilior Lectio Probabilior," which is a partial critique of Barthélemy et al.; McCarter, *Textual Criticism;* and Würthwein, *Text,* 103–17, esp. 116–17. For a comprehensive study on this topic, see Tov, *Textual Criticism.*

Works Cited in This Section

D. Aberbach, "מנה אחת אפים (1 Sam. I 5): A New Interpretation," *VT* 24 (1974): 350–53; **B. Albrektson,** "Difficilior Lectio Probabilior. A Rule of Textual Criticism and its Use in Old Testament Studies," in B. Albrektson et al., *Remembering all the Way* (OTS 21; Leiden: E. J. Brill, 1981), 5–18; **L. Alonso Schökel,** *A Manual of Hebrew Poetics* (Subsidia Biblica 11; Roma: Editrice Pontificio Istituto Biblico, 1988); **F. I. Andersen and A. D. Forbes,** *Spelling in the Hebrew Bible* (BibOr 41; Rome: Biblical Institute Press, 1986); **D. Barthélemy, A. R. Hurst, N. Lohfink, et al.,** *Preliminary and Interim Report on the Hebrew Old Testament Text Project* (5 vols.; New York: United Bible Societies, 1979/80); **A. Berlin,** *The Dynamics of Biblical Parallelism* (Bloomington: Indiana University Press, 1985); **W. Brueggemann,** "I Samuel 1: A Sense of a Beginning," *ZAW* 102 (1990): 33–48; **J. D. Fowler,** *Theophoric Personal Names in Ancient Hebrew* (JSOTSup 49; Sheffield: JSOT Press, 1988); **J. L. Kugel,** *The Idea of Biblical Poetry* (New Haven: Yale University Press, 1981); **P. Kyle McCarter, Jr.,** *1 Samuel* (AB 8; New York: Doubleday, 1980); *Textual Criticism: Recovering the Text of the Hebrew Bible* (Philadelphia: Fortress, 1986); **C. Meyers,** *Discovering Eve: Ancient Israelite Women in Context* (New York and Oxford: Oxford University Press, 1988); **E. Qimron,** *The Hebrew of the Dead Sea Scrolls* (HSS 29; Atlanta: Scholars, 1986); **R. Ratner,** "Three Bulls or One? A Reappraisal of 1 Samuel 1,24," *Bib* 68 (1987): 98–102; **E. Tov,** *Textual Criticism of the Hebrew Bible* (Minneapolis: Fortress; Aassen/Maastricht: Van Gorcum, 1992); **S. D. Walters,** "Hannah and Anna: The Hebrew and Greek Texts of 1 Samuel 1," *JBL* 107 (1988): 385–412; **E. Würthwein,** *The Text of the Old Testament: An Introduction to the Biblia Hebraica* (Grand Rapids, Mich.: Eerdmans, 1979).

1.2   2 Kings 14:23–29

We now move from narrative to a passage of quite formulaic historical writing. This brief summation of the reign of King Jeroboam II is similar to summaries written at the end of the narratives concerning each of the kings of Israel and Judah. Although this passage will challenge your ability to read biblical Hebrew, once you have encountered the style and structure of this kind of historical note, you will have much more confidence in tackling the historical books of the HB/OT.

Most of the accounts about the various kings of Judah and Israel in the Book of Kings follow a basic outline:

(a) an opening and connecting formula, introducing the account and connecting it to the ongoing text (such as "In the second year of King Joash son of Joahaz of Israel, King Amaziah son of Joash became king," in 2 Kgs 14:1);

(b) an evaluative comment, based on the formula, "He [the king] did what was right/evil in the eyes of YHWH";

(c) a report about the deeds of the king concerning the cult (not always given);

(d) reports on special events that occurred during the kingship of the relevant king (not always given);

(e) a concluding and transitional formula, such as "the rest of the acts . . . and X slept with his fathers, and was buried . . . and Y, his son, reigned. . ." (→ Ben Zvi, "Account," esp. 357–58.)

Verse 23.

בִּשְׁנַת חֲמֵשׁ־עֶשְׂרֵה שָׁנָה

This phrase is the opening and connecting formula. The formula "בִּשְׁנַת + number + שָׁנָה" and the related formula "בְּיוֹם + number + יוֹם" are regularly used when the number is higher than ten. (→ WO'C 15.3.2b–c, pp. 285–86.) Beyond the first ten digits Hebrew does not have special ordinal numbers, such as רִאשׁוֹן and עֲשִׂירִי ("first" and "tenth"). Instead, the cardinal numbers are used as ordinals as well. (**?** K. 219; Gr. 180; Ke. 96–100; L. 219, 223, 228; S 203, 205; W. 242–45; → GKC §97, 98, 134; JM §142 o.)

לַאֲמַצְיָהוּ בֶן־יוֹאָשׁ

Why does the text read לַאֲמַצְיָהוּ instead of לְאֲמַצְיָהוּ? (**?** Gr. 28; Ke. 29; L. 22–23; S. 32; W. 10, 27–28; → GKC §102 d; JM §103 b.)

Note the merka (ֽ) in the word אֲמַצְיָהוּ. This is a conjunctive accent that links אֲמַצְיָהוּ and בֶּן־יוֹאָשׁ. Grammatically, בֶּן־יוֹאָשׁ is a definite construct noun chain that identifies Amaziahu. He is not any possible Amaziahu, but a specific one: Amaziahu, the son of Joash.

Note

Many Hebrew names consist of a short verbal sentence. The subject of the sentence tends to be a noun standing for God. When the name yhwh stands at the beginning of a personal name, it appears as either יוֹ or יְהוֹ; when it stands at the end, it appears as either יָהוּ or יָה. The verb in the name is generally in either the affix form or the prefix form. When the verb in the name is affix, it is usually translated by an English present perfect (such as נְתַנְיָהוּ, "yhwh has given"). When the verb in the name is in the prefix form, it is usually translated by an English present tense or by a wish formula (such as יִשְׁמָעֵאל, "God/El hears" or "may God/El hear").

Analyze the name אֲמַצְיָהוּ . . . .

Translate the short verbal sentence that the name אֲמַצְיָהוּ stands for. (? BDB.) . . . .
. . . .

Translate the short verbal sentence that the name יוֹאָשׁ stands for. (The root אושׁ probably means "to bestow.") . . . .
. . . .

Note

The naming of King Amaziahu, son of Joash, at the outset of the summary of the reign of King Jeroboam links this account with that of the deeds of King Amaziahu, which precedes it (vv 17–20). This is one of the ways in which an account is connected to preceding ones and by which the ongoing text is given a measure of unity.

The phrase מֶלֶךְ יְהוּדָה following בֶּן־יוֹאָשׁ is set apart by two disjunctive markers, ṭifḥa and atnaḥ. It should be translated between two commas. The atnaḥ here indicates the end of the temporal clause that opens the account.

מָלַךְ יָרָבְעָם

Analyze מָלַךְ.

Root	Stem	Form	PGN	SF	OS	BRM

מָלַךְ should not be translated as "reigned" but as "became king." מלך (Qal) points either to the status of being a king or to a person's becoming a king (→ JM §111 h, for a more detailed analysis and a slightly different approach).

How should you pronounce the name יָרָבְעָם: *yarob'am* or *yarab'am*? (**?** see our discussion of אָכְלָה in 1 Sam 1:9; → GKC §9 u; JM §6 l–n.) The name יָרָבְעָם stands for a sentence that may mean, "May the people become many." Explain why this is a possible understanding of this name. . . . .

. . . .

אַרְבָּעִים וְאַחַת שָׁנָה

When enumerating items, if the number is between 21 and 99 and the noun follows the number, then the noun tends to occur in the singular, as it does here. You may compare this with שֶׁבַע וְעֶשְׂרִים וּמֵאָה מְדִינָה (Esth 1:1). If, however, the noun precedes the number, then the noun will occur in the plural (e.g., Josh 21:41; cf. עָרִים שֵׁשׁ in Josh 15:59). (→ on these aspects of the use of the Hebrew cardinal numbers, see JM §104 c–k; WO'C 15.2.4–5, pp. 280–83.)

Translate v 23.

┌───┐
│   │
│   │
│   │
│   │
│   │
└───┘

The next verse contains the evaluative comment and reflects on Jeroboam's attitude to the cult. (See [b] and [c] in the outline for formulaic accounts discussed above.)

Verse 24.

וַיַּעַשׂ הָרַע בְּעֵינֵי ה'

This formula occurs word for word eighteen times in the Book of Kings (e.g., 1 Kgs 15:26,34; 22:53, 2 Kgs 8:18; 2 Kgs 24:9,19) and another eight times in accounts that are parallel to those in Kings (e.g., Jer 52:2; 2 Chr 36:9,12).

You might expect to find the definite direct object (hereafter DDO) marker (i.e., אֶת) before הָרַע. In a similar context at Judg 2:11a you will find the DDO. But it is worth remembering that the DDO marker does not always appear before a definite direct object, and that this is the case even in material that cannot be characterized as poetry. (The DDO marker is often missing in biblical Hebrew poetry.) In this frequent formula, the DDO marker does not occur. אֶת also tends to be omitted before other definite abstract nouns, such as הַטּוֹב and הַיָּשָׁר (cf. Deut 6:18). (→ on אֶת, see JM §125 e–ia; for a more comprehensive analysis, see Muraoka, *Emphatic Words*, 146–58.)

For Further Thought

Why does the formula read הָרַע instead of simply רַע? Abstract nouns *may* take the definite article. In some cases, its presence may suggest that the abstract noun itself was seen as determinate, though other explanations for the presence of the article may be possible. In other cases, it signifies that in a certain context a certain abstract noun is determinate. For instance, one reads רָעָה in 1 Kgs 21:21, but הָרָעָה a few verses later in the same section (v 28). Do they convey different meanings? Yes. The first one is indeterminate, but the second one is clearly determinate because it refers to the evil already mentioned in the report. (→ Barr, " 'Determination' and the Definite Article," esp. 318; cf. שׁוֹר in Exod 21:28a, but הַשּׁוֹר in Exod 21:28b.)

The question in 2 Kgs 14:24 is whether הָרַע points to "evil" as an abstract, general term or to "the evil," i.e., a particular evil. Zevit and others think in terms of a specific evil, but most scholars prefer to translate הָרַע בְּעֵינֵי ה' as "what was/is evil in the eyes of the LORD." A decision in this respect has significant implications for the understanding of the Book of Kings, because one cannot disassociate the meaning of הָרַע בְּעֵינֵי ה' in this verse from its meaning in the whole series of occurrences of וַיַּעַשׂ הָרַע בְּעֵינֵי ה'. Only on the basis of a general understanding of the Book of Kings, and against the background of all the occurrences of וַיַּעַשׂ הָרַע בְּעֵינֵי ה' in that book, can one decide whether הָרַע refers to a generalized evil or to a concrete action or set of actions taken by the king.

If you follow most scholars and prefer to translate הָרַע בְּעֵינֵי ה' as "what was/is evil in the eyes of the LORD," would you choose "is" or "was"? On what grounds? Would this choice make a difference in your understanding of the religious thought of the writer of the text?

Analyze סָר (**?** K. 129–31; Gr. 78–80; Ke. 316–22; L. 59–60; S. 103–4; W. 196–98.)

Root	Stem	Form	PGN	SF	OS	BRM

Notice the way the אֲשֶׁר clause functions to achieve rhetorical emphasis. אֲשֶׁר clauses usually answer the question, "which?" In this case, the identity of Jeroboam, the son of Nebat, is clear. The answer to the implied question "which/who?" by the אֲשֶׁר clause serves a clear rhetorical purpose: *which* Jeroboam, the son of Nebat is this? "The one who . . . "

Analyze הֶחֱטִיא (**?** K. 137, 394; Gr. 108–11; Ke. 225–29; L. 213–14; S. 122; W. 157.)

Root	Stem	Form	PGN	SF	OS	BRM

Why does the ה in הָרְמִיא have a composite shewa (ḥaṭaf-segol)? (❓ K. 230; Gr. 22; Ke. 23–24; L. xx–xxi; S. 11; W. 10; → GKC §22 m–p.)

Notice the use of the affix form in the אֲשֶׁר clause. It points to a pluperfect past, that is, to actions or states seen as completed at or before a past time to which the speaker is referring.

Translate v 24.

For Further Thought

"Israel" in v 24 certainly refers to the people of the northern kingdom. What other connotations might the term have? How might the text be read differently depending upon which specific connotation is foregrounded?

The account of Jeroboam now moves on to a report of significant events during his reign (vv 25–27). A reference is made to his military success, with a theological explanation of its causes and results.

Verse 25.

Analyze הֵשִׁיב (❓ K. 137; Gr. 81; Ke. 324; L. 231–32; S. 126; W. 200.)

Root	Stem	Form	PGN	SF	OS	BRM

How do you translate מִלְּבוֹא חֲמָת?

Note

There are two main ways of understanding מִלְּבוֹא חֲמָת:

(a) It may be translated as "from Lebo-hamath," where Lebo-hamath points to a city in the northern Beqaa valley which stood at the place of modern Lebweh, close to the southern border of Hamath with Aram and well north from Damascus (about 40 miles; → Aharoni, *Land of the Bible,* 72–73; Cogan and Tadmor, *II Kings,* 160–61).

(b) It may be translated as "from the entrance/entering (לבוא) of Hamath" (cf. 1 Chr 5:9; 2 Chr 26:8; → WO'C 36.2.3.d, pp. 607–8) which may be understood as "from the entrance of (the city of) Hamath," but more likely refers to the southern border of Hamath in general or, perhaps more precisely, to the Beqaa valley, which leads north to Hamath. In the latter case מִלְּבוֹא חֲמָת would point to the southern border of the valley, to a place relatively close to biblical Dan many miles south of Lebo-hamath (→ Miller and Hayes, *History*, 307–8).

Translate literally יָם הָעֲרָבָה . . . .

The article before עֲרָבָה changes it from a common noun into a definite, "unique" noun which functions as a proper name. (See גִּבְעָה, hill; הַגִּבְעָה, The Hill = Giveah; → WO'C 13.6, p. 249; cf. JM §137 b). The sea referred to here is most likely the Dead Sea. Can you identify another instance in this verse of naming a place by means of the definite article? . . . .
. . . .

There are two אֲשֶׁר clauses, the second standing within the first. The idea, of course, is to identify clearly "the word of the Lord" referred to by the text, first by showing its relation to a certain prophet and then by specifying who this prophet is.

Translate v 25.

For Further Thought

The writer(s) of this text explicitly refer to Jeroboam's conquests in terms of restoration (הֵשִׁיב). In other words, they claim that Jeroboam (and perhaps indirectly God, since Jeroboam is only fulfilling a prophecy) is not conquering foreign lands but bringing back to Israel territories that had been and should be its. When, according to the narrative, had these territories been Israel's? (**?** 1 Kgs 8:65.)

Verses 26–27.

These verses explain what may have seemed to the audience of this text to be absurd, namely, that the Lord would lead a sinful king, Jeroboam II, to great military success. On the surface, the explanation is that Jeroboam's military success is the fulfillment of a divine word given to a legitimate prophet. But is this the real reason, according to the writer(s) of this text, that God allowed Jeroboam to succeed? The answer to this question is in these two verses.

עֱנִי

This is a noun. What is the root? . . . .

If you have trouble finding the root, mark the consonants in this word. How many are there? . . . .

Is one consonant "missing"? . . . . Which may it be? . . . .

Now write the root. . . . .

Go to BDB and learn about the general meaning of this root. You will find that BDB mentions four **homonymic roots** (i.e., roots that are written the same but whose meanings differ from one another). The root you are working with is the third one (III) in BDB. Homonymic roots occur a significant number of times in biblical Hebrew. In most cases, context reveals to which of two or more homonymic roots a certain word belongs. (For more on homonyms, see our discussion of Prov 3:24; → on עֱנִי, from a grammatical perspective, see JM §88E b, 96D c.)

Analyze מֹרֶה

Root	Stem	Form	PGN	SF	OS	BRM

If you thought that this is an hif'il participle of ירה you have not made a grammatical error. But in this case מֹרֶה is a participle from another root. Try again. (**?** K. 127; Gr. 88–91; Ke. 287; L. 35; S. 46–47; W. 217.) . . . .

If you render this מֹרֶה as "rebellious," you may find your translation of the full sentence to be somewhat awkward. Many scholars have suggested emendations to the text at this point. The translators of the Septuagint, who are supported by most of the ancient versions, may have had a Hebrew text that reads differently from the present text—perhaps מר הוא (that is מָר הוּא) instead of מרה (that is מֹרֶה)—remember that the biblical text had no vowel markers, except those signaled by consonants, until about the seventh century CE; → JM §1 a–b; WO'C 1.5, pp. 15–22, esp. 1.5.4d, pp. 21–22.

How would you translate מָר הוּא? . . . .

Compare your "new" translation to the one in the English Bible you are using. (→ Cogan and Tadmor, *II Kings*, 161; Hobbs, *2 Kings*, 176.)

Analyze עָצוּר (**?** K. 179; Gr. 56; Ke. 195; L. 157–58; S. 214–16; W. 84–85; → JM §88E c, 121 o; WO'C 5.3d, p. 88.)

Root	Stem	Form	PGN	SF	OS	BRM

Analyze עָזוּב

Root	Stem	Form	PGN	SF	OS	BRM

Analyze עֵזֶר

Root	Stem	Form	PGN	SF	OS	BRM

עָזוּב occurs only five times in the OT/HB, and always as the second element in the pair עָצוּר - עָזוּב. The pair is generally translated as "bound and free" and is understood as a **merismus,** a literary device by which the mention of two representative components of a whole stands for the whole itself: "old and young," for example, may represent the entire range of age (→ Alonso Schökel, *Manual*, 83–84). Thus, it is considered to be a reference to the full spectrum of Israelite society.

Note

Talmon and Fields, in "The Collocation משתין בקיר ועצור ועזוב and Its Meaning," challenge this consensus and propose that this pair should be understood as a **hendiadys,** the use of two apparently separate words to express an idea (as in the English expression "nice and warm"). They claim that the pair should be understood together as "ruler" or "leader."

Translate vv 25–26:

Before going on, please take time to notice the pattern of alliteration of dominant sounds and the rhyme within this series of three participles (→ Alonso Schökel, *Manual*, 20–26), as well as the emphatic repetition of the word אֶפֶס. Do you think that these features helped the text to convey its message? Please also take into account the movement from passive participles to a final active participle at the end of the verse. What is the effect of this grammatical shift? Isn't the closing expression of the verse ("there was no helper for [no one to help] Israel") a kind of invitation to the response of v 27, namely, that the Lord is Israel's helper?

Verse 27.

Analyze לִמְחוֹת (**?** K. 123; Gr. 89; Ke. 287; L. 143–44; S. 188; W. 216–18.)

Root	Stem	Form	PGN	SF	OS	BRM

Analyze וַיּוֹשִׁיעֵם (**?** K. 148–49, 215; Gr. 71, 93–95; Ke. 157–58, 343–44; L. 222, 271; S. 180, 210; W. 130, 189–91.)

Root	Stem	Form	PGN	SF	OS	BRM

Translate v 27.

Notice the theological precision of this verse. Jeroboam may have won battles, but he is not the savior of Israel; the Lord is the one who delivers Israel. Jeroboam's success only shows that the Lord may deliver Israel even "by the hand" of a king who does what is evil in the Lord's sight.

Verses 28–29.

The account of the reign of Jeroboam II now comes to an end. Verses 28–29 contain the concluding and transitional formula of this report.

Translate וְיֶתֶר דִּבְרֵי יָרָבְעָם וְכָל־אֲשֶׁר עָשָׂה

This is the most common way of introducing the citation formula, which concludes most of the individual reports in the Book of Kings, where it occurs twenty times (e.g., 1 Kgs 11:41; 14:29;

22:39; 2 Kgs 8:23; 12:20; 15:6,21,26,31). This formula includes the introduction, which you have just translated, a short reference to a characteristic feature of the reign of the specific king, and a reference to the "book of chronicles of the kings of Israel/Judah" (→ Long, *2 Kings*, 320).

The language of the rest of v 28 remains formulaic. Concluding notes in the accounts of the different kings may include a reference to גְּבוּרָתוֹ אֲשֶׁר־נִלְחָם (see 1 Kgs 22:46; 2 Kgs 13:12; 14:15; cf. 1 Kgs 16:5; 2 Kgs 10:34; 20:20).

Note

גְּבוּרָה is a feminine noun following the קְטוּל pattern of nouns (cf. אֱמוּנָה, "faithfulness"; → GKC 84 p; JM §88E h). Many feminine nouns express abstract ideas, such as גְּבוּרָה, "might." There is a group of feminine nouns including many abstract and collective names that has the same vowels as גְּבוּרָה and a doubling of the last consonant, e.g., יְרֻשָּׁה, "possession" (→ JM §88C k; WO'C 5.5.b, p. 90; Mettinger, "Nominal Pattern *qᵉtulla*"). Does גְּבוּרָה belong to this group? Remember that ר, as a rule, cannot be doubled. If גְּבוּרָה does belong to the same group as יְרֻשָּׁה, what compensatory change in the vowel preceding the ר would you expect? (**?** analyze מְבֹרָךְ; K. 347, 360, 380, 399; Gr. 108; Ke. 23, 250; L. xx–xxi, 205–6; S. 22, 246; W. 16, 20, 168–69; → GKC §64 e; JM §69 a.)

Translate גְּבוּרָתוֹ אֲשֶׁר־נִלְחָם ....

הֲלֹא־הֵם . . .

הֲלֹא is a combination of the interrogative הֲ and לֹא. A literal translation of הֲלֹא־הֵם . . . would be "are they not . . .?" This is a rhetorical question. הֲלֹא is meant to convey an emphatic statement, something like, "They are indeed . . . "

Translate v 28b (from the atnaḥ to the sof-pasuq).

> [empty box]

Verse 28b consists of another formulaic expression that occurs many times in Kings (for exactly the same wording, see 1 Kgs 15:31; 16:5; 16:20,27; 2 Kgs 14:15; → concerning the nature of the chronicle, see Jones, *1 and 2 Kings* I, 61–64).

For Further Thought

Do you find a difference between the claims made in vv 28 and 25? Is the reference to "for Judah in Israel" awkward? (→ Jones, *1 and 2 Kings*, II, 516–17; Cogan and Tadmor, *II Kings*, 161–62.)

Translate v 29.

Verse 29 contains a variant of the typical closing and transitional formula found in Kings. Compare v 29 with a number of other formulaic closings (**?** 1 Kgs 16:28; 22:40; 2 Kgs 10:35; 14:16; 15:22; 20:21). What elements are included in v 29 that some of the other passages do not contain, and vice versa? . . . .

Translate the entire text of 2 Kgs 14:23–29.

Works Cited in This Section

Y. Aharoni, *The Land of the Bible* (Philadelphia: Westminster, 1979); **L. Alonso Schökel,** *A Manual of Hebrew Poetics* (Subsidia Biblica 11; Roma: Editrice Pontificio Istituto Biblico, 1988); **J. Barr,** " 'Determination' and the Definite Article in Biblical Hebrew," *JSS* 34 (1989): 307–37; **E. Ben Zvi,** "The Account of the Reign of Manasseh in II Reg 21,1–18 and the Redactional History of the Book of Kings," *ZAW* 103 (1991): 355–74; **M. Cogan and H. Tadmor,** *II Kings* (AB 11; Garden City, N.Y.: Doubleday, 1988); **T. R. Hobbs,** *2 Kings* (WBC; Waco, Tex.: Word Book, 1985); **G. H. Jones,** *1 and 2 Kings* (2 vols., NCB; Grand Rapids, Mich.: Eerdmans, 1984); **B. O. Long,** *2 Kings* (FOTL 10; Grand Rapids, Mich.: Eerdmans, 1991); **J. Maxwell Miller and J. H. Hayes,** *A History of Ancient Israel and Judah* (Philadelphia: Westminster, 1986); **T. N. D. Mettinger,** "The Nominal Pattern *qᵉtulla* in Biblical Hebrew," *JSS* 16 (1971): 2–14; **T. Muraoka,** *Emphatic Words and Structures in Biblical Hebrew* (Jerusalem/Leiden: Magnes/E. J. Brill, 1985); **Sh. Talmon and W. W. Fields,** "The Collocation משתין בקיר ועצור ועזוב and Its Meaning," *ZAW* 101 (1989): 85–112; **Z. Zevit,** "Deuteronomistic Historiography in 1 Kings 12–2 Kings 17 and the Reinvestiture of the Israelian Cult," *JSOT* 32 (1985): 57–73.

2. Readings in Legal Literature

2.1 Exodus 21:28–36

Our first reading in biblical law is a portion concerning the responsibility for the actions of a dangerous animal: the goring ox. It points out some important elements of the concept of society which underlies many biblical laws. As such, the laws regarding the goring ox provide a fine introduction to the literature of biblical law (→ Patrick, "Studying Biblical Law as Humanities," 27–47).

Legal principles and laws are generally presented in two forms in the OT/HB:

—by an unqualified statement of the governing rule (**apodeictic** formulation), such as "he who strikes his father or his mother shall be put to death" (Exod 21:15);

—by a case (**casuistic** formulation), such as "if a man gives money or goods to another for safekeeping, and they are stolen . . . if the thief is caught, then . . . if the thief is not caught, then . . . " (Exod 22:6–7) (→ Rendtorff, *Old Testament*, 90–94).

Exod 21:28–36 is a good example of a casuistic formulation. Such a formulation in English would be structured in terms of "if" (or "when") clauses and "then" clauses. In biblical Hebrew, the main "if" (or "when") clause is marked by כִּי; the secondary or subsidiary "if" clauses are generally introduced by אִם. Context, often in addition to some grammatical markers, indicates the beginning of the "then" clause. In many cases, the separation between the "if" clause (**protasis**) and the "then" clause (**apodosis**) is also marked by atnaḥ or by another main disjunctive marker.

Verse 28.

וְכִי־יִגַּח שׁוֹר

The vav provides a link between the new section and the preceding one. כִּי points to the beginning of the main "if" clause. In this kind of legal material, a verb in the prefix form and in the third person immediately follows כִּי (here יִגַּח). The subject governing this verb is explicitly mentioned after it.

Analyze יִגַּח (**?** K. 77–80; Gr. 103–4; Ke. 304; L. 133–34; S. 150–51; W. 141–42.)

Root	Stem	Form	PGN	SF	OS	BRM

אֶת־אִישׁ אוֹ אֶת־אִשָּׁה

Should אִשָּׁה be translated as "woman" or "his wife"? Is there any grammatical indication of the correct reading, in the form of the presence or absence of markers? . . . .
. . . .
(**?** K. 65, 248; Gr. 20 n.1, 67; Ke. 436; L. xxv, 31; S. 9, 54; W. 17, 52; see also our discussion of וַיַּחְשְׁבֶהָ in 1 Sam 1:13.)

Note that this Hebrew equivalent of the English "either . . . or . . . " two-member formula contains only one אוֹ. A multimember formula would have אוֹ before every member but the first (e.g., Exod 22:9; → on biblical Hebrew equivalents to "either . . . or . . . " and related expressions, see JM §175). In general within the legal material the אוֹ formula may be seen as a supplementary note whose aim is to clarify the scope of the law. For instance, had this text been וְכִי־יִגַּח שׁוֹר אֶת־אִישׁ וָמֵת, one could have interpreted it as referring only to the case in which an ox gores a man, not covering a case in which an ox gores a woman. (→ Num 30:3–4; → Fishbane, *Biblical Interpretation*, 170–71).

Are אִישׁ and אִשָּׁה definite nouns? If not, how do you explain the presence of the DDO marker, אֶת־ (or אֵת)? Remember that אֵת does not occur before every definite direct object (**?** see our discussion of 2 Kgs 14:24), and that it may occur before some non-definite direct objects, as is the case here.

Note

The occurrence of אֵת in this verse has been explained in various ways. It has been proposed that the reason for its presence is that

(a) it preempts the reading שׁוֹר אִישׁ, "an ox of a man";
(b) it clearly differentiates between the subject (in this case, the ox) and the direct object (in this case, a man or a woman);
(c) it keeps "a man" and "a woman" from becoming abstract terms and emphasizes that they are individuals
(→ Kahn, "Object Markers and Agreement Pronouns," esp. 469–72).

The protasis concludes with another formulaic note (vav + verb in the affix form) bringing the main consequence of the situation just mentioned to the forefront, namely, וָמֵת (→WO'C 32.2.1c, pp. 526–27).

Analyze the verb.

Root	Stem	Form	PGN	SF	OS	BRM

Why does the text read וָמֵת and not וְמֵת? (**?** Gr. 183; Ke. 209; S. 35; W. 41; → GKC §104 g; and our discussion of Prov 3:23.) ....

Who is the subject governing וָמֵת? ....

Translate the protasis (v 28a).

```
┌─────────────────────────────────────────────────────────────────────────┐
│                                                                           │
│                                                                           │
│                                                                           │
│                                                                           │
│                                                                           │
└─────────────────────────────────────────────────────────────────────────┘
```

Notice how the focus of the protasis shifts from the ox, at the beginning, to the (human) victim, at its conclusion. Do you think that this shift helps the text to convey its message?

The second part of this verse consists of the apodosis, the "then" part of the discussion. The apodosis is set apart from the protasis by atnaḥ.

Analyze סָקוֹל יִסָּקֵל

Root	Stem	Form	PGN	SF	OS	BRM

The first verb is in the qal stem, the second in the nif'al stem. When you find a combination of an infinitive absolute and a finite verb of the same root, the chances are that both verbs are in the same stem, but this is not always the case. Our example here points to a significant number of instances in which the verbs are in different stems. (→ GKC §113 w; JM §123 p; WO'C 35.2.1d, p. 582.)

Translate סָקוֹל יִסָּקֵל ....

If you wrote, "It shall be stoned," you are following a long tradition of interpretation (e.g., JM §113 m). This reading is grammatically correct. Nonetheless, in our verse and in similar legal texts, the combination "infinitive absolute + prefix," as well as prefix alone, most likely conveyed the sense of "it is liable to be" or "it may be." Therefore, it is preferable to translate סָקוֹל יִסָּקֵל as "it is liable to be stoned" or "it may be stoned." In other words, the law allows the stoning of the ox, but the punishment is not obligatory.

Note

סָקוֹל יִסָּקֵל is formally similar to another common expression in legal texts, מוֹת־יוּמַת (e.g., Lev. 20:10). מוֹת־יוּמַת is generally translated as "he shall be put to death." But it was likely understood as "he is liable to execution." Hence, if an adulterer and an adulteress—to whom the law of Lev 20:10 applies—were not put to death but pardoned, this pardoning would not involve a transgression of any absolute divine law. (See Jer 3:12–13; → Buss, "Distinction between Civil and Criminal Law," esp. 55–57.)

In the first part of this verse the text reads שׁוֹר, in the second part הַשּׁוֹר. Can you suggest an explanation? . . . .

. . . .

וְלֹא יֵאָכֵל אֶת־בְּשָׂרוֹ

Translate this sentence.

What is the subject of this sentence? . . . .

How is the subject introduced? . . . .

In this example אֶת points to the recipient or passive character of the subject of the sentence.

Translate v 28.

For Further Thought

Stoning is not the easiest way of killing a dangerous animal, but it is a form of capital punishment. Why is the ox punished? Does the author consider the ox to have free will to choose to gore or not to gore? Most likely not. Instead, it seems that the reason for the execution is that the ox transgressed the hierarchy of being (God-humanity-animals-plants), and whoever does so, intentionally or unintentionally, is liable to capital punishment. (On this issue, see Patrick, "Studying Biblical Law.") In this case, the owner of the ox is free from guilt (נָקִי); but under other circumstances, as we shall see in the next verse, the owner may be held accountable.

Verse 29.

אִם introduces a subcase. It may be translated as "but if, in addition" (WO'C 3.8.2d, p. 637) or "if" provided that the initial וְכִי (v 28) is translated as "when" (e.g., NRSV).

שׁוֹר נַגָּח הוּא

Is נַגָּח a predicate adjective? (**?** K. 70; Gr. 32; Ke. 46–67; L. 13–14; S. 40–41; for contrast with attributive adjectives, see our discussion of 1 Sam 1:3.) If so, where is the verb in this clause?

. . . .

שׁוֹר נַגָּח הוּא is a **verbless clause of classification.** Such a clause focuses on one subject—here, "the ox"—in order to classify it, to answer such questions as, What kind of ox is it? or, What is the ox like? The answer to these questions is provided by the predicate, in our case, נַגָּח. Thus, the text tells us that this ox is not a simple one, but is classifiable as "a goring ox." The pronoun הוּא at the end of the clause returns the reader's focus to the ox, as it is now classified, while at the same time emphasizing the predicate (i.e., נַגָּח) and therefore the message of the entire clause.

The structure of the clause, subject-predicate-pronoun, is the one generally attested in verbless clauses of classification that conclude with a pronoun. If the pronoun is absent, the regular structure is predicate-subject, but the exceptions are many. (→ clauses of classification, see WO'C 8.4.2, pp. 132–35, esp. 132–33, 16.3.3d, pp. 298–99; see also Muraoka, *Emphatic Words*, 75–77; for a major study of the verbless clauses, see Andersen, *Hebrew Verbless Clause*.)

Note
Verbless clauses of classification tell us to which class something or someone belongs. In contrast, **verbless clauses of identification** tell us about the identity of someone or something (e.g., אֲנִי ה', "I am the Lord"). These clauses generally have the pronoun before the predicate. (→ WO'C 8.4.1, pp. 130–32, 16.3.3b–c, pp. 297–98; see also our discussion of Ezek 37:11.)

נַגָּח shows a doubled ג. The nominal pattern קַטָּל is well attested for occupations and professions (e.g., גַּנָּב, "thief"; צַיָּד, "hunter"; and דַּיָּן, "judge"), and it suggests someone who is repeatedly doing something. (→ S. 264; GKC §84ᵇ b; JM §88H a; WO'C 5.4.a, p. 89.)

מִתְּמֹל שִׁלְשֹׁם
This is an adverbial idiomatic time phrase legally qualifying the attribute נַגָּח. It conveys the sense of "in the past."

Translate it literally. . . . .
Notice that the words תְּמֹל ,אֶתְמֹל (1 Sam 10:11), and אֶתְמוּל (Isa 30:33) are equivalent.

Analyze הוּעַד (**?** K. 185–86, 401; Gr. 82, 212; Ke. 325–26; L. 243–44; S. 247–50; W. 200; → GKC §72 d; JM §80 g.)

Root	Stem	Form	PGN	SF	OS	BRM

Analyze יִשְׁמְרֶנּוּ (**?** think of יִשׁמר + נ + הוּ—cf. יִשְׁמְרֵהוּ in Ps 41:3; K. 214–15, 248, 356; Gr. 61; Ke. 159; L. 271–72; S. 181; W. 131; → GKC §58 i; JM §61 f, 63 a.)

Root	Stem	Form	PGN	SF	OS	BRM

Analyze הֵמִית (**?** see our discussion of הֵשִׁיב in 2 Kgs 14:25.)

Root	Stem	Form	PGN	SF	OS	BRM

Two of these verbs are in affix and one is in prefix form. How would you explain this contrast?

. . . .

Translate v 29a.

Verse 29a presents the protasis ("if" clause); the next part of the verse, 29b, is the apodosis ("then" clause).

Analyze יוּמָת (**?** see our discussion of הוּעַד; had this verb been in a non-pausal location, it would have been written יוּמַת; on the contrast between pausal and non-pausal forms, see K. 95; Gr. 135–36; Ke. i7, 240–41; L. 201–02; S. 290; W. 137; → GKC 629 i–w; JM §32.)

Root	Stem	Form	PGN	SF	OS	BRM

Translate all of v 29.

```
┌─────────────────────────────────────────────────────────────────┐
│                                                                   │
│                                                                   │
│                                                                   │
│                                                                   │
│                                                                   │
└─────────────────────────────────────────────────────────────────┘
```

Does this law *require* the execution of the owner of the goring ox? (**?** see our discussion of v 28.)

. . . .

In the case described in v 28, the owner of the ox is not liable, but in the case described in v 29 the owner is liable through negligence. The assumption is that the owner could have prevented the death of a human being by restraining an ox already known to be dangerous. As a legal issue, negligence here is restricted by two preconditions:

—the ox had been known as a goring ox before the event;
—the owner had been explicitly warned concerning the goring character of the ox and the danger posed to the community.

Should either of these preconditions not obtain, the owner would not be liable. Yet a legal issue still remains. However negligent the owner may have been, one may assume that he or she did not intend to murder the gored man or woman. Biblical law allows the execution of an intentional killer, but provides an escape for the unintentional one (→ Patrick, "Studying Biblical Law"), as the next verse shows.

Verse 30.

Analyze יוּשַׁת

Clue: Although the vowel markers point to the hof'al stem (cf. יוּמַת), it is most likely a qal passive; **?** L. 253; S. 250; W. 151; → GKC §53 u; JM §58; WO'C 22.6, pp. 373–76 and esp. 22.6b, p. 375.

Root	Stem	Form	PGN	SF	OS	BRM

Translate v 30.

```
┌─────────────────────────────────────────────────────────────────┐
│                                                                   │
│                                                                   │
│                                                                   │
│                                                                   │
│                                                                   │
│                                                                   │
└─────────────────────────────────────────────────────────────────┘
```

Thus, this law provides a possible escape for the negligent but unintentional killer. It is interesting that in the legal biblical material, in contrast to other ancient Near Eastern material, there is never any mention of monetary compensation for a murdered person. The murderer cannot pay for the victim of his or her negligence. This prevents the establishment of any scale of value based on the social status of persons, with the exception of slaves. (On slavery, see v 32.) The murderer can only pay ransom for his or her own life, not compensation for the murdered person's life. (→ Patrick, "Studying Biblical Law.")

For Further Thought

The text does not say who will decide the actual amount of the ransom. Certainly, the owner of the goring ox is not a candidate, as יוּשַׁת עָלָיו makes clear. Who may be involved in making this decision?

Verse 31.

Analyze יֵעָשֶׂה (? K. 197–98, 205; Gr. 88, 110; Ke. 224, 287; L. 185; S. 222, 224; W. 156, 217; → GKC 63 h; JM §68 c.)

Root	Stem	Form	PGN	SF	OS	BRM

The dagesh forte in לֹּ is just a conjunctive dagesh that brings יֵעָשֶׂה and לֹּ closer but does not alter their meaning (→ Gr. 145 n1; Ke. 147; L. 208).

Note

This kind of dagesh should be expected to occur when a monosyllabic word such as לֹּ (or a word that is accented in its first syllable) occurs immediately after and in close connection to a word ending with segol (or qamets) in which the next-to-last syllable is accented. This conjunctive dagesh emphasizes the close relationship between the two words. (→ JM §18 j; and esp. Yeivin, *Introduction*, 289–92.)

Translate v 31.

The אוֹ formula may be seen as a supplementary note whose aim is to clarify the scope of the law.

In this verse the issue is whether the goring of a male or female child should be treated in the same way as that of an adult male or female, or more leniently. The answer here is categorical: כַּמִּשְׁפָּט הַזֶּה יֵעָשֶׂה לּוֹ. Does the same apply for a slave, male or female? The next verse provides the answer.

Verse 32.

The first word of the verse, אִם, points to a new subcase.

Translate v 32.

```
┌─────────────────────────────────────────────────────────────────┐
│                                                                   │
│                                                                   │
│                                                                   │
│                                                                   │
│                                                                   │
│                                                                   │
│                                                                   │
└─────────────────────────────────────────────────────────────────┘
```

The rules that apply to free human beings do not apply to slaves in this society. (The society described here is certainly an ancient one; slavery was accepted by Christianity and Judaism for many centuries.) The ox is still liable to death because it has trespassed the hierarchy of being, but the owner is liable to a monetary payment rather than to death. The slave is human enough that his or her death calls for the stoning of the ox, but is also a commodity worth a fixed price for which restitution could be paid to the owner in case of damage. Interestingly, in this case the value of male and female slaves is considered to be the same.

Verse 33.

This verse does not open with a new subclause but rather with a main independent clause. How can you know that? ....

As we would expect (see discussion of v 28), a verb in the prefix form and in the third person immediately follows וְכִי, and the subject of this verb is explicitly mentioned afterward.

Analyze the verb. **Write down** its subject.

Root	Stem	Form	PGN	SF	OS	BRM

In v 33 one finds another case of an אוֹ clause. In this case, however, it does not provide supplementary information concerning the recipient of the action described in the main כִּי clause (as in v 28). Instead, it supplements the main clause itself, introducing a parallel כִּי clause. Now the two clauses turn into one semantic unit (v 33aa) which is marked by a ṭifḥa (**?** see note on 1 Sam 1:21).

Analyze יִכְרֶה

Root	Stem	Form	PGN	SF	OS	BRM

Following the ṭifḥa one finds a וְלֹא legal formula (as in v 21; cf. Exod 21:18,22). Its function is to restrict the scope of the case under discussion by defining certain delimiting circumstances that must obtain. In our case, as in v 21, the main legal issue is whether the accused owner was negligent.

Analyze יְכַסֶּנּוּ (**?** יִשְׁמְרֶנּוּ in v 29.)

Root	Stem	Form	PGN	SF	OS	BRM

As in vv 28 and 29, the protasis ends with another formulaic note (vav + verb in the affix form) describing the final result of the situation.

Translate v 33.

For Further Thought

Compare the spelling of the word בֹּר in its two occurrences in this verse. Although this word is generally spelled בּוֹר, the evidence suggests that the scribes responsible for the present form of this text did not consider consistent spelling to be important.

Verse 34.

Whereas v 33 contains the protasis, this verse contains the apodosis. You might call v 34 the prescriptive statement for such a case.

Analyze the verbs in v 34.

יְשַׁלֵּם

Root	Stem	Form	PGN	SF	OS	BRM

יָשִׁיב

Root	Stem	Form	PGN	SF	OS	BRM

יִהְיֶה

Root	Stem	Form	PGN	SF	OS	BRM

Translate v 34 up to the zaqef qaṭan. (**?** שלם in the pi'el is to be translated here as "to make restitution.")

The question now is, How should the owner of the pit make restitution? In kind? In silver? The answer to the question immediately follows.

Translate v 34 from the zaqef qaṭan to the atnaḥ.

The question now is what to do with the dead animal.

Translate v 34 from the atnaḥ to the sof-pasuq.

```

```

Verses 33 and 34 move away from the discussion of a goring ox. Perhaps they are an interpolation into the text, for v 35 goes back to the goring ox. But these verses are certainly related to the issue of negligence. Moreover, by separating vv 28–32 from vv 35–36, a strong message is conveyed: the goring of a human being (even of a male or female slave) is a completely different case from the goring of another animal. In vv 28–32 we are dealing with a clear trespassing of a hierarchy of living creatures, whereas in vv 35–36 there is no such trespassing. In accordance with that significant difference in the object of the goring, the fate of the goring ox is in each case different. (→ Patrick, "Studying Biblical Law.")

Verses 35–36.

The atnaḥ separates the protasis from the apodosis. As we would expect, the new legal case begins with וְכִי followed by a verb in the prefix form and in the third person, and then the subject. After the ṭifḥa and before the atnaḥ, we find a report concerning the result of the circumstances just mentioned. This short report contains, as we would expect, a verb in the third-person affix form.

Translate v 35.

```

```

In this case, the ox is neither to be punished (it did not violate the hierarchy of life) nor is the owner personally liable (he or she could not be held negligent, because the goring nature of the ox was not known). All that remains, therefore, is to achieve an equitable formula for the distribution of the monetary loss. Such an arrangement, of course, cannot be made in the case of a negligent owner, as we see in v 36. The protasis of the case of a negligent owner in v 36 is strongly reminiscent of that of v 29.

Translate v 36.

For Further Thought

List the legal cases in Exod 21:28–36 in which words from the root שלם in the pi'el occur, and those in which they do not occur. Do you think that the distribution of words conveying the meaning "to make restitution" is haphazard? What does your list tell you about practical ways of making restitution (in kind, in silver, etc.)?

Translate the whole of Exod 21:28–36.

For Further Thought

In the Babylonian code of Hammurabi it is written:

—"If an ox, when it was walking along the street, gored a seignior (a freeman) to death, that case is not subject to claim."

—"If a seignior's ox was a gorer and his city council made it known to him that it was a gorer, but he did not pad its horns (or) tie up his ox, and that ox gored to death a member of the aristocracy, he shall give one mina of silver."

—"If it was a seignior's slave, he (the seignior) shall give one-third mina of silver." (*ANET* 176b; see laws 250–52)

In another ancient Near Eastern legal code, the code of Eshnunna, one reads:

—"If an ox gores an(other) ox and causes (its) death, both ox owners shall divide (among themselves) the price of the live ox and also the equivalent of the dead ox."

—"If an ox is known to gore habitually and the authorities have brought the fact to the knowledge of the owner, but he does not have his ox dehorned, (if) it gores a man and causes (his) death, then the owner of the ox shall pay two-thirds of a mina of silver."

—"If it gores a slave and causes (his) death, he shall pay fifteen shekels of silver." (*ANET* 163b; see laws 53–55)

For Further Reading

On Exod 21:28–36, see Finkelstein, "Ox That Gored," esp. 5–47; and Patrick, "Studying Biblical Law."

Works Cited in This Section

F. I. Andersen, *The Hebrew Verbless Clause in the Pentateuch* (Nashville: Abingdon, 1970); **M. J. Buss,** "The Distinction between Civil and Criminal Law in Ancient Israel," *Proceedings of* *the Sixth World Congress of Jewish Studies* (Jerusalem: Academic Press, 1977), 1:51–62; **D. Patrick,** "Studying Biblical Law as Humanities," *Semeia* 45 (1989): 27–47; **J. J. Finkelstein,** "The Ox That Gored," *Transactions of the American Philosophical Society* 71, part 2 (Philadelphia: American Philosophical Society, 1981); **M. Fishbane,** *Biblical Interpretation in Ancient Israel* (Oxford: Clarendon Press, 1988); **G. A. Kahn,** "Object Markers and Agreement Pronouns in Semitic Languages," *BSO[A]S* 47 (1984): 468–500; **T. Muraoka,** *Emphatic Words and Structures in Biblical Hebrew* (Jerusalem/Leiden: Magnes/E. J. Brill, 1985); **J. B. Pritchard,** ed., *Ancient Near Eastern Texts relating to the Old Testament* (ANET, 2d ed.; Princeton, N.J.: Princeton University Press, 1955); **R. Rendtorff,** *The Old Testament: An Introduction* (Philadelphia: Fortress, 1986); **I. Yeivin,** *Introduction to the Tiberian Masorah* (Masoretic Studies 5; Missoula, Mont.: Scholars Press, 1980).

2.2   Leviticus 5:20–26

We turn our attention to the literature of the priestly laws. This passage (found in English translations as Lev 6:1–7) presents you with the opportunity to encounter priestly terminology and expressions. In addition, you will be introduced to some aspects of priestly thought.

Verse 20.

Translate וַיְדַבֵּר ה' אֶל־מֹשֶׁה לֵּאמֹר

```


```

Note

You may have noticed the dagesh in the ל of לֵּאמֹר. You can be quite certain that this is not a dagesh lene. How do you know? (**?** K. 13; Gr. 22–23; Ke. 3, 12–13; L. xxiv–xxv; S. 5; W. 14–17.) The doubled ל stands at the beginning of לֵּאמֹר when it follows the word מֹשֶׁה with a conjunctive accent (such as merka). Its original role may have been to call for a pronunciation that clearly distinguishes the two words from one another (→ Yevin, *Introduction*, 294). Do you remember why the א in לֵּאמֹר has no vowel marks? (**?** K. 4, 273; Gr. 98, 100; Ke. 182; L. xxiv; S. 13; W. 18–19.)

The expression וַיְדַבֵּר ה' אֶל־מֹשֶׁה לֵּאמֹר is very common in priestly writings. Usually, it indicates the beginning of a new topical unit in the priestly writings (e.g., Lev 4; Lev 5:14). In addition to demarcating a unit, it also claims the highest possible legitimacy—God's direct speech to Moses—for the instructions that follow. (For variants of this expression, see, e.g., Lev 13:1; 25:1.)

Sof-pasuq sets this expression apart from the subsequent material. In Leviticus, a command to speak usually follows this introductory formula, usually in the next verse. Such a command is commonly expressed by a verbal chain consisting of one imperative followed by either a vav-affix form or another imperative. (In such a case, the vav-affix should be translated as imperative; **?** K. 274, 293, 305, 309; Ke. 214–15; L. 119; S. 174; → JM §119 1; WO'C 32.2.2, pp. 529–30.)

The command to speak usually follows the formula . . . דַּבֵּר אֶל . . . וְאָמַרְתָּ אֶל (e.g., Lev 17:2). Alternatively, phrases like . . . דַּבֵּר אֶל . . . לֵאמֹר may occur (e.g., Lev 4:2; 12:2), and in a relatively few instances the text shows צַו אֶת־ instead of דַּבֵּר אֶל (Lev 6:1–2; Num 28:1–2; 34:1–2). On the basis of the form you encounter in v 20, you might expect v 21 to begin with the command to speak. But is this actually the case?

Verse 21.

נֶפֶשׁ כִּי תֶחֱטָא וּמָעֲלָה מַעַל בַּה'

The verse does not begin with דַּבֵּר אֶל or any other verb in the imperative. Instead, it opens with a noun, נֶפֶשׁ, followed by כִּי + verb in the prefix form. In many instances this opening is the third structural unit following the formulaic introduction וַיְדַבֵּר ה' אֶל־מֹשֶׁה לֵּאמֹר and the command to speak (e.g., Lev 1:1–2; 4:1–2; 12:1–2; 15:1–2; 27:1–2). This is the case most often at the beginning of a large topical unit, marked in modern versions of the Bible by the beginning of a new chapter. But in a number of instances, the medial command to speak is omitted (as here; see also Lev 5:14–15; 13:1–2; 22:26–27).

נֶפֶשׁ is sometimes translated as "soul." Here it means "any person," whether male or female, similar to אִישׁ אוֹ־אִשָּׁה (e.g., Num 5:6) or אָדָם (e.g., Lev 1:2) (→ Milgrom, *Leviticus 1–16*, 171–72; see also p. 145).

The word כִּי in this verse introduces the protasis, the "if" or "when" part of an "if/when . . . then . . ." unit. You have seen this use of כִּי in the legal material in Exod 21:28–36. Notice, however, that here and many other times in Leviticus (e.g., Lev 1:2; 5:1; 13:2; 22:14) it follows the noun (the subject/agent) and precedes the verb in the prefix form, whereas in Exod 21:28 (as well as in Exod 21:14,18,20,22,26,33,35) the word order is כִּי, then a verb in the prefix, and then a noun.

For Further Thought

The formulaic legal expression that opens v 21 (נֶפֶשׁ כִּי + verb in prefix form) is frequent in the laws in Leviticus 5 (Lev 5:1,4,15,17,21). Elsewhere in the OT/HB it occurs only in Lev 2:1; 4:2; 7:21. What does this evidence suggest about the redaction of these laws?

Analyze תֶחֱטָא (**?** K. 394, 406; Gr. 99, 109–110; Ke. 225, 275–77; L. 115; S. 148–49; W. 155, 178–79.)

Root	Stem	Form	PGN	SF	OS	BRM

Analyze מָעֲלָה

Root	Stem	Form	PGN	SF	OS	BRM

Translate v 21a.

The first verb is in the prefix form, the second in the affix form. In such a sequence, the vav-affix verb may point to what follows, temporally or logically, from the situation described by the verb in the prefix form. It may also clarify the meaning conveyed by the prefix verb, as it does here. In any case, the vav-affix here is translated as if it were a prefix form. (**?** Ke. 212–14; L. 180; S. 160; → WO'C 32.1.3–32.2.1, pp. 523–29, esp. 32.2.1c–d, pp. 526–29, and cf. 32.2.3e, p. 533; also JM §119.)

וּמָעֲלָה מַעַל בַּה' is usually translated as "commits a trespass against the Lord," but it may be better to follow Milgrom (*Leviticus 1–16*, 319–320, 345–56) and translate וּמָעֲלָה מַעַל in cultic context as "commits a sacrilege" (the opposite of "sanctifies"). This half-verse than translates as, "When a person sins by committing a sacrilege against the Lord . . . "

The strong **assonance** (repetition of vowels; → Alonso Schökel, *Manual*, 20–29, esp. p. 25) and the stress on the sounds represented by the letters ל, ע, and מ in וּמָעֲלָה מַעַל are stylistic devices to turn the readers'/listeners' attention to the main focus: the committing of a sacrilege. But what kind of sacrilege is this? What actions would make a person the referent of this law? The beginning of the answer is in the second part of this verse.

וְכִחֵשׁ בַּעֲמִיתוֹ

Analyze כִחֵשׁ

Root	Stem	Form	PGN	SF	OS	BRM

You may be perplexed about the subject of this verb. Can it be the same as the subject of מָעֲלָה and תֶחֱטָא, though one is a "he" (3rd masc. sg.) and the other a "she" (3rd fem. sg.)? Yes, it can.

Moreover, in many cases the strength of the congruency with a feminine subject seems to ebb with distance from the feminine noun (e.g., Lev 2:1; 5:1; 20:6; Job 1:19; → GKC 145 t). Of course, the lack of congruency does not change the nature of the subject; here, the fact remains that נֶפֶשׁ refers to any person, male or female.

You may translate כָּחַשׁ as "deceiving" or "denying falsely." Keep in mind that here this term suggests "speaking a false oath (by the Lord)." This understanding becomes explicit in the next verse. (→ Milgrom, *Leviticus 1–16*, 335, 337–38, 365–73.)

The use of the term עָמִית ("fellow") underscores the existence of a relationship between two people, for it never appears without a possessive suffix. That is to say, it is always "my/your/his/her fellow," never "the/a fellow." Note that if the Hebrew וֹ- looks back to נֶפֶשׁ, as it does here, it may refer to a woman as well as a man. Notice, too, the lack of agreement between נֶפֶשׁ, a feminine noun, and the pronominal suffix וֹ-.

For Further Thought

The pattern of occurrence of what was possibly a technical term, עָמִית, is worth noting. עָמִית occurs nine times in legal-cultic material found in Leviticus. Outside Leviticus it occurs nowhere in biblical laws, and elsewhere only once, in Zech 13:7. What does this evidence suggest about the legal material embedded in Leviticus?

Following בַּעֲמִיתוֹ one finds a series of three specific cases of a person's deceiving his or her fellow. The structure of this subsection is simple: each example is presented by a noun (or a construct chain) preceded by -בְּ. The entire subsection is brought together by אוֹ clauses. You have seen אוֹ clauses in Exod 21:28–36. In a legal context they provide additional material whose aim is to clarify the scope of the law. Here they provide characteristic examples so that one may understand what cases of deception the law talks about. Deception is seen not only as an act against one's fellow human, but also against God, as suggested by וְכִחֵשׁ.

Notice the play on the use of -בְּ; compare this -בְּ with the one before "fellow" and "the Lord." . . . .

בִּתְשׂוּמֶת יָד may be translated either as "loan/investment" or "partnership" (Milgrom, *Leviticus 1–16*, 335). The root עשׁק in the qal stem, in legal texts, indicates the illegal withholding by X of something that rightfully belongs to Y, but which came into X's hands legally (e.g., withholding salaries or a pledge after the repayment of a loan). In the same kind of texts, גזל, in the qal, points to the illegal withholding by force of something that belongs to someone else and was obtained illegally from the outset, that is, to an act of outright robbery. (→ Milgrom, *Cult and Conscience*, 89–104; *Leviticus 1–16*, 335–37.)

Translate v 21 up to the second and last zaqef qatan of the verse.

After the zaqef qaṭan you will find another אוֹ clause. But this one is different from the preceding ones. Does it clarify what is meant by וְכִחֵשׁ בַּעֲמִיתוֹ or by וּמָעֲלָה מַעַל בַּה' ? Take into account the structure of the sentence and its clauses, as well as the masoretic accents, and explain your choice. . . . .

. . . .

. . . .

Note

The play on the word עֲמִיתוֹ is worthy of mention. It occurs first as an indirect object (preceded by -בְּ), and then as a definite direct object (preceded by אֶת־). Moreover, the text insists that the reader/listener focus attention on עֲמִיתוֹ by the concluding position of the word in this verse, according to the received masoretic text.

Verse 22.

The verse opens with another אוֹ clause linked to the preceding one. This clause is relatively easy to read, so you may use this as an opportunity to check your ability to apply what you have learned.

Analyze מָצָא

Root	Stem	Form	PGN	SF	OS	BRM

Do you remember why the vowel marker underneath the צ is qamets and not pataḥ? (? K. 61; Gr. 98; Ke. 275–76; L. 47; S. 101–2; W. 178–79.)

וְכִחֵשׁ בָּהּ

You have already analyzed this verbal form (v 21). In this case of middle-guttural pi'el affix, the vowel changes you might have expected do not take place (? K. 71–72; Gr. 114; Ke. 251; L. 195; S. 113; W. 167–68; → GKC §64 d–e). In fact, the form כִּחֵשׁ is almost identical to the strong verb form. The "expected" change in the vowel of the first consonant of the root, from hireq to tsere, occurs regularly in middle ר roots and in many (but not all) middle א roots (→ GKC §64 e). It does not occur in other middle-guttural roots. In such cases, since there is neither actual doubling nor lengthening of the preceding vowel, the middle-guttural letters are said to be "virtually doubled" (→ JM §69 a).

Note

You may have noticed the accent on the next-to-last syllable and the related change from tsere to segol in וְכִחֵשׁ בָּהּ, none of which occurs in וְכִחֵשׁ בַּעֲמִיתוֹ. (→ GKC §64 g and §29 e–f and esp. 29 g.)

Do you remember why the text reads וְכִחֵשׁ בָּהּ and not וְכִחֵשׁ בָּהּ? (**?** K. 65, 248; Gr. 20 n.1, 67; Ke. 436; L. xxv, 31; S. 9, 54; W. 17, 52; see also our discussion of וַיַּחְשְׁבֶהָ in 1 Sam 1:13.)

. . . .

Translate vv 21–22 up to the first ṭifḥa in v 22.

```
┌─────────────────────────────────────────────────────┐
│                                                       │
│                                                       │
│                                                       │
│                                                       │
└─────────────────────────────────────────────────────┘
```

Notice the chiasmus: וְכִחֵשׁ בַּעֲמִיתוֹ, וְכִחֵשׁ בָּהּ. This chiasmus not only sets a subunit apart but also underscores the importance of the action described by וְכִחֵשׁ. Significantly, וְכִחֵשׁ here suggests "to speak a false oath by the Lord." In addition, there seems to be a movement of attention from "one's fellow" to the object of the false swearing, from בַּעֲמִיתוֹ to בָּהּ.

Analyze נִשְׁבַּע

Root	Stem	Form	PGN	SF	OS	BRM

וְנִשְׁבַּע עַל־שָׁקֶר

Is this the opening of an additional אוֹ clause, in which the case that follows would give another example of wrongdoing? . . . .

If not, how do you think that it relates to the material connected by אוֹ clauses, which points to different cases of illegal taking of what rightfully belongs to one's fellow? (**?** our discussion of וְכִחֵשׁ) . . . .

. . . .

Translate עַל־אַחַת מִכֹּל אֲשֶׁר־יַעֲשֶׂה הָאָדָם

```
┌─────────────────────────────────────────────────────┐
│                                                       │
│                                                       │
│                                                       │
│                                                       │
└─────────────────────────────────────────────────────┘
```

Notice the use of הָאָדָם (cf. Gen 1:27) equivalent to נֶפֶשׁ in v 21. Since here it means "*a human being*," you may wonder why the text reads הָאָדָם instead of simply אָדָם. The answer is that here, as in a number of other instances, -הַ (or -הָ) does not have its most common function of definite article. Its use here might be related to the generic character of the attached noun (אָדָם); compare it with הַכֶּלֶב in Judg 7:5, which must be translated as "a dog" (→ Williams, *Hebrew Syntax*, 19; cf. JM §13 m–o, and for an advanced study on the article in Hebrew, see Barr, "'Determination' and the Definite Article"). This use of -הַ (or -הָ) is similar to the generic use of the English "the" in a phrase like "The lion is the king of the forest." The idiom does not refer to a specific, definite lion in a specific forest; neither does הָאָדָם refer to a specific, definite person.

For Further Thought

The expression . . . עַל־אַחַת מִכֹּל אֲשֶׁר־יַעֲשֶׂה looks like legal boilerplate. But in fact it occurs nowhere else in the OT/HB but here, in vv 22 and 26. Even the expression ". . . אַחַת מִכֹּל," which seems useful as a formulaic introduction of a summary reference to a full category of either wrong deeds or commandments (מִצְוֹת), occurs only in Lev 4:13,22; 5:17,22,26 (cf. Lev 7:14). A related expression, אַחַת מֵאֵלֶּה, is attested in Lev 5:4,5,13, and elsewhere only in Ezek 16:5. What does this pattern of occurrence suggest?

לַחֲטֹא בָהֵנָּה

Can you explain why לַחֲטֹא contains these vowels? (**?** see our discussion of לַאֲמַצְיָהוּ in 2 Kgs 14:23.) . . . .

Analyze לַחֲטֹא

Root	Stem	Form	PGN	SF	OS	BRM

As you know, the preposition -בְּ may convey different sets of meanings. Here in בָהֵנָּה it may be translated as "with regard to." Accordingly, one may translate בָהֵנָּה as "with regard to those (actions)." (→ WO'C 11.2.5e, p. 198.)

Translate vv 21–22.

For Further Thought

Milgrom (*Leviticus 1–16*, 338) claims that the atnaḥ under שָׁקֶר should be placed under בָּהּ. Do you agree with him? What difference does this make in translation? What justification do you see for Milgrom's position?

Verse 23.

This verse first describes quite succinctly the condition of the wrongdoer. Then the protasis is brought to its conclusion, underscoring the last, and perhaps most significant, condition for the applicability of the apodosis that follows (**?** see our discussion of Exod 21:28–36). Finally, it begins to describe the apodosis.

Translate וְהָיָה כִּי־יֶחֱטָא

| |
| |

This short subunit encapsulates the situation of the wrongdoer on the basis of his or her deeds. The next word concludes the protasis by bringing to the text a necessary condition that is directly related to the wrongdoer's own appraisal of his or her deeds.

Analyze וְאָשֵׁם

Root	Stem	Form	PGN	SF	OS	BRM

Translate v 23 up to the first zaqef qaṭan, that is, up to the end of the protasis.

| |
| |

The meaning of אָשֵׁם here is not "to be guilty" or "to be held guilty" but rather "to feel guilty" or "to realize one's guilt." Robbers and defrauders, however, are most likely aware of their sinning.

The issue, therefore, is not if they come to know that they were doing wrong, but rather if they feel remorse for their wrongdoing. (→ Milgrom, *Leviticus 1–16*, 334, 38, 39–45.)

The condition of feeling remorse for one's guilt is the regular conclusion of the protasis in Lev 4:13,22,27; 5:2,3,4,5,17,23. These priestly texts claim that there is no possible ritual expiation for a sinner unless he or she feels remorse. In other words, sacrifices are not seen as a mechanical gate to purification; on the contrary, the right attitude of the heart—repentance—is essential for the efficacy of the ritual.

Moreover, the sacrifice is only the last of a series of actions that a person should take upon feeling guilty. One assumption on which a text such as Lev 5:20–26 rests is that a person cannot expect expiation and forgiveness while retaining the fruits of misbehavior. Thus, the first actions to be taken are those concerned with restitution and the rectification of the wrong. The description of these actions opens the apodosis of our text immediately following וְאָשֵׁם. (→ Milgrom, *Leviticus 1–16*, 334, 38, 44–45.)

Analyze הֵפְקַד. (Pronounce this word aloud. **?** see our discussion of אָכְלָה in 1 Sam 1:9.)

Root	Stem	Form	PGN	SF	OS	BRM

Translate v 23 from the first zaqef qaṭan to the atnaḥ.

Note

As to contents, this portion of the verse clearly points to a reversal of the actions mentioned in Lev 5:21–22. But, most likely as a matter of style, the writer did not choose to follow fully the order of actions found in vv 21–22. The *a-b-c-d* order of vv 21–22 has become *b-c-a-d* in v 23 (i.e., the actions referred to at the beginning and at the end of the series in vv 21–22 are brought together as a conclusion to the series in v 23).

It may seem strange that there is no second reference to תְּשׂוּמֶת יָד, but one can hardly think that this case was therefore considered to be exempted. It is included in the general statement opening the next verse.

Verse 24.

Analyze יִשָּׁבַע

Root	Stem	Form	PGN	SF	OS	BRM

Translate v 24 up to the segolta (֒).

Note

Segolta is an important disjunctive (separating) marker that looks like an inverted segol. It generally marks the first major division of the first half of a verse (which in turn is marked by atnaḥ). How does segolta relate to zaqef? Zaqef cannot precede segolta but may follow it. When following, zaqef marks the two main subdivisions of the clause set apart by segolta (at the beginning) and atnaḥ (at the end). (→ Yeivin, *Introduction*, 188–90; see also pp. 171–72.)

For Further Thought

The expression מִכֹּל אֲשֶׁר־X, followed by a verb in the prefix form, is used in the pentateuchal legal material only in Lev 5:22,24,26, and in Num 6:4. Does this infrequent occurrence surprise you? Why, or why not?

וְשִׁלַּם אֹתוֹ בְּרֹאשׁוֹ וַחֲמִשִׁתָיו יֹסֵף עָלָיו

Analyze יֹסֵף (**?** K. 203; Gr. 95; K. 343; L. 222; S. 214; W. 188–89.)

Root	Stem	Form	PGN	SF	OS	BRM

Notice the shift from a vav-affix form (וְשִׁלַּם) to a prefix form (יֹסֵף), and from the pi'el to the hif'il stem. Such shifts provide some variety of expression and are relatively common in biblical prose and verse (→ Berlin, *Dynamics*, 35–40). Notice also the fourfold repetition of the pronominal suffix (אֹתוֹ‎, בְּרֹאשׁוֹ‎, וַחֲמִשִׁתָיו‎, and עָלָיו‎). How does this choice of expression support the message of the text?

Before translating v 24 from the segolta to the atnaḥ, remember what you have learned about the technical use of שלם‎ in the pi'el in legal texts (Exod 21:34,36). Here בְּרֹאשׁוֹ‎ is to be translated as "its principal" or "according to its principal" (→ Milgrom, *Cult and Conscience*, 137–40). Translate חֲמִשִׁתָיו‎ just as you would translate חֲמִשִׁתוֹ‎ (which is attested a few verses earlier, in Lev 5:16).

Translate v 24 from the segolta to the atnaḥ.

```
```

For Further Thought

—Is restitution made in kind or in silver in this case?

—A fine of 20 percent is relatively low in biblical times. Why does this law prescribe such a low fine? The only possible judicial proceeding against the kind of offender mentioned would have required him or her to take an oath before the Lord. How does the level of the fine relate to the nature of the evidence available against such an offender? (→ Phillips, "Undetectable Offender," 146–50.)

The next legal issue to be decided in the law we are looking at is to whom restitution should be made, and when.

Analyze יִתְּנֶנּוּ‎ (recall your work on Exod 21:29).

Root	Stem	Form	PGN	SF	OS	BRM

A literal translation of בְּיוֹם אַשְׁמָתוֹ‎ would not convey its sense here, "as soon as he or she [remember to whom נֶפֶשׁ‎ refers] feels guilty."

Translate v 24 b.

```
```

The transgressor has now made restitution to the wronged person, but this is not enough. He or she has caused monetary or material damage to another person, has disturbed the social order, and has strayed from the way of life commanded by God. In addition, the transgressor has explicitly sworn falsely by the Lord, desecrating the Holy Name. In other words, this person has committed a sacrilege. He or she knows and feels that. It is not surprising, therefore, that although making amends for the material damage is considered to be the first and absolutely necessary step for healing the relationship between the sacrileger and God, more is considered to be needed: a ritual is prescribed. The purpose of this ritual is to signify that the relationship between God and the sacrileger is mended. The next two verses concern themselves with this ritual.

Verses 25–26.

אָשָׁם in v 25 refers to the offering prescribed in cases of מַעַל. The term conveys the sense of a "reparation offering" as well as a "feeling-guilty offering."

Translate v 25a.

בְּעֶרְכְּךָ לְאָשָׁם

One may literally render עֶרְכְּךָ as "your value" or "your valuation." But here we are dealing with an extremely rare case of a possessive suffix devoid of any possessive meaning. Here, as well as in Lev 5:15,18, Lev 27 *passim*, and Num 18:16, the possessive suffix of עֶרְכְּךָ seems to have lost all of its original function and meaning. Accordingly, "your value/valuation" turns out to be understood as an external valuation.

Note

Evidence that the possessive suffix has lost its value and function in these verses is found in what would have been a serious grammatical irregularity in Lev 27:12,23 had the suffix retained its function as a possessive (**?** WO'C 13.6b, pp. 249–50). Can you identify the above-mentioned irregularity? The ךָ is most likely a "fossilized" form (→ Speiser, "Leviticus and the Critics," 30–31).

If one renders עֶרְכְּךָ as "valuation," it seems reasonable to translate the phrase בְּעֶרְכְּךָ לְאָשָׁם as "according to the valuation of the אָשָׁם." In such a case, אָשָׁם probably points to both the ram to be offered as אָשָׁם and the set of meanings conveyed by "reparation" and "feeling guilty."

Translate v 25b according to this line of thought.

[blank box]

Some scholars would agree with this translation (→ Wright, "MKR," esp. 446–47). They propose that "the priest had to place a value on the ram to insure that the worth of the beast matched the seriousness of the offerer's infraction" (Wright, "MKR," 446). But many other scholars (→ Milgrom, *Leviticus 1–16*, esp. 326–27) question the actual feasibility of this matching. These scholars underscore the fact that עֶרְכְּךָ is, in most cases, explicitly associated with discerning the monetary equivalent that may be presented in the place of an animal offering. If you accept the position of those scholars who agree with or follow Milgrom, how would you translate v 25b?

[blank box]

How many verbal forms are in v 26?

If you answered three (וְנִסְלַח, וְכִפֶּר, and יַעֲשֶׂה), you have missed one: לְאַשְׁמָה. This is a feminine form of the qal infinitive construct of the root אשם. It points to both the wrongdoing and its consequences: the feeling of guilt and the liability for reparation and for the reparation/feeling-guilty offering. Milgrom (*Leviticus 1–16*, 319) translates v 26b as, "for whatever he has done to feel guilty thereby."

Compare Milgrom's translation with the one in the English Bible you usually consult. Remember that with very few exceptions, English Bibles translate Lev 5:20–26 as Lev 6:1–7. For a useful list of differences between Hebrew and English biblical references, see Rendtorff, *Old Testament*, 303–4.

Translate vv 25–26.

[blank box]

Translate the whole passage, Lev 5:20–26.

For Further Reading

To learn more about Lev 5:20–26, begin by reading Milgrom, "Priestly Doctrine of Repentance," and his treatment of this section in his commentary on Leviticus (Milgrom, *Leviticus 1–16*).

Works Cited in This Section

L. Alonso Schökel, *A Manual of Hebrew Poetics* (Subsidia Biblica 11; Roma: Editrice Pontificio Istituto Biblico, 1988); **J. Barr,** "'Determination' and the Definite Article in Biblical Hebrew," *JSS* 34 (1989): 307–37; **A. Berlin,** *The Dynamics of Biblical Parallelism* (Bloomington: Indiana University Press, 1985); **J. Milgrom,** *Cult and Conscience* (Leiden: E. J. Brill, 1976); "The Priestly Doctrine of Repentance," in J. Milgrom, *Studies in Cultic Theology and Terminology* (Leiden: E. J. Brill, 1983), 47–66; *Leviticus 1–16* (AB 3; New York: Doubleday, 1991); **A. Phillips,** "The Undetectable Offender and the Priestly Legislators," *JThS* 35 (1985): 146–50; **R. Rendtorff,** *The Old Testament: An Introduction* (Philadelphia: Fortress, 1986); **E. A. Speiser,** "Leviticus and the Critics," in M. Haran, ed., *Y. Kaufmann Jubilee Volume* (Jerusalem: Magnes, 1960): 29–45; **R. J. Williams,** *Hebrew Syntax: An Outline* (2d ed.; Toronto: University of Toronto Press, 1984); **L. S. Wright,** "MKR in 2 Kings xii 5–17 and Deuteronomy xviii 8," *VT* 39 (1989): 438–48; **I. Yeivin,** *Introduction to the Tiberian Masorah* (Masoretic Studies 5; Missoula, Mont.: Scholars Press, 1980).

2.3 Deuteronomy 24:14–22

The Book of Deuteronomy asks the reader to overhear the reported exhortation of Moses to the Israelites. Its main instruction can be summarized briefly: *Always follow the way of the Lord, which is shown to you by means of this text.* The "you" of the text refers to the Israelites who were listening to Moses, but certainly not only to them. The readers of the book are asked to identify with those Israelites, and accordingly to hear or see the exhortation as if it were a direct message of Moses to them (→ McEvenue, *Interpreting the Pentateuch*, 128–33). This sense of direct message is strongly conveyed by the conspicuous use of the language of direct address, as exemplified in this portion. You will come to recognize some other stylistic features that are characteristic of Deuteronomy and of other biblical texts that are strongly influenced by its language and thought, i.e., deuteronomistic texts, such as Josh 1:1–9 and Jer 7:1–15. Moreover, it is widely accepted that the historical books, from Joshua to Kings, were written and edited within deuteronomistic circles.

This passage divides itself into several subunits: vv 14–15, v 16, vv 17–18, v 19, and vv 20–22 (or, v 20, vv 21–22). That these divisions have long been recognized may be seen by their being marked in the masoretic text. Our discussion will be based on these units of thought within the passage.

Subunit 1: vv 14–15.

Verse 14.

לֹא־תַעֲשֹׁק שָׂכִיר עָנִי וְאֶבְיוֹן

The form לֹא־X, where X is a verb in the prefix form, expresses prohibition. It occurs, for instance, several times in the Ten Commandments (e.g., לֹא תִרְצָח, "you shall not murder," Exod 20:13; Deut 5:17). There is also a related form of expressing a negative command with אַל־ instead of לֹא. אַל־X generally points to a specific situation in which someone is asked, commanded, or warned not to do something or not to be in a certain state, as in אַל־תִּירָא, "do not be afraid." לֹא־X, on the other hand, is generally used in laws and edicts to set down an absolute rule. אַל־X is close to the English expression "do not . . .", and לֹא־X is more like "you shall not . . ." Another difference between אַל and לֹא concerns the negation of the jussive and cohortative. אַל may precede and negate verbs in the jussive and the cohortative, but לֹא, with very few exceptions (e.g., 1 Kgs 2:6), is not used in this way. Remember that neither אַל nor לֹא negates the imperative verb form itself. The grammatical imperative form cannot be negated. (**?** Ke. 173–74; L. 114; S. 144, 173; W. 77, 114–15; → GKC §49 a, 107 o–p, 109 c–e; WO'C 34.2.1b–e, p. 567, esp. n.6, 34.4a, p. 571.)

לֹא־תַעֲשֹׁק is sometimes translated as "you shall not oppress/abuse," But "to abuse" and "to oppress" are vague terms, whereas the root עשׁק in the qal and in legal texts points to a more precise meaning, as we saw in Lev 5:21.

The expression עָנִי וְאֶבְיֹון occurs fairly often in the OT/HB. Although there is some controversy about the exact meaning of each of these terms within different biblical genres, עָנִי וְאֶבְיֹון can reasonably be translated as "poor and needy" or "needy poor," as most translations do. (→ Gillingham, "Poor in the Psalms," 15–19; Whybray, "Poverty, Wealth, and Point of View in Proverbs," 332–36.)

אֶבְיֹון is a good example of a relatively frequent nominal pattern characterized by the ending וֹן or ֹן, (e.g., קָרְבָּן, "offering"; עִצָּבֹון, "pain"). Adjectives may follow this pattern (e.g., רִאשֹׁון, "first"; אֶבְיֹון, "needy"). (→ L. 296; S. 265–66; and esp. GKC §85 u–v; JM §88M a–e; WO'C 92.)

Translate v 14a.

Notice that whereas לֹא־תַעֲשֹׁק is linked to the next word by the conjunctive marker merka (**?** see our discussion of 2 Kgs 14:23), שָׂכִיר is separated from the expression עָנִי וְאֶבְיֹון by ṭifḥa (**?** see our discussion of 1 Sam 1:21).

The second part of the verse consists of a clause that further defines the social group referred to in the first part. This clause contains another example of an inclusive legal אֹו clause (**?** see our discussion of Exod 21 *passim*), and in some ways it may be compared to a modern expression such as, "This regulation applies equally to citizens and permanent residents of . . . "

The term גֵּר in this verse, and in Deuteronomy in general, refers to a landless, powerless, most likely very poor non-Israelite (except when the referent is Israel in Egypt) who resides either permanently or temporarily in the land of Israel. This range of meanings is conveyed neither by "sojourner" nor by "alien," which are the most common English translations of גֵּר; you may simply write *ger* in yours.

Translate v 14.

```




```

Note

This verse is rich in terms and concepts that are common in deuteronomic or deuteronomistic literature, such as אָחִיךָ pointing to a fellow Israelite, the reference to שְׁעָרֶיךָ and אַרְצֶךָ, the expression וְגֵרְךָ אֲשֶׁר בִּשְׁעָרֶיךָ (Deut 5:14; 31:12), and the tendency to bring the *ger* and the Israelites under one law in terms of responsibilities and protection (e.g., Deut 1:16; 5:14; 16:11; 31:12). This tendency is further developed in such priestly writings as Lev 24:22 and Exod 12:49. (See also Lev 16:29; 17:8–10; 19:34–35 cf. Lev 19:18; → Mayes, *Deuteronomy* 124–25.)

For Further Thought

In social terms, how would you describe the "you" in this text?

Verse 14 commands the addressees not to withhold what is due to a hired poor and needy worker. But such a command leads the "you" in the text to ask, What is meant by withholding? In other words, when should we pay such a laborer? The answer comes in the first half of the next verse.

Verse 15.

Since the main issue here is time, references to time introduce and close the first portion of the verse.

Translate לֹא־תָבוֹא עָלָיו הַשֶּׁמֶשׁ . . . בְּיוֹמוֹ

```




```

The next part of v 15a answers a different question: *Why* is paying such a worker on a daily basis so important that not doing so is absolutely prohibited?

Note

The shift in the implied question being answered by the text is mirrored in the way in which the text refers to the poor and needy worker. When the text discusses the question of *when* payment should be made, time is discussed in relation to the worker—it is the central issue of בְּיוֹמוֹ . . . לֹא־תָבוֹא עָלָיו. Accordingly, in this portion, pronominal suffixes point to the worker. But when the issue at stake is *why* to pay daily, it is the workers themselves whose concerns are central, and so the independent pronoun הוּא stands for the poor and needy laborer.

כִּי עָנִי הוּא

Is this an identifying or a classifying clause? (**?** see our discussion of Exod 21:29.)

Translate v 15a.

Verse 15b brings this section to a conclusion with a direct warning.

וְלֹא־יִקְרָא עָלֶיךָ אֶל־ה' וְהָיָה בְךָ חֵטְא

Translate v 15b.

The verse clearly implies that if this rule is neglected, the Lord will hear the call of the poor and needy hired worker and will punish those who withhold the worker's wages (cf. Exod 22:20–23). This assumes that the Lord is the King in accordance with the ancient Near Eastern image of the ideal monarch as the protector of the weak in society, such as widows and orphans (→ Boyce, *Cry to God*).

For Further Thought

The withholder is warned of divine justice, but no worldly justice is mentioned. What does this text suggest concerning the actual capacity of the poor and needy hired worker to get the daily salary from a recalcitrant employer before evening?

These verses bear a formal resemblance to other legal texts you have read, but they do not contain a law, in the sense of a judicial (or cultic) law. They are basically an exhortation to behave in a socially responsible way—an exhortation that is rhetorically buttressed by a warning that the powerful God will defend those who seem to be powerless (cf. Prov 22:22–23)?

Translate vv 14–15.

```



```

Subunit 2: v 16.

This verse is to be considered a parenthetical comment related formally to the text by a catchword. *Find* this catchword. . . . .

Note

Verse 16 presents an issue that seems to be only remotely related, namely the restriction of capital punishment to the person who is guilty. And by the way in which the reader is addressed, this verse sets itself apart from its textual surround, for it is not formulated as a direct address to the Israelites as are other parts of this section from Deuteronomy (for vv 14–15, see בְּךָ, לֹא־תַעֲשֹׁק; for vv 17–22, see below). It has been proposed that this verse was included here as a theological response to Exod 22:20–23, which addresses many of the same issues that our reading from Deuteronomy deals with.

Analyze יוּמְתוּ (**?** K. 185, 362, 401; Gr. 62, 82; Ke. 318, 325–26; L. 243–44; S. 247–50; W. 115, 199–200.)

Root	Stem	Form	PGN	SF	OS	BRM

Analyze יוּמָתוּ

Clue: How does this form relate to the preceding one? Take into account the position of this verb in the verse (**?** see our discussion of Lev 5:22).

Root	Stem	Form	PGN	SF	OS	BRM

Is the subject of יוּמָתוּ singular or plural? . . . .

You may wonder about a possible noncorrespondence between the number (singular or plural) of the noun and that of the verbal form. But אִישׁ here means "every person." When אִישׁ is used in this form, it shows a strong tendency to take verbs in the plural (→ GKC §139 b; JM §147 d).

Translate v 16.

Clue: עַל here may be translated as either "for" or "together with"; probably both meanings were intended.

```
```

For Further Thought

Read the quotation from סֵפֶר תּוֹרַת־מֹשֶׁה in 2 Kgs 14:6, according to both the qere and the ketiv (**?** see below). Compare with Deut 24:16. What conclusions do you reach from this comparison?

In most printed editions the qere is indicated by a ק marker in the margins of the text. The edition published by the British and Foreign Bible Society (ed. Snaith) is an exception. There the qere is indicated at the bottom of the page by a ק׳ marker.

The qere represents the "reading" tradition of a word, i.e., the way in which it is to be read; the ketiv represents the "written" tradition, i.e., the way in which it is to be written. We will see qere/ketiv variants in other texts, e.g., Isa 49:5. (→ on ketiv-qere, see GKC §17 a–c, and JM §16 e; for more advanced readings, see Yeivin, *Introduction*, 52–64, and Barr, "New Look at Kethibh-Qere.")

Subunit 3: vv 17–18.

Verse 17.

Analyze תַּטֶּה (**?** K. 150; Gr. 105; Ke. 306; L. 227; S. 209–11; W. 224–25.)

Root	Stem	Form	PGN	SF	OS	BRM

Analyze תַּחֲבֹל

Root	Stem	Form	PGN	SF	OS	BRM

In legal texts, the root חבל in the qal stem points to seizing goods as a pledge or, more likely, as a distress after a loan has not been repaid (→ Milgrom, *Cult and Conscience*, 95–98). לֹא תַחֲבֹל may be translated as "you (the creditor) shall not confiscate."

Translate v 17.

```



```

Following the interlude of v 16, the text goes back to the prohibitions of seemingly "profitable" actions by people in positions of strength against the weak. In v 17, as in v 14, the negative command is explicitly introduced; in both verses, there is an implicit description of the addressees as those who are in positions of social strength (judges and creditors in v 17, employers of poor and needy hired workers in v 14); and both verses explicitly refer to the protection of the weak within society. Verse 17 contains the typical list of the powerless in society, namely widows, orphans, and *gerim* (see Deut 10:18; 14:29; 16:11; 24:17,19,20,21; 26:12,13; 27:19; Jer 7:6; 22:3; Ezek 22:7; Zech 7:10; Mal 3:5). Verse 14 mentions another weak element in society, the hired laborer who is poor and needy. This element is included in the typical list found in Mal 3:5.

The structural parallelism between vv 14 and 17 suggests that we might expect v 18 to be parallel to v 15 in explaining why the addressees should behave in this way and in containing a clear, implicit warning.

Verse 18.

Analyze וַיִּפְדְּךָ

Root	Stem	Form	PGN	SF	OS	BRM

Analyze מְצַוְּךָ. Is the root of מְצַוְּךָ hollow? . . . . (? K. 159; Gr. 90; Ke. 80–81; L. 143; S. 181; W. 202.)

Root	Stem	Form	PGN	SF	OS	BRM

Translate v 18.

```
┌─────────────────────────────────────────────────────────────┐
│                                                             │
│                                                             │
│                                                             │
│                                                             │
│                                                             │
└─────────────────────────────────────────────────────────────┘
```

Both the language and contents of v 18 are strongly characteristic of Deuteronomy (see Deut 5:15; 15:15; 16:12; 24:22).

Does the atnaḥ in v 18 point to a significant semantic distinction within the verse? If so, *explain.* . . . .

Note

The apodosis opens with . . . עַל־כֵּן אָנֹכִי מְצַוְּךָ, which is usually translated as "therefore I command you." Since כֵּן refers to something mentioned earlier in the text (i.e., it has an anaphoric function), its role in the expression may be compared to that of the English "fore" in "therefore." One must remember that two כֵּן forms, עַל־כֵּן and לָכֵן, are usually translated by the English "therefore," though they are not fully interchangeable. The expression עַל־כֵּן אָנֹכִי מְצַוְּךָ occurs several times in Deuteronomy (Deut 15:11,15; 19:7; 24:18,22), whereas לָכֵן אָנֹכִי מְצַוְּךָ is not attested in Deuteronomy or anywhere else in the OT/HB.

Waltke and O'Connor summarize the difference between עַל־כֵּן and לָכֵן as follows: "The first of these (לָכֵן) usually introduces a proposed or anticipated response after a statement of certain conditions. . . . In contrast, עַל־כֵּן usually introduces a statement of later effects, notably the adoption of a name or a custom" (WO'C 39.3.4e, p. 666). In our case, the state of affairs introduced by עַל־כֵּן consists of a new and lasting commandment.

Neither לָכֵן nor עַל־כֵּן should be mechanically translated as "therefore." Although they always refer a new situation or impending action to a set of circumstances mentioned earlier in the text, the relation between them expressed by לָכֵן and עַל־כֵּן is not always one of cause and effect (see, for instance, Judg 11:8). In many cases, a more general paraphrase of the text, such as "taking all this into account," is perhaps preferable to the much more explicit "therefore." (→ Jongelin, "LAKEN dans l'Ancient Testament.")

Subunit 4: v 19.

This verse contains both the law and the rhetorical argument for its keeping. The rhetorical argument is set apart from the law by atnaḥ, and not by sof-pasuq, as in vv 17–18.

Translate כִּי תִקְצֹר קְצִירְךָ בְשָׂדֶךָ

```
┌─────────────────────────────────────────────────────┐
│                                                       │
│                                                       │
│                                                       │
│                                                       │
│                                                       │
└─────────────────────────────────────────────────────┘
```

Does כִּי תִקְצֹר קְצִירְךָ בְשָׂדֶךָ help to characterize the following text in terms of the two formulations in which legal principles and laws are generally presented in the OT/HB (i.e., apodeictic and casuistic formulations; **?** see the introductory discussion of chapter 2.1)? . . . .

. . . .

Compare the opening phrase of this verse (כִּי תִקְצֹר קְצִירְךָ בְשָׂדֶךָ) with that of vv 14 and 17.

. . . .

Can you point to the repetitions of sound in כִּי תִקְצֹר קְצִירְךָ בְשָׂדֶךָ? What do they empha-size? . . . .

If קְצִירְךָ is a definite noun and the direct object of תִקְצֹר (**?** K. 22; Ke. 71; L. 90; S. 70; W. 53), one may expect to read כִּי תִקְצֹר אֶת־קְצִירְךָ. Certainly, the writer was free to choose between these two alternatives. Would you like to suggest a possible explanation for the writer's choice? (**?** 1 Sam 8:12.) . . . .

. . . .

The protasis in v 19a ends with a note that opens with a vav-affix verb. You have already seen similar cases, for instance, in Exod 21:28a. There, the closing note pointed to the relevant consequence (or result) of the described situation; but this closing note can hardly be understood in such a way. Nonetheless, one can easily find a common denominator for these two notes, for they both describe a situation that follows (either chronologically or logically or both) the one just mentioned and is introduced by a verb in the prefix form (→ WO'C 32.2.1c, pp. 526–27; cf. JM §176 c–d).

Translate וְשָׁכַחְתָּ עֹמֶר בַּשָׂדֶה

```
┌─────────────────────────────────────────────────────┐
│                                                       │
│                                                       │
│                                                       │
│                                                       │
│                                                       │
└─────────────────────────────────────────────────────┘
```

The word שָׂדֶה (notice the repetition) shows a disjunctive marker that we have not discussed as yet. It is called revia, and many times it divides a zaqef clause (→ Yeivin, *Introduction*, 187). Here it points to the end of the protasis.

לֹא תָשׁוּב לְקַחְתּוֹ

In this verse the negative command (לֹא + prefix) that the addressees should obey comes in the apodosis rather than opening the unit as in vv 14 and 17. The difference goes back to the main division about the way in which laws are presented: v 19 (and vv 20 and 21) follow a casuistic model, vv 14 and 17 an apodeictic one.

Analyze לְקַחְתּוֹ **?** (K. 123; Gr. 105; Ke. 302, 305–07; L. 134; S. 188–89; W. 149–50.)

Root	Stem	Form	PGN	SF	OS	BRM

(→ on the verbal patterns of the root לקח, see our note on Ps 15:5.)

Translate לֹא תָשׁוּב לְקַחְתּוֹ

The contents of the next section of v 19a are quite expected. The previous units include an explicit reference to the direct beneficiaries of these commandments, namely, the weak. Moreover, this law could have hardly concluded with the command not to go back to get the sheaf without an explanation. The social and humanitarian function of leaving the sheaf needs to be spelled out.

Translate לַגֵּר לַיָּתוֹם וְלָאַלְמָנָה יִהְיֶה (Notice the inverted and repeated form of היה ל)

Exactly the same expression concludes vv 20 and 21, each of which presents a similar instruction to the one in v 19. This triple repetition not only unifies these three units, but also underscores the main message: the goods we are talking about belong to the *ger*, the orphan, and the widow, and to no one else, including "you," the owner of the field.

As in the other units, this unit concludes with the response given to the addressees' implied questions: Why should we follow this law which will certainly diminish our profits? Does the ownership of sheaves reaped in our fields depend upon whether we momentarily forget them? Verse 19b answers these questions.

לְמַעַן may indicate either purpose or result in biblical Hebrew (→ Williams, *Hebrew Syntax*, 61–62; JM §168 d, 169 g, i; WO'C 38.3a–c, pp. 638–40). In v 19b, לְמַעַן should be translated as "so that."

Analyze יְבָרֶכְךָ (? K. 73; Gr. 108, 113; Ke. 250; L. 195; S. 201; W. 167–68.)

Root	Stem	Form	PGN	SF	OS	BRM

Translate v 19b.

The contents as well as the language of v 19b are attested elsewhere in Deuteronomy (Deut 14:29; 23:21). The exhortation conveyed by this and similar expressions is clear, namely, that "you" should share a relatively small portion of your profit with those in need so that the Lord will keep providing for you. Of course, this message contains an implied warning, reminding the reader of the explicit one in v 15b. As mentioned above, the theological background against which these warnings are made is the image of the Lord as ideal monarch (→ discussion of v 15b).

The text does not mention any worldly legal action against the owner of a field who would go back and get the sheaves; the possible punishment for such an action seems to be within the realm of divine rather than human justice. Hence the exhortative function of these laws comes again to the forefront.

Translate v 19.

Subunit 5: vv 20–22.

The aim of the law in v 19 is to convince the owner of the field to share some of his or her grain with the weak. As part of the persuasive appeal of this law, the owner is offered a reassurance that not only will this action not result in a loss, but it is actually a necessary action even from the landholder's perspective, for, according to Deuteronomy, there is no blessing without sharing.

Of course, the land (or, according to the theological discourse of the Book of Deuteronomy, the blessing of God through the land) provides more than just grain. It also brings forth other goods, especially olives and grapes, which are turned into oil and wine. The production of the fields is usually characterized as grain, wine, and oil. (See, for instance, Num 18:12; Deut 7:13; 11:14; 12:17; 14:23; 18:4; 28:51; Jer 31:12; Hos 2:10,24; 2 Kgs 18:32; Neh 5:11; 10:40; 13:5,12.) The laws in the next verses (vv 20 and 21) deal with ways in which owners of vineyards and olive groves are supposed to share their production with the weak in society.

Verse 20.

Analyze and **translate** תְּפָאֵר and תַחְבֹּט

Root	Stem	Form	PGN	SF	OS	BRM

Root	Stem	Form	PGN	SF	OS	BRM

Explain the pataḥ of the first verb (❓ K. 85; Gr. 109–10; L. 114–15; S. 148; W. 155) and the qamets of the second (❓ see your analysis of יְבָרֶכְךָ in v 19). . . . .
. . . .

Verse 21.

Analyze and **translate** תְּבֹצֵר and תְעוֹלֵל (❓ K. 209; Gr. 138; Ke. 326–27; L. 253–54; S. 253–54; W. 201–2.)

Root	Stem	Form	PGN	SF	OS	BRM

Root	Stem	Form	PGN	SF	OS	BRM

Translate vv 20–21.

Verse 22.

Verse 22 completes the pattern we have seen in vv 14–19: it answers their implied question: Why should we follow this law (vv 20–21), which certainly diminishes our profit?

Translate v 22.

Have you read a similar verse before? Where? . . . .

    Some attention to stylistic considerations is now in order. How would you characterize the relationship between vv 20 and 21, and between both of these verses and v 19? *Map* the patterns of repetition (be they entire sentences, words, sounds, endings, or structural shaping of verses) and *relate* them to the message of these verses. . . . .

. . . .

. . . .

For Further Thought

How does the withholder of wages (vv 14–16) relate to the creditor (vv 17–18), and the creditor in turn to the landholder (vv 19–21)? Is there a gradual heightening of the moral demand throughout the passage? Does the placement of stylistic markers support your position?

    Translate the whole passage, Deut 24:14–22.

Works Cited in This Section

J. Barr, "A New Look at Kethibh-Qere," in B. Albrektson et al., *Remembering All the Way* (OTS 21; Leiden: E. J. Brill, 1981), 19–37; **R. N. Boyce,** *The Cry to God in the Old Testament* (SBLDS 103; Atlanta: Scholars Press, 1988); **S. McEvenue,** *Interpreting the Pentateuch* (OTS 4; Collegeville, Minn.: Glazier, 1990), 128–33; **S. Gillingham,** "The Poor in the Psalms," *ExpT* 100 (1988): 15–19; **B. Jongelin,** "LAKEN dans l'Ancient Testament," in B. Albrektson et al., *Remembering All the Way* (OTS 21; Leiden: E. J. Brill, 1981), 190–200; **A. D. H. Mayes,** *Deuteronomy* (NCB; Grand Rapids, Mich./London: Eerdmans/Marshall Morgan & Scott, 1981); **R. N. Whybray,** "Poverty, Wealth and Point of View in Proverbs," *ExpT* 100 (1989): 332–36; **R. J. Williams,** *Hebrew Syntax: An Outline* (2d ed.; Toronto: University of Toronto Press, 1984); **I. Yeivin,** *Introduction to the Tiberian Masorah* (Masoretic Studies 5; Missoula, Mont.: Scholars Press, 1980).

3.   Readings in Prophetic Literature

3.1   Jeremiah 22:1–5

We will begin our readings from the prophetic books with a passage from the Book of Jeremiah that shows social concerns reminiscent of biblical texts we have already read, and a theological perspective similar to that found in Deuteronomy. But unlike Deuteronomy, in which the speaker claims to report events and laws from Moses' time, the divine speech reported in Jer 22:1–5 is anchored in the last days of the Judean monarchy, on the eve of the destruction of the Temple, the razing of Jerusalem, and the downfall of the monarchy.

Verse 1.

Translate כֹּה אָמַר ה' ....

כֹּה אָמַר ה' is a very common formula in prophetic literature and is called "the messenger formula." In Jer 22, it sets apart the following speech from the preceding material and (as is always the case) characterizes the following material as divine speech. The formula by itself does not claim to be divine speech (the Lord is referred to in the third person).

Who do you think is the speaker here? ....
Why is this formula called the messenger formula? ....
....

כֹּה אָמַר ה' reflects the way in which political messengers used to present the words of their lords (e.g., 2 Kgs 18:19). Thus, prophetic texts introduced by this formula conveyed an analogy between prophets and messengers of a worldly king. What are the possible implications of this similitude? (→ Hals, *Ezekiel*, 361; Rendtorff, *Old Testament*, 116.)

כֹּה has a **cataphoric** function; that is, it calls attention to something that is mentioned later in the text. Do you remember a word that points to something mentioned earlier in the text? (**?** see our note in Deut 24:18.)

Analyze רֵד

Root	Stem	Form	PGN	SF	OS	BRM

Translate v 1. (**?** on how to translate the "imperative/vav-affix" sequence, see K. 274; Ke. 214–15; L. 118–19; S. 174; and our discussion of Lev 5:20.)

```
┌─────────────────────────────────────────────────────────────────────┐
│                                                                       │
│                                                                       │
│                                                                       │
│                                                                       │
│                                                                       │
└─────────────────────────────────────────────────────────────────────┘
```

Here we find a verb from the root ירד which is not followed by a preposition. Though it is not usually the case, sometimes an expected preposition is omitted (for another example, see Jer 36:12). Your translation should not be affected by this "missing" preposition.

For Further Thought

According to this verse, when the prophet received this divine message he stood in a place which was geographically higher than the royal palace. One may speculate that he was in the Temple, but many other places (especially on the Western Hill of Jerusalem) are also possible. In any case, the writer did not tell us where the prophet stood, nor when he proclaimed these words, nor even to which of the last kings of Judah they are addressed. The text is written in such a way that a clear attachment to a specific moment is avoided.

When you finish this section (3.1), come back to this issue and suggest a possible relation between the contents of this passage and its generalized setting.

In contrast to the vague temporal reference, the text clearly specifies the place in which the prophet is supposed to deliver this divine message. The emphatic use of שָׁם seems to underscore this point.

After reading the entire passage (Jer 22:1–5), be prepared to offer a possible explanation for the singling out of the palace.

Verse 2.

אָמַרְתָּ֙

Note

The disjunctive marker pashṭa (תָּ֙) is one of the markers that divide zaqef clauses into two main sections. (Revia is another marker that does so; **?** see our discussion of Deut 24:19.) Pashṭa is attested when the main division occurs one word before the zaqef. It is likely to be present when the division stands two words before the zaqef (as in our case; → Yeivin, *Introduction*, 186). In v 2, it signals the end of the divine speech addressed to the prophet. The text immediately following it claims to be a quotation of the divine speech that the prophet is supposed to proclaim at the palace.

What is the function of the metheg underneath the א in אָמַרְתָּ? (**?** K. 370; Gr. 133; Ke. 17–18; L. xxvii; S. 291; W. 7–8; → GKC §16 c–i; JM §14.)

Neither the Hebrew manuscripts nor the printed versions are consistent in regard to the use of this kind of metheg, or ga'ya, as it is also called. It often fails when expected. (→ Yeivin, *Introduction*, 248–52.) As a reader you should not be troubled by its absence; but if it is present, you should know what it is signaling.

Analyze שְׁמַע

Root	Stem	Form	PGN	SF	OS	BRM

Who is to listen?

Translate v 2a in order to answer this question.

Clue: The article in הַיֹּשֵׁב has the function of a relative, which is a quite common case before participles. You should translate it as either "who . . . " or "the one who . . . " → WO'C 13.5.2d, p. 248.

One cannot consider the king to be the subject of the sentence for he is the person addressed in the speech. A noun that identifies the addressee of an imperative is called **vocative** (→ WO'C 4.7d, p. 77; 8.3d, p. 130).

If a clause follows a vocative noun, it is usually phrased in the third person, as in our case . . . הַיֹּשֵׁב. The expression יֹשֵׁב . . . כִּסֵּא דָוִד occurs also in Jer 17:25; 22:30, and 36:30 but nowhere else in the Latter Prophets (the books from Isaiah to Malachi).

As you will see, the Book of Jeremiah, like other books in the OT/HB, shows a certain degree of "characteristic" language, especially in its prose sections (see, for instance, the expression הַבָּאִים בַּשְּׁעָרִים הָאֵלֶּה in this verse and in Jer 7:2 and 17:20; → Stulman, *Prose Sermons*).

Note

דְּבַר־ה' and מֶלֶךְ יְהוּדָה show the same grammatical structure, namely a construct chain. Nevertheless the masoretes (**?** K. 369; Gr. 177–79; Ke. 436; L. xiv; S. x) indicate a difference between them that is reflected in the written text. In the first case, ה' and דְּבַר are linked by maqqef (**?** K. 10, 21, 368; Gr. 132, 145 n.1; Ke. 12, 436; L. 5; S. 33, 71, 291; W.

12.) Therefore, they are considered as if they were one word; they have one accent which is marked by the zaqef. Since zaqef is a disjunctive marker, it also sets דְּבַר־ה׳ apart from what follows. On the other end, דְּבַר־ה׳ is linked to what precedes it by a main conjunctive marker under שְׁמַע. This marker (מַ) is called munaḥ (→ Yeivin, *Introduction*, 179; note that in Kelley, *Grammar*, munaḥ "has been adopted as the standard accent for words accented on any syllable other than their final syllable" [437]). Another munaḥ is attested between מֶלֶךְ and יְהוּדָה. Since munaḥ is not maqqef, each of these two nouns has its own accent (which is marked by the munaḥ in מֶלֶךְ and the zaqef in יְהוּדָה). Thus, they are linked one to the other but not so closely as to be read as if they were a single word. Remember that munaḥ is a very common marker in construct chains. *Find* a munaḥ other than the one in מֶלֶךְ יְהוּדָה in v 2a.

The range of the people to be addressed by the prophet grows in the second part of the verse, while at the same time the speech becomes more personally directed to the king.

Translate אַתָּה וַעֲבָדֶיךָ וְעַמְּךָ הַבָּאִים בַּשְּׁעָרִים הָאֵלֶּה

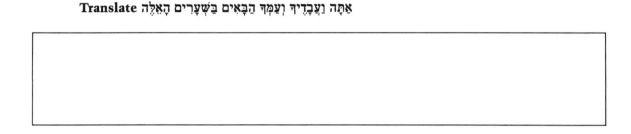

You probably translated עַמְּךָ as "your people," but what do you think the writer would have meant by that? All the people of Judah? If so, your translation would imply that anyone among the people of Judah would be welcome to come to the palace. On the other hand, you may interpret עַמְּךָ as pointing specifically to the people of the king, those who are faithful to him and carry out his orders—in short, the people of the court. A third possibility is to understand עַמְּךָ as pointing to a certain social and political group that is presented as representative of the people of Judah (see, for instance, 2 Kgs 11:13–20; 21:4; Jer 26:11–19). This way of understanding "people" is similar to the modern journalistic use of the names of nations. For instance, one may read, "The United States proposes . . . ," whereas in fact the referent is the government of the United States. A fourth possibility is that עַמְּךָ refers to "your army" (for הָעָם, "the army," see Deut 20:1; 1 Kgs 16:16; 20:10). According to the last three options, those referred to as עַמְּךָ have at least some degree of authority and social power.

The next verse will help us understand what is meant by עַמְּךָ in this text. But, first some grammatical issues in this half-verse are worthy of special consideration:

—This half-verse contains an example of the article functioning as if it were a relative pronoun. *Find* it.

—The addressees are clearly many, so why does the text read שְׁמַע and not שִׁמְעוּ in v 2a? (**?** read Gen 13:1.)

—Five out of the six separate words that compose this half-verse contain a letter with dagesh forte. *Explain* why each of these words shows a doubled letter.

Translate all of v 2.

```



```

Verse 3.

כֹּה אָמַר ה'

We have seen this prophetic formula before. Here it marks the opening words the prophet is asked to say to the king and his officers. Its rhetorical function within the prophetic speech is to provide the audience with an important interpretative key, namely, that this speech is God's (not the prophet's) and therefore its truthfulness is beyond dispute.

The reported message of God is, of course, written in the first person. It begins after the revia (**?** see our discussion of Deut 24:19) and ends in v 5. It is divided into three main sections, which correspond to vv 3, 4, and 5, respectively. The section in v 3 consists of four sentences set apart by disjunctive markers.

(a) עֲשֹׂו מִשְׁפָּט וּצְדָקָה

עֲשֹׂו in this verse, עָשֹׂו (in v 4), and the relatively common עָשֹׂו look very similar at first glance, but they are quite different.

Analyze and differentiate עֲשֹׂו, עָשֹׂו, and עָשֹׂו

Root	Stem	Form	PGN	SF	OS	BRM

Root	Stem	Form	PGN	SF	OS	BRM

Root	Stem	Form	PGN	SF	OS	BRM

מִשְׁפָּט וּצְדָקָה is a typical instance of hendiadys (**?** see our discussion of 2 Kgs 14:26). The two nouns have a single referent, which may be translated as "justice and righteousness," "what is just and right," or "righteous justice." Notice that "righteous" in the latter is closer to "according to the divine/moral law" than to any meaning of "righteous" in modern English.

Note
It is worth remembering some of the ways in which hendiadys is used:

—the same hendiadic pair may occur in the inverse position; compare מִשְׁפָּט וּצְדָקָה in our verse with צְדָקָה וּמִשְׁפָּט in Ps 33:5;

—the ו may be omitted. One reads שָׁלוֹם וֶאֱמֶת in 2 Kgs 20:19 but שָׁלוֹם אֱמֶת in Jer 14:13;

—the two nouns do not necessarily stand next to one another in the sentence, as שִׁמְרוּ מִשְׁפָּט וַעֲשׂוּ צְדָקָה in Isa 56:1 clearly illustrates.

Translate sentence (a).

```



```

The next three sentences tell the reader what the command "to do what is right and just" entails.

(b) וְהַצִּילוּ גָזוּל מִיַּד עָשׁוֹק

Analyze וְהַצִּילוּ and גָזוּל

Root	Stem	Form	PGN	SF	OS	BRM

Root	Stem	Form	PGN	SF	OS	BRM

Should וְהַצִּילוּ be translated as if it were another imperative (i.e., "do . . . and deliver . . . ")? If so, why? (**?** see our discussion of Jer 22:1.)

We have learned that terms from the root עשק in legal texts refer specifically to withholding someone else's property, the possession of which was gained by legal means (**?** see our discussion of Lev 5 and Deut 24). In the same kind of texts, terms from the root גזל cover the case of a withholder who took possession of property by illegal use of force. Since both terms convey a sense of robbery, in non-legal texts they may be used as synonyms (→ Milgrom, *Cult and Conscience*, 98–99). It is worth remembering that in biblical Hebrew, as in English, words may have one meaning in the legal sphere and another in common language; moreover, the actual meaning of a word is always dependent on its context and on the genre of the text.

Translate sentence (b).

```

```

Note

The word עָשׁוֹק occurs only once in the OT/HB. (The technical term for a word attested by a single occurrence is **hapax legomenon**. → For a substantial work on biblical *hapax legomena*, see Greenspahn, *Hapax legomena*.) This עָשׁוֹק may well be the result of the work of a scribe who wrote עשׁוק instead of עושׁק in a text that predated the masoretic vocalized text (**?** see our discussion of 2 Kgs 14:26). If so, the original עושׁק would have stood for the word עוֹשֵׁק and our sentence would have read וְהַצִּילוּ גָזוּל מִיַּד עוֹשֵׁק exactly as in Jer 21:12. The alternative is to keep עָשׁוֹק and compare it with such adjectives as גָּדוֹל and קָרוֹב (as was done by Radaq more than seven hundred years ago). These adjectives may occasionally be used as nouns. Significantly, the pattern קָטוֹל for *nomen agentis* is quite common in mishnaic Hebrew, for instance טָחוֹן, "miller," and לָקוֹחַ, "buyer." (→ Segal, *Grammar of Mishnaic Hebrew*, 106; JM §88E a.)

According to this text, to do justice and righteousness entails more than administering fair justice in the court. The addressees of this speech are asked to rescue the oppressed from the hands of the oppressor. It follows, then, that they themselves should not act as oppressors. This is the main issue of sentences (c) and (d). These two sentences are related to one another not only by their respective contents but also by a common emphatic word order in which the object heads the sentence (→ Muraoka, *Emphatic Words*, 37–41). They are also related by the use of the negative command, אַל + prefix, which stands in sharp contrast to the positive commands expressed in sentences (a) and (b).

(c) וְגֵר יָתוֹם וְאַלְמָנָה אַל־תֹּנוּ אַל־תַּחְמֹסוּ

We have discussed the expression וְגֵר יָתוֹם וְאַלְמָנָה in Deut 24:17. This locution occurs many times in Deuteronomy, and in the Book of Jeremiah, in Jer 7:6a, a verse whose language is very much like that of Jer 22:3.

אַל־תֹּנוּ may be considered a somewhat difficult verb to analyze because only one consonant of the root is present. The ת and the וּ provide you with the information needed to decide the person, gender, and number of the verb as well as its form. The ḥolem immediately after the ת gives you information concerning the stem and the first letter of the root. How can you find the third letter of the root?

Analyze אַל־תֹּנוּ **(?** K. 148–49, 150; Gr. 90, 93; Ke. 288, 343–44; L. 222–23; S. 208–10; W. 190, 219.)

Root	Stem	Form	PGN	SF	OS	BRM

Analyze אַל־תַּחְמֹסוּ

Root	Stem	Form	PGN	SF	OS	BRM

Translate sentence (c).

(d) וְדָם נָקִי אַל־תִּשְׁפְּכוּ בַּמָּקוֹם הַזֶּה

Translate sentence (d).

This sentence occurs word for word in Jer 7:6a. There בַּמָּקוֹם הַזֶּה refers to the Temple. Is this the case in Jer 22:3? . . . .

וְדָם נָקִי אַל־תִּשְׁפְּכוּ is considered a deuteronomistic phrase, i.e., a locution characteristic of writers who were strongly influenced by the contents and language of the Book of Deuteronomy (→ Stulman, *Prose Sermons*). The use of such phrases as גֵּר יָתוֹם וְאַלְמָנָה is consistent with this influence.

Translate all of verse 3.

```



```

For Further Thought

How would you describe the addressees of this verse? Who, do you think, is "your people" in v 2?

> **"Jeremiah 22:4–5 contains a quite symmetrical statement concerning the assured gains and losses related to the imperatives of v 3. This unit is arranged in two parallel 'if . . . then' structures, one positive and one negative. . . . The 'if . . . then' structure is remarkable, for this rhetoric makes the monarchy explicitly conditional" (Brueggemann, *Jeremiah 1–25*, 188).**

Verse 4.

This verse contains the first of the "if . . . then . . ." structures mentioned by Brueggemann. *Identify* the protasis. . . . .

The range of the possible meanings conveyed by כִּי is certainly not narrow. But in this sentence it is clearly an asseverative כִּי and should be translated as "indeed" or "truly" or "surely." The use of כִּי as an asseverative is probably related to its use in oaths (Williams, *Hebrew Syntax*, 73). In any case, this use of כִּי in v 4 is reminiscent of the language of an oath (cf. JM §165 e). Significantly, the negative "if . . . then . . ." structure in v 5 explicitly contains an oath in its apodosis.

Translate v 4a. (**?** see your analysis of עָשׂוֹ)

```



```

The apodosis begins, as in many other instances and especially after a protasis beginning with כִּי or אִם, with vav-affix. (→ JM §176 d; WO'C 32.2.1b, p. 526.)

Translate v 4b up to the zaqef. (**?** write the phrase introduced by the revia within commas.)

```
┌─────────────────────────────────────────────────────────────────────────┐
│                                                                           │
│                                                                           │
│                                                                           │
│                                                                           │
│                                                                           │
└─────────────────────────────────────────────────────────────────────────┘
```

You may wonder why the text reads בָרֶכֶב וּבְסוּסִים instead of בְּרֶכֶב וּבְסוּסִים. Of course, the reference is not a specific group of horses (i.e., "*the* horses") or chariots (רֶכֶב here has a collective meaning). The presence of the article here may be related to the generic character of the attached nouns, as expressed by translations such as "(riding) in chariots and on horses." (→ Williams, *Hebrew Syntax*, 19; cf. our discussion of Lev 5:22.)

The reference to "sitting on the throne of David" links this verse to v 2, and within the discourse of the speech, points to the addressees already identified in v 2. Nonetheless, up to this point only the main addressee (i.e., the king) is referred to. The conclusion of the verse (from zaqef to sof-pasuq) includes the "servants/officials" of the king and his "people."

Translate v 4 from the zaqef to the sof-pasuq.

```
┌─────────────────────────────────────────────────────────────────────────┐
│                                                                           │
│                                                                           │
│                                                                           │
│                                                                           │
│                                                                           │
└─────────────────────────────────────────────────────────────────────────┘
```

Perhaps you expected the text to read הֵם וְעַבְדֵיהֶם וְעַמָּם instead of הוּא וַעֲבָדָו וְעַמּוֹ, because of the plural מְלָכִים. If so, you may be glad to know that many scholars have thought as you did (→ McKane, *Jeremiah*, I, 514) and that ancient versions seem to point to this reading. As it stands, perhaps the best approach entails a distributive understanding: "each king with his . . . and his . . ."

For Further Thought

The qere shows עבדיו; the consonantal ketiv shows עבדו. To which reading of this phrase may the ketiv point? ....

Some scholars have suggested that the singular in the Hebrew text is due to a messianic interpretation. Is the ketiv congruent with this position?

Verse 5.

This verse contains the second of the "if . . . then . . ." structures mentioned by Brueggemann.

Identify and **translate** the protasis. (**?** remember that וְ may mean either "and" or "but.") . . . .

כִּי נִשְׁבַּעְתִּי נְאֻם־ה'

Analyze and **translate** כִּי נִשְׁבַּעְתִּי (**?** כִּי should be translated as "by myself.")

Root	Stem	Form	PGN	SF	OS	BRM

. . . .

כִּי נִשְׁבַּעְתִּי introduces an oath. Such expressions are generally followed either by ". . . כִּי" in case of a positive formulation ("I will . . .") or by ". . . אִם" if the formulation is negative ("I will not . . ."). (→ JM §165 b–d). Significantly, in v 5, the expression נְאֻם־ה' stands between כִּי נִשְׁבַּעְתִּי and the expected ". . . כִּי."

נְאֻם־ה' is a common formula in prophetic literature. It is called the "prophetic utterance formula" and is attested more than two hundred times in prophetic books, not counting closely related locutions such as נְאֻם ה' צְבָאוֹת. It is generally translated by "says the Lord" or "declares the Lord"; a more literal translation would be "utterance of the Lord." The function of the prophetic utterance formula is to legitimize a speech by explicitly attributing it to the Lord. In this sense it is similar to the messenger formula.

The prophetic utterance formula tends to occur at the end of a unit or a significant subunit within a prophetic speech (→ Hals, *Ezekiel*, 361–62). In Jer 22:1–5 it occurs only once, just before the Lord announces what will happen if the ruling elite do not do what is right and just. After reading this announcement of potential judgment, think about the reasons for introducing נְאֻם־ה' just here.

Note

There is another and perhaps more common way of introducing oaths, namely, by means of the "oath formula": חַי־X (where X may be God, the Lord, or a human lord such as Pharaoh. See our discussion of 1 Sam 1:26). This formula is also generally followed by . . . כִּי, if the formulation is positive, and by . . . אִם, if it is negative. (→ JM §165 e–f.)

כִּי־לְחָרְבָּה יִהְיֶה הַבַּיִת הַזֶּה

Following נְאֻם־ה' one finds the usual structure of the oath, though not an expression such as "I will . . .". Rather than emphasizing the action of the subject, the text wishes to stress the future situation of the object.

Translate כִּי־לְחָרְבָּה יִהְיֶה הַבַּיִת הַזֶּה

[blank box]

Translate all of Jer 22:1–5.

[blank box]

To some extent the message of the five-verse unit is encapsulated by the change within the similar conclusions of the first, middle, and last sections: הַדָּבָר הַזֶּה (v 1), בַּמָּקוֹם הַזֶּה (v 3), and הַבַּיִת הַזֶּה (v 5). Try to elaborate on this point. (**?** הַבַּיִת הַזֶּה refers directly to the royal palace, but in the context of this unit the connotation "House of David" is very likely.)

Please go back to the questions about the relationship of generalized and specified temporal and spatial settings to the message of this passage (see discussion of v 1). Are you able to make a statement about this now?

For Further Reading
On Jer 22:1–5, see McKane, *Jeremiah*, 514–17; Carroll, *Jeremiah*, 416–18; Holladay, *Jeremiah 1*, 580–82; and Brueggemann, *Jeremiah 1–25*, 187–89.

Works Cited in This Section
W. Brueggemann, *Jeremiah 1–25: To Pluck Up, to Tear Down* (ITC; Grand Rapids, Mich.: Eerdmans, 1988); **R. P. Carroll,** *Jeremiah* (OTL; Philadelphia: Westminster, 1986); **G. E. Greenspahn,** *Hapax legomena in Biblical Hebrew* (SBLDS 74; Chico, Calif.: Scholars Press, 1984); **R. M. Hals,** *Ezekiel* (FOTL 19; Grand Rapids, Mich.: Eerdmans, 1989); **W. L. Holladay,** *Jeremiah 1* (Hermeneia; Philadelphia: Fortress, 1986); **W. McKane,** *Jeremiah*, vol. 1 (ICC; Edinburgh: T. & T. Clark, 1986); **J. Milgrom,** *Cult and Conscience* (Leiden: E. J. Brill, 1976); **T. Muraoka,** *Emphatic Words and Structures in Biblical Hebrew* (Jerusalem/Leiden: Magnes/E. J. Brill, 1985); **R. Rendtorff,** *The Old Testament: An Introduction* (Philadelphia: Fortress, 1986); **M. H. Segal,** *A Gram-*

mar of Mishnaic Hebrew (Oxford: Clarendon Press, 1958); **L. Stulman,** *The Prose Sermons of the Book of Jeremiah* (SBLDS 83; Atlanta: Scholars Press, 1986); **R. J. Williams,** *Hebrew Syntax: An Outline* (2d ed.; Toronto: University of Toronto Press, 1984); **I. Yeivin,** *Introduction to the Tiberian Masorah* (Masoretic Studies 5; Missoula, Mont.: Scholars Press, 1980).

3.2 Ezekiel 37:1–14

This is one of the best-known pieces of prophetic literature, the vision of the valley of dry bones. The background of Ezek 37:1–14 is the situation of the Judean deportees in Babylonia. The powerful imagery of the passage, together with a tradition of interpretation that relates it to the issue of resurrection—whether national or personal—have significantly contributed to its popularity. As you read this passage, you will become more aware of the ways in which the text supports the flow of the argument. You will see how direct speech is integrated into a report written in the first person. And you will become acquainted with some additional formulaic expressions that not only characterize prophetic books but also strongly contribute to their communicative message. This reading will give you a chance to savor the characteristic language of the Book of Ezekiel. Thus, this text will challenge and help develop your ability to read Ezekiel and other prophetic texts.

Verse 1.

Translate up to the segolta. (**?** see our discussion of Lev 5:24.)

You probably translated יָד as "hand." This is its most common translation. But in fact there is no English word for יָד. Literally, יָד is the part of the body from the elbow to the tip of the fingers, not just the hand (→ WO'C 7.1b, p. 111). Metaphorically, יָד means "strength" (e.g., Josh 8:20), or even actions that are done through "strength" (see Exod 14:31; → BDB).

For Further Thought

Do you think that the historical audience of this text understood יָד literally or metaphorically? The expression הָיְתָה עָלַי יַד־ה' is the basic form of a formula relatively common in Ezekiel, sometimes called "the hand of the Lord revelatory formula" (→ Hals, *Ezekiel*, 360–61). In Ezekiel, this formula usually introduces a first-person account of a vision, either by itself or as the concluding element of a more complex introduction (Ezek 1:3; 3:22; 8:1; 33:22; 37:1; 40:1). Of course, these references to the hand of the Lord serve not only as markers of the beginning of a new unit but also as their main interpretive key. They signal that the message of the following text should be considered to be of divine origin and therefore extremely convincing.

Compare the use and message of the hand of the Lord revelatory formula with that of the messenger formula, 'כֹּה אָמַר ה (**?** see our discussion of Jer 22:1). . . . .
. . . .
. . . .

Compare the use and message of the hand of the Lord revelatory formula with that of the "prophetic utterance formula," i.e., נְאֻם־ה' (**?** our discussion of Jer 22:5). Point out the similarities and differences between the two. . . . .
. . . .
. . . .

Note

The most common marker of a new unit in Ezekiel is not the hand of the Lord revelatory formula but rather the prophetic word formula (וַיְהִי דְבַר־ה' אֵלַי לֵאמֹר). (→ on this formula, see Hals, *Ezekiel*, 362; Rendtorff, *Old Testament*, 116–17.)

The hand of the Lord revelatory formula, here and elsewhere in Ezekiel, is set apart from the following text by a main disjunctive marker (in most cases either sof-pasuq, atnaḥ, or segolta, and in a few cases zaqef). Can you explain why? . . . .
. . . .
. . . .

Immediately after this formula and its disjunctive marker, here and in its other occurrences, the narrative turns to a vav conversive–prefix verbal form (Ezek 1:4; 3:22; 8:2; 33:22; 37:1; 40:1).

Analyze וַיּוֹצִאֵנִי

Root	Stem	Form	PGN	SF	OS	BRM

Analyze וַיְנִיחֵנִי

Root	Stem	Form	PGN	SF	OS	BRM

There are two conjugations of נוח in the hif'il, and they differ in meaning. One of them is called hif'il A in BDB and means "cause to/give rest," whereas the other, hif'il B, means "set/lay down." The most conspicuous difference between the two is that the first letter of the radical is doubled in hif'il B. Which pattern does וַיְנִיחֵנִי follow? . . . . Double patterns in hif'il (and in nif'al) are attested for several hollow verbs (middle י/ו) although they do not always lead to differences in meaning. (→ GKC §72 ee; JM §80 p; for a similar situation concerning geminates, see GKC §67 g; JM §82 h.)

For Further Thought

Some scholars propose to emend the Hebrew text from וַיְנִיחֵנִי to וַיַּנִּיחֵנִי (e.g., Zimmerli, *Ezekiel 2*, 254). How would this emendation change the meaning of the text?

Translate v 1 from the segolta to the atnaḥ.

Who is the subject of וַיְנִיחֵנִי and וַיּוֹצִאֵנִי? . . . . *Clue:* יַד־ה' and רוּחַ ה' are unlikely candidates because יַד and רוּחַ are feminine nouns; יַד is considered to be masculine only in Exod 17:12. Also notice that רוּחַ is preceded by a preposition.

   If you find that within v 1 there is no easy answer to this question, you are right. You may follow one of these two alternatives:

(a) You may relate this vav conversive–prefix chain to that in v 3, as the context suggests. If so, who is the subject of the chain in v 1?

(b) You may consider these expressions impersonal and therefore translate the third-person masculine singular as an indefinite personal subject, "one" (→ GKC §144 d; JM §155 a–d; WO'C 4.4.2.a, pp. 70–71). If you follow this alternative, you may translate the phrase as, "one brought me out . . ." or, to make it more acceptable in English, "I was brought out . . ." (→ Wever, *Ezekiel*, 195.)

The repetition of sounds (which is continued in v 2a) points to the first person of the report, who is represented by a pronominal suffix. The rhetorical function of this repetition seems clear; both to bring to the forefront the first person of the report and to stress that the "I" of the report (the direct object) is not bringing about the change of circumstances described here, but rather is being affected by another agent. Thus far the identity of this agent is unclear, but the repetitive structure of רוּחַ ה' – יַד־ה' may be suggestive (cf. Ezek 3:22–27; 40:1–3).

   In our verse רוּחַ ה' is also related to the prophet's being moved by a force external to himself. Since רוּחַ may also mean wind (e.g., Gen 3:8), the image of wind moving the prophet (see also וְהֶעֱבִירַנִי in v 2a) is certainly alluded to (cf. Ezek 11:1,24; see also 1 Kgs 18:12; 2 Kgs 2:16). But this is not just any wind, for it is רוּחַ ה', a wind from the Lord.

The expression רוּחַ ה' has other connotations. In biblical Hebrew, divine names may provide a sense of the superlative. For instance, הַרְרֵי־אֵל in Ps 36:7 does not refer to "the mountains of God" but to "mighty mountains" (→ JM §141 n; WO'C 14.5b, p. 268). Thus, רוּחַ ה' in Ezek 37:1 suggests an image of a mighty wind.

The reference to רוּחַ ה' in this verse, immediately following הָיְתָה עָלַי יַד־ה', also suggests God's endowment of Ezekiel with a special and uncommon power or capacity, so that the prophet may fulfill a certain task (cf. Gen 41:38; Exod 31:3; 35:31; Num 24:2–3; Judg. 3:10; 6:34; 11:29; 14:6; 1 Sam 10:6,10; 16:13; 1 Kgs 22:24; Isa 11:2; 42:1; Ezek 3:24; 11:5; Mic 3:8). In the OT/HB the expression רוּחַ-X may well refer to the vital powers of X (e.g., Zech 12:1; the common English translation "spirit of X" reflects this understanding). Thus רוּחַ ה' in this verse suggests that Ezekiel's new capacity and his strange experience are intrinsically related to the divine vital power.

Of course, in your English translation, you are not expected to reflect the full range of meanings conveyed by the phrase רוּחַ ה'. (→ on the meanings of רוּחַ and רוּחַ ה' in the OT/HB, see Wolff, *Anthropology*, 32–39.)

In sharp contrast to the series of vav conversive–prefix forms, the second part of v 1 opens with vav + independent pronoun. Such a vav + (pro)noun sequence frequently has a disjunctive value, that is, it separates the clause or sentence from what is preceding it (**?** see our discussion of 1 Sam 1:9; for another instance of this disjunctive vav, see Isa 49:4). In this case, it marks an important change of focus in the narrative. The narrative moves from describing what happened to the prophet Ezekiel to describing the valley he saw, and then to the most significant feature of that valley: its being full of bones. Moreover, the narrative moves from a temporal and logical sequence of specific actions to a description of the already existing state of the valley.

Translate v 1b.

As you may observe, the new unit (v 1b) is linked to the preceding one (v 1ab) by the anchoring reference to its last word, הַבִּקְעָה ← הִיא. Here the pronoun reference also points to the main topic to which the text turns its attention. The same stylistic device is attested in v 2.

Verse 2.

וְהַעֲבִירַנִי עֲלֵיהֶם סָבִיב סָבִיב

Analyze וְהַעֲבִירַנִי

Root	Stem	Form	PGN	SF	OS	BRM

וְהַעֲבִירַנִי is a vav-affix form. It follows a series of vav conversive–prefix forms (interrupted by the clarifying comment on the main feature of the valley, v 1a), and shares with them a common ending, the reference to the direct object, "me." The main question is whether וְהַעֲבִירַנִי is the third component of a series of sequential actions (namely, "brought me out . . ." "caused me to rest/set me down . . ." "led me . . .") or not.

The same question may be phrased differently: Is the change from vav conversive–prefix forms to a vav-affix form merely a matter of style in Ezek 37:2? This may well be the case. First, such a use of the vav-affix form is not unthinkable. Indeed, it is well known that there was a tendency to use vav-affix rather than vav conversive–prefix in what is called late biblical Hebrew (hereafter, LBH; as in the Book of Chronicles) and in postbiblical Hebrew literature. Second, there are many instances in Ezekiel in which a vav-affix form stands where one might have expected a vav conversive–prefix. Following this data, Rooker claims that in this respect the Book of Ezekiel is a precursor of the late biblical Hebrew use of vav-affix forms (→ Rooker, *Biblical Hebrew in Transition*, 100–102).

Alternatively, וְהַעֲבִירַנִי may introduce a clarifying comment in the midst of a vav conversive–prefix chain (notice the resumption of the vav conversive–prefix chain following this comment, in v 3). In such a case, וְהַעֲבִירַנִי would not refer to the third of a series of actions as proposed above; it would, rather, explain the circumstances within which the action develops: "he brought me out . . ." "he caused me to rest/set me down . . ." "he would lead me out . . . and . . ." or less literally "he brought me out . . ." "he caused me to rest/set me down . . ." "when he led me out . . ." Such a use of the vav-affix form would be consistent with its use in classical biblical Hebrew (→ WO'C 32.2.3e, pp. 533–34; Zimmerli, *Ezekiel 2*, 254).

עֲלֵיהֶם

To whom does the pronominal suffix refer? . . . .

If you think that it refers to עֲצָמוֹת mentioned in v 1b, you are right. But notice that it implies that עֶצֶם is treated as if it were a masculine noun, although everywhere in the OT/HB except Ezek 37:1–8 it is considered to be a feminine noun (? BDB). Moreover, as you read further in this unit, you will find that pronominal suffixes referring to עֲצָמוֹת are consistently those of the third-person or second-person masculine plural (e.g., עֲלֵיכֶם v 2; אֲלֵיהֶם v 4; בָּכֶם v 5; עֲלֵיכֶם three times in v 6; בָּכֶם v 6; עֲלֵיהֶם twice in v 8; בָּהֶם v 8).

Two observations are in order:

—A tendency to use the masculine pronominal suffix where the feminine is expected is well, although not consistently, attested in Ezekiel (e.g., Ezek 1:6,7,8,9; 23:37; 34:23; 42:4,11). This tendency is seen as one of the traits that relate the language of this book to the corpus of LBH literature (→ Rooker, *Biblical Hebrew in Transition*, 78–81).

—The blurring of some grammatical distinctions between feminine nouns and masculine nouns enabled the writer to use masculine instead of feminine forms, but did not compel the writer to do so, as the evidence of the Book of Ezekiel clearly shows. Hence the use of masculine suffixes, and other masculine references to עֲצָמוֹת (see v 4), may well be related to the communicative message of this text. We shall return to this question later, but now keep observing the attributed gender of עֶצֶם/עֲצָמוֹת in the verses that follow.

סָבִיב סָבִיב

The pair סָבִיב סָבִיב occurs twenty-five times in Ezekiel (twenty-two of which occur in Ezek 40 and 41) but elsewhere only in 2 Chr 4:3. The repetition of the word סָבִיב is meant to provide emphasis (→ GKC §123e, 133 k; cf. JM §141 k). סָבִיב סָבִיב may be translated either literally, "around, around," or as "all around."

Note

When a word is doubled for emphasis, the two instances of the term are related to one another by a conjunctive marker. Which marker relates סָבִיב to סָבִיב in this verse? (**?** see our discussion of Jer 22:2.) The vertical stroke you see between them indicates a short pause and is called paseq. It is used to separate two similar or identical words (e.g., Gen 22:11; Isa 6:3; Ezek 8:10; 40:5). (→ on this and the other uses of paseq, see Yeivin, *Introduction*, 217; cf. JM §15 m.)

וְהִנֵּה רַבּוֹת מְאֹד עַל־פְּנֵי הַבִּקְעָה וְהִנֵּה יְבֵשׁוֹת מְאֹד

The narrative that was slowed by the emphatic repetition of סָבִיב suddenly shifts from the point of view of Ezekiel as narrator to that of Ezekiel as the one who is going all around these bones. The narrative turns, as it were, to what the eyes of Ezekiel see: many, many (bones); dry, very dry (bones). The common marker of a shift to the perception of the character in the narrative (to what his or her eyes are "actually" seeing at a certain point in the story) is הִנֵּה (→ on this use of הִנֵּה, see Berlin, *Poetics*, 62–64).

For Further Thought

Notice the parallel structure and the repetition of sounds between וְהִנֵּה רַבּוֹת מְאֹד and וְהִנֵּה יְבֵשׁוֹת מְאֹד. Do you think that these features help to shape a certain message? *Explain*.

Translate all of v 2.

Verse 3.

One of the most idiosyncratic features of the Book of Ezekiel is God's usual address to the prophet as בֶּן־אָדָם, "human being." In many cases, the expression X־בֶּן is used in the sense of belonging to the category or the realm of X (e.g., בְּנֵי־הָאֱלֹהִים, divine beings in Gen 6:2; → JM §129 j; WO'C 9.5.3b, p. 150; Westermann, *Genesis 1–11*, 371–72). In our case, the term בֶּן־אָדָם means belonging to the realm or category of humans.

For Further Thought

Every description of a talk between God and a human may be seen as building a bridge between the two, as narrowing the distance between the two. Against this background, how do you understand the theological point made by this vocative? What does it emphasize?

Since בֶּן־אָדָם constitutes the opening vocative of an account presented as direct speech from the deity to the prophet, it is usually preceded by the formula וַיֹּאמֶר אֵלַי (e.g., Ezek 2:1,3; 3:1,3,4,10; 4:16; 8:5,6,8,12,15,17), as in our verse.

Note

Vocative expressions are set apart from the text that follows (the message addressed by the vocative) by disjunctive markers. The marker above בֶּן־אָדָם is a variant of zaqef, called zaqef gadol (→ Yeivin, *Introduction*, 184–85). For our purposes here, you may consider all the forms of zaqef as identical.

Analyze הֲתְחַיֶּינָה. Look carefully. What kind of (consonantal) ה is this? (**?** K. 134; Gr. 141; Ke. 94–95, 432; L. 48; S. 64–65; W. 80.) Note that one י is a consonant, the other a vowel marker.

Root	Stem	Form	PGN	SF	OS	BRM

Translate v 3a.

Within the limits of normal human experience, the question you wrote calls for an immediate response in the negative. But Ezekiel is talking to the Lord, so . . .

Analyze וַיֹּאמֶר (**?** K. 273; Gr. 100; Ke. 237–39; L. 119–20; S. 148; W. 161–62.)

Root	Stem	Form	PGN	SF	OS	BRM

Note

The double divine name/title אֲדֹנָי ה' occurs 280 times in the OT/HB, and 230 of those instances are in Ezekiel. Some scholars have proposed that the present reading אֲדֹנָי ה' is the result of relatively late pious additions of the perpetual qere of ה' to the text (**?** K. 6; Ke. 32; L. 52–53; S. 37, 291; W. 22–23; → JM §16 f; Yeivin, *Introduction*, 58–59), but this proposal remains unconvincing (→ Zimmerli, *Ezekiel 2*, 558–61; McGregor, *Greek Text of Ezekiel*, 57–93; Ben Zvi, *Zephaniah*, 86–87). Note that the distribution of the attestations of ה' and אֲדֹנָי ה' is not random. For instance, only one of the several occurrences of the hand of the Lord revelatory formula in Ezekiel reads יַד אֲדֹנָי ה' (Ezek 8:1); all the others read יַד־ה'.

Translate יָדַעְתָּ. Remember that affix forms of verbs that point to perceptions, feelings, experiences, or knowledge may convey a meaning that should be translated in the present tense. To illustrate, אֲשֶׁר־אָהַבְתָּ in Gen 22:2 cannot be translated as "whom you loved" (once, in the past), but should be "whom you love." (→ K. 233; S. 93; and esp. M §112 a; WO'C 30.5.3, pp. 491–93.)

[ ]

Translate v 3.

[ ]

Verse 4.

Analyze הִנָּבֵא

Clue: Notice that the first letter of the root is doubled, but not the second.

Root	Stem	Form	PGN	SF	OS	BRM

הִנָּבֵא עַל-X generally means "prophesy against X" (e.g., Am 7:16; Jer 25:13; Ezek 4:7; 11:4; 13:17; 25:2; 28:21; 36:6; 39:1), but in our verse it can hardly have this meaning. Nonetheless, readers of (or listeners to) this text cannot realize that this הִנָּבֵא עַל-X means "prophesy to" rather than "prophesy against" until they reach v 5b. They cannot be sure whether the divine speech entails judgment against or salvation for these bones on the basis of v 4. They expect and need further information. This is another example of the use of ambiguity in prophetic literature to channel the attention of the audience to the main point of this section, here the fate of the "many, very dry bones." (→ Ben Zvi, *Zephaniah*, 185–87.)

Note
Although there is no doubt that הִנָּבֵא is in the nif'al stem, it is not clear how the regular meanings of nif'al (i.e., middle, passive, reflexive, reciprocal, tolerative, and stative) relate to נבא in the nif'al. Moreover, this is certainly a case of denominative use of the nif'al, but such cases are rare. So, why did the language develop in such a way that נבא is attested in the nif'al? Are the other attested meanings of nif'al irrelevant to our understanding of נבא in the nif'al? One way of approaching this issue is to relate the meaning of נבא in the nif'al to either the ingressive-stative character of some instances of nif'al (→ WO'C 23.3c, p. 386) or the causative-reflexive sense of several nif'al verbs (→ WO'C 23.4h, pp. 390–92). (The term *ingressive-stative* points to verbs describing "coming" into a certain state rather than "being" in such a state; *causative-reflexive* points to meanings generally conveyed in English by "to cause/make oneself . . .").

In either case, whether הִנָּבֵא originally conveyed the sense of "come into the *state* of being a prophet," or "make yourself a prophet," hitpa'el forms of נבא, which are well attested in the OT/HB, could have conveyed a similar meaning, namely: (a) "to behave as a prophet/show the behavior of a prophet" (→ WO'C 26.2f, pp. 430–31) or (b) "to cause oneself to be a prophet" (→ 26.2b–c, pp. 429–30). If so, the meanings conveyed by נבא in the nif'al and the hitpa'el should be considered as overlapping. (→ on the issue of נבא in the hitpa'el and the nif'al, see Blenkinsopp, *History*, 37.)

The idiom הִנָּבֵא . . . וְאָמַרְתָּ is quite common in Ezekiel (e.g., Ezek 6:2–3; 13:2; 21:14,33; 30:2; 34:2; 36:3; 37:4,9,12). How would you translate it? . . . .

Where does the direct speech of the prophet begin? ....

Is there a disjunctive marker supporting your decision? Which? Is הָעֲצָמוֹת הַיְבֵשׁוֹת a

vocative? ....

....

Remember that the definite article is expressed in many (but not all) vocative expressions. (→ Concerning the use of the article in vocative expressions and its possible implications, see Barr, " 'Determination' and the Definite Article," 307–37, esp. 319–21.)

Analyze שִׁמְעוּ

Root	Stem	Form	PGN	SF	OS	BRM

Is this the verbal form you expected to find in an address to הָעֲצָמוֹת הַיְבֵשׁוֹת? (**?** Isa 32:9; Jer 9:19). If not, do you detect any tension between the gender of הָעֲצָמוֹת הַיְבֵשׁוֹת and that implied by שִׁמְעוּ?

Translate v 4.

Verse 5.

The first part of v 5a consists of a variant of the messenger formula (**?** see our discussion of Jer 22:1). It includes the double divine name/title (see v 3) and a comment identifying again those to whom this speech is addressed (cf. Ezek 6:3).

For Further Thought

Do you think that the seemingly unnecessary repetition made by לָעֲצָמוֹת fulfills any communicative role in the text (cf. Jer 2:4–5; 7:2–3; 10:1–2; 17:20–21; 19:3; 42:15)? *Explain.* (→ for a similar but not identical case, see Ezek 6:3; 36:4).

הִנֵּה אֲנִי מֵבִיא

הִנֵּה אֲנִי מֵבִיא is a variant of a more common expression, הִנְנִי מֵבִיא (e.g., 2 Kgs 21:12; Jer 5:15; 11:11; 19:3; 31:8; 35:17; 39:16; 45:5; Ezek 26:7; 28:7; 29:8). The idiom הִנֵּה אֲנִי + participle occurs several times in chapter 37 of Ezekiel in places where one may have expected the more common

הִנְנִי + participle (Ezek 37:5,12,19,21), and in 2 Chr 2:3. These variations should not influence your translation. Remember that הִנְנִי + participle conveys a sense of immediate and assured action, something like "I am about to . . ." or "I am going to . . ." (→ JM §121 e; WO'C 37.6f, pp. 627–28).

Note

The tendency to use אֲנִי rather than אָנֹכִי is still another trait of LBH (→ Rooker, *Biblical Hebrew in Transition*, 72–74).

Translate v 5 up to the last ṭifḥa in the verse, the one that stands just before silluq. (**?** about these disjunctive markers, see our discussion of 1 Sam 1:21.)

```
┌─────────────────────────────────────────────────────────────┐
│                                                               │
│                                                               │
│                                                               │
│                                                               │
│                                                               │
└─────────────────────────────────────────────────────────────┘
```

To analyze וִחְיִיתֶם you need to know that וְחִ stands for וְחָ. Prefixed prepositions (such as מִ, כִּ, לְ, בְּ) and prefixed vav (וְ) take hireq (defectiva) before verbs from the roots היה and חיה in which either the first ה or ח takes shewa (e.g., לִהְיוֹת; → GKC §63 q, 104 f; JM §79 s). The rest of the analysis will be relatively simple. *Analyze* and *translate* וִחְיִיתֶם. . . . .

Root	Stem	Form	PGN	SF	OS	BRM

Who is the subject of this verb? . . . .
    The change of subject moves the focus from the coming divine action to its results as seen from the perspective of the new subject, those who will be affected by the action. But the focus returns to God and God's imminent actions in the next verse.

Verse 6.

In this verse the message conveyed by the formula from v 5, הִנְנִי + participle, is further developed by a series of vav-affix forms which should be translated in the same way as הִנְנִי (or הִנֵּה אֲנִי) + participle. This series is set apart by an inclusio. *Identify* it. . . . .
    . . . .

Translate v 6a.

```



```

Analyze וִידַעְתֶּם and **explain** its vocalization.

Root	Stem	Form	PGN	SF	OS	BRM

. . . .

Translate v 6b.

```



```

Verse 6b consists of a formula occurring more than fifty times in the first thirty-nine chapters of Ezekiel (e.g., Ezek 6:10,14; 7:4,9,27). This formula is used to express the purpose of many of the actions of the Lord and, for obvious reasons, is called the "recognition formula" (→ Hals, *Ezekiel*, 362).

Note

Although this formula is attested elsewhere in the OT/HB, and especially in Exodus (e.g., Exod 6:7; 7:5; 10:2; 14:4,18; 1 Kgs 20:28; Isa 49:23; 60:16), the frequency in which it occurs in Ezekiel has no parallel in any other biblical book. Most likely, the formula was extensively used in Ezekiel because of its sharp contribution to the general theological message of this book (or at least of its first thirty-nine chapters).

The divine speech ends in v 6. The text now returns to the prophet and to his response to the divine speech addressed to him beginning with וַיֹּאמֶר אֵלַי in v 4.

Verse 7.

Analyze וְנִבֵּאתִי

Clue: this verb is *not* in the pi'el stem; **?** K. 191, 406; Gr. 98–99, 103–04; Ke. 275–77, 302–03; L. 183–84; S. 221; W. 185, 297.

Root	Stem	Form	PGN	SF	OS	BRM

Analyze צִוֵּיתִי (**?** K. 188; Gr. 88, 213; Ke. 287–89; L. 205–06; S. 246–47; W. 218.)

Root	Stem	Form	PGN	SF	OS	BRM

Translate v 7a.

The contrast between the two affix forms in v 7a is noteworthy. One of them is in the passive voice, the other in the active voice. Despite the fact that both are in the same grammatical form and both point to something that occurred in the past, they do not refer to actions occurring at the same time in the past.

Spell out the differences and similarities between the two verbs, **explain** how they are grounded in Hebrew grammar and in the syntax of v 7a, and **indicate** how they contribute to the message of the text. . . . .
. . . .
. . . .
. . . .

The text emphasizes that the prophet did exactly what he was commanded. (For the identical formulation, see Ezek 12:7; 24:18; cf. Ezek 37:10.) The audience expects now that some event will take place. The beginning of a new subunit is marked by וַיְהִי. This expression is regularly followed by a temporal clause, but in here the word קוֹל separates וַיְהִי and כְּהִנָּבְאִי.

Analyze and **translate** כְּהִנָּבְאִי . . . .

Root	Stem	Form	PGN	SF	OS	BRM

Translate וַיְהִי־קוֹל כְּהִנָּבְאִי.

וְהִנֵּה־רַעַשׁ

The referent of this locution is probably the same as וַיְהִי־קוֹל כְּהִנָּבְאִי, but וְהִנֵּה־רַעַשׁ introduces the point of view of the person experiencing these events (see our discussion of v 2).

Analyze וַתִּקְרְבוּ

Root	Stem	Form	PGN	SF	OS	BRM

Although analyzing this verb may be relatively easy, making sense of it in its textual context is more complicated. It is the second-person masculine plural, qal vav conversive–prefix form. The subject governing this verb must be עֲצָמוֹת. At this point of your reading of this passage, you should not be surprised that עֲצָמוֹת is treated as a masculine noun, but why is the verb in the second person rather than the third? This question has been answered by scholars in several different ways, among them:

(a) This is a rare instance of ת as the prefix marker for the third-person masculine plural, as in Ugaritic (cf. Deut 5:23,24). This position is most likely to be rejected (→ Ratner, "Does a t-Preformative Third Person Masculine Plural Verbal Form Exist in Hebrew?" 80–88; WO'C 497 n 2).

(b) This is a rare instance of a ת–וּ third-person feminine plural prefix form, i.e., a counterpart to the י–וּ third-person masculine plural (cf. וְאַלְמְנֹתֶיךָ עָלַי תִּבְטָחוּ in Jer 49:11; → Zimmerli, *Ezekiel 2*, 255).

(c) The text should be emended to וַיִּקְרְבוּ as proposed in the critical apparatus of BHS.

In any case, because of the context in the verse, the meaning of וַתִּקְרְבוּ עֲצָמוֹת seems evident, namely, "and bones came together." Verse 7 ends with a clarifying clause concerning this coming together and with a stylistic repetition that underscores the word "bone."

Translate all of v 7.

```
┌─────────────────────────────────────────────────────────────────────┐
│                                                                       │
│                                                                       │
│                                                                       │
│                                                                       │
│                                                                       │
└─────────────────────────────────────────────────────────────────────┘
```

Verse 8.

וְרָאִיתִי at the beginning of this verse is the second link of a chain of vav-affix forms indicating the actions or activities of the prophet after he heard the divine speech of vv 4–6. The first link of this chain is וְנִבֵּאתִי at the beginning of v 7.

Verse 8 continues the report of the fulfillment of the words of the Lord in v 6aa (up to the first zaqef).

Translate v 8a (❓ מִלְמָעְלָה < לְמָעְלָה < מָעְלָה + מִן < מָעְלָה + לְ + מַעַל + ,הַ > מִן > מִן + לְ + מִן; → BDB 583 b; 751 a–b).

```
┌─────────────────────────────────────────────────────────────────────┐
│                                                                       │
│                                                                       │
│                                                                       │
│                                                                       │
│                                                                       │
└─────────────────────────────────────────────────────────────────────┘
```

Note

The root קרם is attested only twice in the OT/HB, both times in the qal and both times in our passage, Ezek 37:6,8. In v 6, the verb is transitive and shows a **fientive** meaning (i.e., answers the implicit question, "What does X do?"), but such a meaning is out of the question in v 8. There, the verb is **stative** (i.e., it describes a state) and intransitive (→ WO'C 22.2.1–2, pp. 363–65). There are roots in the qal that show both a transitive, fientive meaning ("to fill") and a stative, intransitive one ("to be full"); ❓ BDB; → WO'C 22.2.3, pp. 365–66. BDB, the apparatus in BHS, and other scholarly works (e.g., Zimmerli, *Ezekiel 2*, 255; but see Wevers, *Ezekiel*, 195) suggest that וַיִּקְרַם in v 8 should be repointed וַיִּקְרַם. What does this repointing achieve? . . . .
. . . .

Verse 8a reports the fulfillment of the first part of the divine word of v 6a (given in v 6aa). The audience is now expecting a reference to the fulfillment of its second part, v 6ab (also expressed in v 5b). That is, the bones have rejoined and have been covered with flesh. They have yet to be given life.

Translate v 8b.

```
┌─────────────────────────────────────────────────────────────────────────┐
│                                                                           │
│                                                                           │
│                                                                           │
│                                                                           │
│                                                                           │
│                                                                           │
└─────────────────────────────────────────────────────────────────────────┘
```

Verse 9.

In the kind of report we are reading, the word of the Lord is expected to be fulfilled, certainly in its main aspects if not in its entirety. Moreover, in these texts the word of the Lord is usually fulfilled after the prophet does what he has been commanded to do. The text here certainly reinforces this expectation. The bones are actually affected by the divine action only after the prophet has prophesied as commanded. Hence one cannot but notice that the divine word in 6ab has not yet been fulfilled. This word is certainly not of secondary importance, but is the climax of God's announced actions. Indeed, the text itself calls special attention to this event by means of the inclusio between 5b and 6ab, reinforcing the audience's awareness that covering the bones with flesh falls short of reviving them.

In sum, genre conventions explicitly supported by this text lead its audience to a growing expectation of a further action on the part of the prophet in order to realize the announced word of God. But here rests the problem: the prophet has already done what was requested of him. Hence the logic of the situation calls for a new command from God to the prophet.

Verse 9 contains this second command. It is introduced with almost the same wording as the first command (v 4), namely, וַיֹּאמֶר אֵלַי הִנָּבֵא אֶל־X. The only difference is that the expression in v 9 shows the preposition אֶל instead of עַל. In fact, on many occasions in the Book of Ezekiel עַל occurs instead of an expected אֶל. The tendency to show עַל instead of אֶל is another characteristic of LBH that is attested in Ezekiel as well as in postbiblical Hebrew (→ Rooker, *Biblical Hebrew in Transition*, 127–31).

Note

A communicative environment in which the writer is able to interchange these two prepositions makes it possible for the writer to play with possible connotations and double meanings; it does not mean that such interchanges are necessarily meaningless. For instance, as you have seen, the use of עַל in v 4 allows the writer to develop an ambiguity that calls attention to the text's primary focus, namely, the future status of these bones. Taking into account this interchange between prepositions and the play on the multiple possible meanings of the word רוּחַ, it seems clear that exploiting the rhetorical possibilities of terms that can have more than one meaning is one of the literary techniques used by the writer of this text.

Analyze בֹּאִי and וּפְחִי

Root	Stem	Form	PGN	SF	OS	BRM

Root	Stem	Form	PGN	SF	OS	BRM

Analyze and **translate** וְיִחְיוּ (Remember that a nonconversive vav + prefix that stands as the second link in a sequence opened by one or more imperatives should be translated as "so . . ." or "so that . . .")

Root	Stem	Form	PGN	SF	OS	BRM

Analyze and **translate** הֲרוּגִים

Root	Stem	Form	PGN	SF	OS	BRM

Translate all of v 9.

For Further Thought

In v 9 the equation הֲרוּגִים = עֲצָמוֹת becomes evident. Do you think that this equation may have something to do with the writer's referring to עֲצָמוֹת as a masculine noun some of the time but not always?

Are there any elements of the report in vv 8–9 that are reminiscent of the general picture given in Gen 2:7? If so, what point may this reminiscence convey? (**?** think of the emphasis on the term רוּחַ and of its different meanings in this unit.)

Verse 10.

Following the pattern observed in vv 4–6 and 7–8, one expects

(a) the explicit claim of the prophet that he did as he was commanded (parallel to v 7a); and

(b) a dramatic report of the fulfillment of the divine word in 5b and 6ab (parallel to 7b–8a).

Both occur in v 10.

Analyze וְהִנַּבֵּאתִי and צִוָּנִי

Root	Stem	Form	PGN	SF	OS	BRM

Root	Stem	Form	PGN	SF	OS	BRM

Translate v 10a.

Compare v 10a with 7a, pointing out the similarities and differences between them.

. . . .

. . . .

. . . .

Stylistic variation, which allows the writer to convey the same basic message while varying the expression, is evident in v 10. This is even more evident in the description of the fulfillment in v 10b of the divine word given in 5b and 6ab.

Translate v 10b (**?** The repetition of the adverb מְאֹד is emphatic, and much like the English repetition of "very, very . . .").

```
┌─────────────────────────────────────────────────────────────────────────┐
│                                                                           │
│                                                                           │
│                                                                           │
│                                                                           │
│                                                                           │
└─────────────────────────────────────────────────────────────────────────┘
```

Compare v 10b with vv 5b and 6ab. . . . .
. . . .
. . . .

The divine word in vv 5 and 6ab has now been fulfilled, but two issues remain unresolved:

(a) The divine speech in vv 5b–6 does not end in v 6ab. But what happens to וִידַעְתֶּם כִּי־אֲנִי ה' in v 6b? This divine word remains unfulfilled (at least explicitly).

(b) The entire vision reported here centers on the transition of the עֲצָמוֹת from death to life, something that is unreasonable in worldly human terms but is made possible by the enlivening power of רוּחַ and the will and power of ה'. (Notice how the text repeats these Hebrew words again and again in these verses.) But for whom do these bones stand? Who or what is like these bones?

These issues are dealt with by the last three verses of the unit. They explicitly provide the interpretive key for the preceding eleven verses. Moreover, since the text presents this key as direct divine speech, it also claims that the key is to be considered authoritative.

Verse 11.

The divine speech is introduced exactly as in v 3.

Translate v 11 up to the zaqef gadol. (**?** see our discussion of v 3.)

```
┌─────────────────────────────────────────────────────────────────────────┐
│                                                                           │
│                                                                           │
│                                                                           │
│                                                                           │
│                                                                           │
└─────────────────────────────────────────────────────────────────────────┘
```

The remainder of v 11a is a sentence structured according to the pattern *subject* (disjunction) *predicate* (disjunction) *pronoun/pronominal copula*. This is the common structure of clauses of classification. These clauses generally answer such questions as "What is the subject like?" The pronoun at the end emphasizes the predicate and consequently the message of the entire clause. (You have encountered this verbless structure before; **?** see our discussion of Exod 21:29.)

Translate v 11 from the zaqef gadol to the atnaḥ.

```
┌─────────────────────────────────────────────────────────────────────────┐
│                                                                           │
│                                                                           │
│                                                                           │
│                                                                           │
│                                                                           │
└─────────────────────────────────────────────────────────────────────────┘
```

Note

One may take a different approach to this verbless clause (and to identifying and classifying clauses that contain a pronominal copula). Namely, הָעֲצָמוֹת הָאֵלֶּה may be considered a **focus marker** that is syntactically separated from the following clause and, consequently, one may understand the following clause as showing the simple structure *predicate + subject* (הֵמָּה). That is, it is possible to read the sentence as follows: "As for these bones, they are the whole House of Israel." In such a reading, it is self-evident that "these bones" functions as a focus of attention. Some works refer to the focus marker as **nominative absolute** or **casus pendens**. (→ GKC §143 a–d; JM §156; and esp. WO'C 16.3.3, pp. 297–99).

For הִנֵּה see our discussion of v 2.

Who is the subject governing אֹמְרִים? . . . .
The context leaves no doubt about its identity, thereby allowing for its omission.

The reported direct speech of the whole House of Israel follows אֹמְרִים and is set apart from the preceding text by a disjunctive marker. Which one? . . . .

Note

Here we have a case of someone's direct speech (that of the whole House of Israel) quoted within a direct speech of someone else (the Lord), which is itself quoted by someone else (Ezekiel) as part of a narrative written in the first person. Biblical Hebrew is abundant in direct quotations and in dialogues that are presented as a series of direct quotations. Significantly, biblical Hebrew literature shows no tendency to any conversation in which more than two parts actively participate, even when the narrative includes more than two separate parts (for a typical example, see Ruth 1:8–17).

Analyze the verbs and **translate** וְאָבְדָה תִקְוָתֵנוּ ,יָבְשׁוּ עַצְמוֹתֵינוּ, and נִגְזַרְנוּ לָנוּ.

Root	Stem	Form	PGN	SF	OS	BRM

Root	Stem	Form	PGN	SF	OS	BRM

Root	Stem	Form	PGN	SF	OS	BRM

. . . .

. . . .

Notice patterns of structure and repetition, and *explain* their possible significance.

. . . .

. . . .

The presence of לָנוּ in נִגְזַרְנוּ לָנוּ is worthy of note. If the text had read נִגְזַרְנוּ alone, your English translation would probably be the same, something like, "we are destroyed/cut off." If so, what is the function of לָנוּ in the sentence? . . . .

. . . .

לָנוּ underscores the strong significance that the event had for the speakers ("us," that is, "the whole House of Israel"). This use of the preposition לְ (+ pronominal suffix) is sometimes referred to as **dativus ethicus** (or **ethical dative,** → GKC §119 s; JM §133 d, esp. N 2, 3; WO'C 11.2.10d, pp. 208–09).

For Further Thought

The first two verbs are stative qal verbs (see our discussion of v 8). None of them points to any action, but to a state of being. The third verb is a nif'al verb with a passive sense. What do these stylistic choices suggest concerning the whole House of Israel?

Series such as the one in v 11 may contain an ongoing heightening of the message. Can you discern such a heightening in this series?

Translate all of v 11.

Note

Between vv 10 and 11 your text shows a long blank space, in the midst of which is the letter ס. This space marks the end of one "paragraph" and the beginning of a new one. In English there is only one kind of paragraph, set apart by beginning to write on a new line and sometimes by indentation. There are two kinds of paragraphs in the HB/OT. The **open paragraph/parashah** (פָּרָשָׁה פְּתוּחָה) is similar to the English paragraph because it always starts on (opens) a new line. The **closed paragraph/parashah** (פָּרָשָׁה סְתוּמָה) is set apart from the preceding verse by a blank space, as shown between vv 10 and 11 in our text. In some manuscripts and in the printed versions of the Hebrew Bible, the letters פ (standing for פְּתוּחָה) and ס (standing for סְתוּמָה) were added to indicate open and closed paragraphs, respectively. But mistakes and different traditions concerning the nature of a paragraph (i.e., whether it is open or closed) caused confusion and many inconsistencies in the system (→ Würthwein, *Text*, 20–21; and esp. Yeivin, *Introduction*, 39–42).

Verse 12.

The circumstances described in v 11 provide the grounds for the divine actions announced in the next verses.

Verse 12 opens a לָכֵן clause, which is the apodosis of this paragraph. We have learned about this kind of clause in our discussion of Deut 24:18. The protasis consists of v 11b; it is in response to this situation that God commands the prophet to prophesy.

The command to prophesy in v 12 is similar to those in vv 4 and 9; the messenger formula in v 12 with which the prophet is commanded to open his speech repeats the formula as it is found in vv 5 and 9.

Translate v 12aα up to the segolta (remember that segolta always marks the first main division of an atnaḥ section).

The language describing the announced divine actions shares its basic verbal sequence with that of vv 5–6, namely, הִנֵּה אֲנִי + participle, followed by a series of vav-affix forms which eventually leads to a non-conversive vav + prefix form (v 13).

Analyze, explain the vocalization, and **translate** פָּתַח, וְהַעֲלֵיתִי, and וְהֵבֵאתִי . . . .

. . . .

Root	Stem	Form	PGN	SF	OS	BRM

Root	Stem	Form	PGN	SF	OS	BRM

Root	Stem	Form	PGN	SF	OS	BRM

. . . .

. . . .

Translate v 12.

Note

Most likely you have just read and translated the expression אַדְמַת יִשְׂרָאֵל rather easily. This seemingly common expression is in fact a special feature of the language of the Book of Ezekiel. אַדְמַת יִשְׂרָאֵל occurs many times in this book, or more precisely, in its first thirty-nine chapters (e.g., Ezek 7:2; 11:17; 36:6; 38:18–19), but nowhere else in the HB/OT. As you have come to learn, many biblical texts tend to show a certain degree of idiosyncratic language.

For Further Thought

You have no doubt already recognized two contrasting patterns of repetition in this verse, one pointing to the second-person masculine plural and the other to the first-person common singular. *Explain* their possible significance, and the linking function of עַמִּי.

The Septuagint and the Peshitta suggest a Hebrew version of Ezekiel in which the word עַמִּי was not attested. How would such a version be different from the existent Hebrew version?

According to this passage, the *whole* House of Israel has been deported and will be brought back to the land of Israel. This verse does not reflect the historical circumstances of the period, for many Judeans were never deported (→ 2 Kgs 25:12; Jer 39:10; 52:15–16, 28–30; → Mazar, *Archaeology*, 548). What kind of social perspective, however, does this wording reflect?

Verse 13.

The first half of this verse consists of the recognition formula (see v 6b). This formula presents the purpose of the divine action and seems to bring the metaphor of the bones to a close by explicitly referring to the final element in the divine words in vv 5–6, namely, the recognition formula.

Translate v 13a.

Verse 13b provides a temporal (and, within this context, also causal) clause that closely follows the wording of v 12 ab (from segolta to atnaḥ).

Analyze and **translate** בְּפִתְחִי and בְּהַעֲלוֹתִי

Root	Stem	Form	PGN	SF	OS	BRM

. . . .

Root	Stem	Form	PGN	SF	OS	BRM

. . . .

Translate v 13b and **compare** it to all of v 12.

```
┌─────────────────────────────────────────────────────────────────┐
│                                                                   │
│                                                                   │
│                                                                   │
│                                                                   │
│                                                                   │
└─────────────────────────────────────────────────────────────────┘
```

Verse 14.

At first glance, it seems that v 13 brings to completion the comparison between the bones and the whole House of Israel. But a careful reading will show that an important element of the prophecy to the bones and its fulfillment has no explicit parallel in the prophecy to Israel. Which element is that? (**?** vv 5b, 8b, 9–10.) The first part of v 14a solves this tension, and the second part reiterates, with some differences, v 12.

Analyze וְהִנַּחְתִּי (Use the terms hifʻil A and hifʻil B, as explained in our discussion of v 1.)

Root	Stem	Form	PGN	SF	OS	BRM

Translate v 14a.

```
┌─────────────────────────────────────────────────────────────────┐
│                                                                   │
│                                                                   │
│                                                                   │
│                                                                   │
│                                                                   │
└─────────────────────────────────────────────────────────────────┘
```

Note

Two observations should be made concerning the exact language of v 14a. First, the movement from the sequence קִבְרוֹתֵיכֶם > אֶתְכֶם > קִבְרוֹתֵיכֶם (twice in both v 12 and v 13) to אַדְמַתְכֶם > אֶתְכֶם in v 14 encapsulates a substantial part of the message of this text. Second, in v 14a one finds the term רוּחִי, but it does not occur in the divine speeches reported in vv 5–6 and 9. Is this only a matter of style? If not, what is the underlying significance?

Following the patterned announcement of divine action, v 14b opens with the recognition formula (see vv 6b and 13a). It concludes with another formula, the prophetic utterance formula (נְאֻם ה'), which functions as if it were a signature to these divine words (**?** see our discussion of Jer 22:5). A third concluding and legitimizing formula, the conclusion formula for divine speech, stands in the middle, namely, כִּי־אֲנִי ה' דִּבַּרְתִּי. This formula occurs in many places in Ezekiel, sometimes with and sometimes without the כִּי (e.g., Ezek 5:13,15,17; 17:21; 21:22,37; 26:14; 30:12; 37:14). It may follow the recognition formula (e.g., Ezek 5:13; 17:21; 37:14) and may be followed by the prophetic utterance formula (e.g., Ezek 26:14; 37:14; cf. 39:5). On occasion, וְעָשִׂיתִי is attached to כִּי־אֲנִי ה' דִּבַּרְתִּי or אֲנִי ה' דִּבַּרְתִּי, producing an emphatic variant of the conclusion formula for divine speech (e.g., Ezek 17:24; 37:14). (→ on the conclusion formula for divine speech and other formulae, see Hals, *Ezekiel*, 359–63.)

Translate v 14b.

```




```

Notice the remarkable emphasis on the authority of these words, which legitimizes not only this speech but also the message of the entire unit.

Translate all of Ezek 37:1–14.

For Further Thought

There is no doubt that one of the main messages of this text is that just as the bones are revived the whole House of Israel is to be revived, despite their seemingly hopeless situation. The correspondence between the "bones" and "the whole House of Israel" is not only explicitly mentioned but is reinforced again and again by formal correspondences between the account of the bones and its interpretation as an account of the whole House of Israel.

Against this background, one discrepancy is worthy of notice. The announcement of the divine word in the account of the bones includes a command to prophesy. This command is fulfilled by the prophet—exactly as he is commanded, and then an account of the fulfillment of the divine word is attested. The account of the whole House of Israel also contains an announcement of the divine word, which includes a command to prophesy to the whole House of Israel. It does not include a first account of the prophet explicitly saying that he did as commanded, but perhaps the entire account (Ezek 37:1–14) may be seen as fulfilling this condition. Far more important, v 14 is not followed by an account claiming that the divine word has been fulfilled.

The historical/rhetorical situation against which this text was composed now becomes clear. The addressees of the text of Ezek 37:1–14, who most likely identify themselves with the whole House of Israel, have not yet been revived at the time at which they hear the message. The text's purpose is to convince them that just as the bones were revived, so will they be. The text has to compete against a sense of hopelessness derived from a "realistic" way of looking at their situation. It does so not by denying that the deportees' lack of expectation is reasonable. It even agrees that such a lack of expectation is as well founded as that of any person who sees dry bones and doubts that they can be revived. But it claims that the difference between death and life is in the presence or absence of the enlivening רוּחַ, which is not independent of God, and that God has certainly the power and the will to cause "unexpected" and even "unreasonable" events to happen. Moreover, the text claims that God has already decided what is going to happen concerning the revival of the whole House of Israel, so that even if it has not yet happened, it is as if it had, for the divine decision always entails its fulfillment (note the language of v 14). But why would people listen to such an incredible and unprovable claim based on no evidence other than the vision of the prophet Ezekiel? Because of the divine authority hammered home by several divine speeches in the first person and by a variety of prophetic formulae. Since this issue stands at the core of the acceptability of the message, it is no surprise that a reiteration of the divine authorization of the message concludes the entire unit.

For Further Reading

On this unit, see Zimmerli, *Ezekiel 2*, 253–66; Wevers, *Ezekiel*, 194–96; Hals, *Ezekiel*, 266–72; on the rhetoric of this passage, see Fox, "Rhetoric of Ezekiel's Vision."

Works Cited in This Section

J. Barr, "Determination and the Definite Article in Biblical Hebrew," *JSS* 24 (1989): 307–37; **E. Ben Zvi,** *A Historical-Critical Study of the Book of Zephaniah* (Berlin: de Gruyter, 1991); **A. Berlin,** *Poetics and Interpretation of Biblical Narrative* (Sheffield: Almond Press, 1983); **J. Blenkinsopp,** *A History of Prophecy in Israel* (Philadelphia: Westminster, 1983); **M. V. Fox,** "The Rhetoric of Ezekiel's Vision of the Valley of the Bones," *HUCA* 51 (1980): 1–15; **R. M. Hals,** *Ezekiel* (FOTL 19; Grand Rapids, Mich.: Eerdmans, 1989); **A. Mazar,** *Archaeology of the Land of the Bible* (ABRL; New York: Doubleday, 1990); **L. J. McGregor,** *The Greek Text of Ezekiel* (SBLSCS 18; Atlanta: Scholars Press, 1985); **R. Ratner,** "Does a t- Preformative Third Person Masculine Plural Verbal Form Exist in Hebrew?" *VT* 38 (1988): 80–88; **R. Rendtorff,** *The Old Testament: An Introduction* (Philadelphia: Fortress, 1986); **M. F. Rooker,** *Biblical Hebrew in Transition: The Language of the Book of Ezekiel* (JSOTSup 90; Sheffield: JSOT Press, 1990); **C. Westermann,** *Genesis 1–11* (Minneapolis: Augsburg, 1984); **J. W. Wever,** *Ezekiel* (NCB; Grand Rapids, Mich.: Eerdmans/London: Marshall, Morgan & Scott, 1982); **H. W. Wolff,** *Anthropology of the Old Testament* (Philadelphia: Fortress, 1974); **E. Würthwein,** *The Text of the Old Testament: An Introduction to the Biblia Hebraica* (Grand Rapids, Mich.: Eerdmans, 1979); **I. Yeivin,** *Introduction to the Tiberian Masorah* (Masoretic Studies 5; Missoula, Mont.: Scholars Press, 1980); **W. Zimmerli,** *Ezekiel 2* (Philadelphia: Fortress, 1983).

3.3 Isaiah 49:1–6

This reading from the Book of Isaiah will challenge you to use what you have learned so far about reading prophetic writings. It will also give you a chance to study the Hebrew literary device of parallelism within a highly stylized passage in the prophetic writings. Full of nuances and apparently intentional ambiguity, this passage about the relationship of the servant of God to God and to God's purposes has intrigued readers for centuries. This reading will give you a chance to join in the ongoing discussion about this passage and will give you increased confidence in reading complex prophetic texts.

Verse 1.

Analyze שִׁמְעוּ

Root	Stem	Form	PGN	SF	OS	BRM

A plural noun, אִיִּים, immediately follows an imperative in the second-person masculine. You have seen this kind of structure in Jer 22:2. This noun stands in **apposition** ("juxtaposition of a noun [or noun phrase] to another noun [or noun phrase] with the same reference and in the same grammatical slot," WO'C, p. 689) to the second-person pronoun (the "you") implied in the imperative. In such a case, the noun is a vocative and designates the addressees of the command שִׁמְעוּ. (**?** see our discussion of Jer 22:2; WO'C 4.7d, p. 77, 8.3d, p. 130.)

You will find אִיִּים under the root אוה I in BDB. But in fact אִי, the singular form, is more likely a monoradical noun (having one consonantal root letter, like פֶּה). There are very few such nouns in Hebrew (→ JM §88A). אִי is most likely a Egyptian loanword.

Analyze הַקְשִׁיבוּ

Root	Stem	Form	PGN	SF	OS	BRM

Is לְאֻמִּים in this sentence a vocative? ....

Translate v 1a.

If you wrote something like, "Listen to me coastlands, attend (to me), distant peoples," your translation is literally correct. But are you sure that it actually conveys the communicative meaning of the text?

Notice that the references to coastlands and distant peoples here should not be interpreted narrowly, as pointing *only* to these peoples. In fact, the opposite is true: this expression points to an extreme case in order to include every possible instance, any imaginable people among the nations (cf. Isa 41:1; 42:10; 43:9; 51:4–5).

On Parallelism

No literary technique is so ubiquitous in biblical Hebrew poetry as parallelism. Parallelism also may lend an elevated character to biblical Hebrew prose. Through this reading you will begin to trace the intricacies of this seemingly simple technique. (For an introduction to parallelism, see Miller, *Interpreting*, 29–47; and esp. Petersen and Richards, *Interpreting*, 21–35.) Even a cursory reading of v 1a may reveal that it contains two parallel versets, which are set apart by the zaqef. In terms of contents, one verset echoes the other. This kind of parallelism is generally called **synonymous parallelism.** Sometimes the relationship of contents is one of contrast (e.g., Ps 90:6; → our discussion of Prov 10:1). In these cases, the term usually used is **antithetic parallelism.** Most cases of parallelism are neither synonymous nor antithetic. When one verset substantially develops the idea or image presented by the preceding one, the second is said to complete the first verset. In such a case, many scholars speak of **synthetic parallelism** (e.g., Ps 1:3; → K. 221; Kaiser, *Introduction*, 321–23). Not being as clearly defined as synonymous or antithetic parallelism, the term *synthetic parallelism* has caused some controversy among scholars (→ Petersen and Richards, *Interpreting*, 26).

The term *synonymous parallelism* must not mislead you: two (or more) versets in synonymous parallelism rarely mean the same and are rarely fully parallel to one another.

The two versets in Isa 49:1a are a good example. On the surface, they look very similar. Certainly, they show a parallel grammatical structure (imperative + vocative + prepositional clause). The two imperatives are in the same person, gender, and number and constitute a common lexical pair (e.g., Hos 5:1; Zech 1:4; Prov 4:1; 7:24; Job 13:6; see our discussion of Prov 3:13). Nonetheless, this pair shows a well-attested contrast between stems (qal vs. hif'il). You will find the same (morphological) contrast in the next three half-verses (Isa 49:1b; 49:2a; 49:2b; → Berlin, *The Dynamics*, 36–40). The two nouns are masculine plural, and are attested elsewhere in Isa 41–66 as a pair (Isa 41:1). We will study their relation later on, following the analysis of the prepositional clauses.

The two "parallel" prepositional clauses share only one feature: they open with a preposition. The two prepositions are different, and so are the words following them. One calls attention to the speaker, the other modifies the noun. Thus, although from a formal (grammatical) point of view אִיִּים is parallel to לְאֻמִּים, semantically לְאֻמִּים מֵרָחוֹק is the "equivalent" of אִיִּים. Moreover, לְאֻמִּים מֵרָחוֹק narrows the meaning of אִיִּים by actualizing some of its possible conveyed meanings. The word אִי is correctly translated as "coastland," and sometimes may be translated as "island." But it also connotes a sense of a remote place, and may refer not only to a geographical body of land but also to the people living there. These possible connotations are actualized and brought to the forefront in Isa 49:1 by לְאֻמִּים מֵרָחוֹק.

Turning our attention again to the correspondence between the prepositional clauses, it is worth noting that the clause that is semantically parallel (equivalent insofar as it concerns meaning) to אֵלַי in the first verset is the elliptic (unwritten but implied) אֵלַי in the second, for the verse is to be understood: "listen to me, coastlands, attend (to me), distant peoples."

To sum up, synonymous parallelism must not be thought of as one verset repeating the other. Moreover, grammatical parallel structures may show much more complexity than one might think after a cursory reading of the text.

A final observation: In your reading of Isa 49:1 you have encountered an instance of parallelism involving grammatically parallel structures (imperative + vocative + prepositional phrase), lexical pairs (הַקְשִׁיבוּ and שִׁמְעוּ), morphological contrasts (such as qal vs. hif'il stem), and semantic equivalencies (אִיִּים and לְאֻמִּים מֵרָחוֹק). There are many such instances in the HB/OT.

Following the command to listen to the speaker, to attend to "me," we find the message to be listened to. This message is presented in the first person and begins in v 1b.

Analyze קְרָאָנִי (? K. 164; Gr. 71; Ke. 155; L. 260–61; S. 133; W. 123–25) and הִזְכִּיר.

Root	Stem	Form	PGN	SF	OS	BRM

Root	Stem	Form	PGN	SF	OS	BRM

Translate v 1b.

```
┌─────────────────────────────────────────────────────────────────┐
│                                                                   │
│                                                                   │
│                                                                   │
│                                                                   │
│                                                                   │
│                                                                   │
└─────────────────────────────────────────────────────────────────┘
```

קְרָאָֽנִי here has the sense of "appointed me." The expression opens with מִבֶּטֶן to underscore that it is "from birth" that the speaker was appointed (cf. Jer 1:5; cf. v 5).

On Parallelism

The two versets in this half-verse are another good example of what is called synonymous parallelism. We will examine the style and structure of this specific instance of parallelism so that you may respond to the next one with more sensitivity to its possibilities.

The first verset is headed by the subject, the Lord. Who is the subject in the second verset? Is the subject actually written? . . . .

The prepositional clause in both versets is headed by מִ. In the first one, the noun that follows is בֶּטֶן, while in the second it is מְעֵי אִמִּי (cf. Ps 71:6). In both cases, the idiom headed by מִ signifies "from birth." The two expressions correspond to each other, but the latter is more explicit. This is, after all, a definite construct chain. How do we know this? . . . .

מִבֶּטֶן and אִמִּי tend to go together in the expression מִבֶּטֶן אִמִּי (e.g., Judg 16:17; Job 31:18). This relation between מִבֶּטֶן and אִמִּי strengthens the semantic correspondence between בֶּטֶן and מְעֵי אִמִּי, yet the grammatical contrast between the two expressions is rather obvious. Here the writer has chosen to contrast not only singular and plural forms (a frequent contrast, → Berlin, *Dynamics*, 44–50), but also a concise form (one single noun) in the first verset with an expanded form (a construct chain) in the second. This writer has chosen to contrast an object pronominal suffix in the first verset (a concise form) with a separate direct object in the second (an expanded form). Notice additional instances of grammatical contrast against the background of general correspondence:

—The verb in the qal stem in the first verset is contrasted with a semantically similar verb but in the hif'il stem;

—the first verset concludes with an object pronominal suffix (the equivalent of "me"), but the second ends with a possessive pronominal subject (the equivalent of "mine"), both having the same referent, the speaker.

The writer points in an additional way to the relationship between the verbs from the roots קרא and זכר and that between בֶּטֶן and מְעֵי אִמִּי. The first member in each pair calls up, as it were, an element closely related to the second member, in this case the word "name" (see Isa 43:1, where the referent is Israel, and Isa 45:3, where the referent is Cyrus).

Yet another stylistic observation: this and the next two half-verses open with a reference to the Lord and conclude with a reference to the speaker. This feature encapsulates the issue of this unit, which deals with the special relationship between God and the speaker.

What do you think of the following translation?
"The Lord, from the womb he has called me, from my mother's bowels has pronounced my name." . . . .
. . . .

(This translation is similar to Merendino's German translation; → Merendino, "Jes 49 1–6: ein Gottesknechtslied?" 237.)

For Further Thought

To say that the speaker received a specific appointment from birth and by God is to undermine rival claims, whether potential or actual, based on deeds, lineage, ideas, political and social authority, and the like. In the ancient Near East, several kings claimed to have been appointed to the kingship while still in their mother's womb (e.g., Assurbanipal of Assyria and Pianchi of Egypt). Whenever such an assertion is forcefully made, one may wonder if it does not reflect a real need to sustain the legitimacy of the appointee.

Verse 2.

Analyze וַיְשִׂימֵנִי, הֶחְבִּיאָנִי, and הִסְתִּירָנִי

Root	Stem	Form	PGN	SF	OS	BRM

Root	Stem	Form	PGN	SF	OS	BRM

Root	Stem	Form	PGN	SF	OS	BRM

Notice that the affix forms take qamets as the connecting vowel between the verb and the pronominal suffix, in contrast to the prefix form, which uses tsere for this purpose. As a general rule, affix forms take either qamets or pataḥ as their connecting vowel, and prefix forms take either tsere or segol (→ Ke. 155, 157–58; JM §61 d).

Who is the subject governing these four verbs? . . . .

Analyze בָּרוּר

Root	Stem	Form	PGN	SF	OS	BRM

חֵץ בָּרוּר may be translated as "polished arrow" (BDB) or "sharpened arrow" (e.g., de Boer, *Second Isaiah's Message*, 25), but also as "chosen arrow" (e.g., McKenzie, *Second Isaiah*, 103; see meaning 2 in BDB). Perhaps it conveys all these meanings.

To whom does the pronominal suffix in יָדוֹ and בְּאַשְׁפָּתוֹ (בְּאַשְׁפָּתוֹ > וֹ + אַשְׁפָּה + בְּ) refer?

Translate v 2.

```



```

On Parallelism

Verse 2a is parallel to v 2b. What kind of parallelism is it—synonymous, antithetic, or synthetic parallelism? . . . .

Analyze the correspondence between versets 2a and 2b, **spell out** grammatical contrasts, and **point out** elliptic words, if any. . . . .
. . . .
. . . .

Does the first half of each verset relate to the second half of each verset in the same way? . . .
. . . .

Do the two parts of each verset (2a and 2b) relate to each other in the same way as the two parts of the first verset (1aa and 1ab)? If not, *explain* the differences in correspondence. . . . .
. . . .
. . . .

For Further Thought

These two versets convey a clear message, namely, that (a) the speaker is potentially very powerful as a result of God's election; and (b) the potential of the speaker has not been actualized, that is, it remains hidden.

But to convince anyone of a hidden potential is a tricky thing, because there is no tangible evidence. The problem of the speaker is, therefore, to make a convincing case that would resolve the tension between a powerful future potential and a powerless situation in the present. The solution suggested in v 2 is based on the practical (and personal) knowledge of God's will and actions claimed by the speaker; namely, it is certainly God's will that the potential exists (see וַיְשִׂימֵנִי and וַיָּשֶׂם) and that it has not yet been manifested (see הֶחְבִּיאָנִי and הִסְתִּירָנִי). To be sure, to claim to be powerful when to all appearances one is powerless demands a good rhetorical argument. The two next verses also concern themselves with tension between the lofty actual status of the speaker and its lack of manifestation.

Verse 3.

This verse consists of a new link in the chain of vav conversive–prefix that goes back to vv 2a and 2b (cf. the similar openings of vv 2a, 2b, and 3). But in this case, the described action of the Lord is to talk to the speaker. The next verses deal with the contents of their "conversation." The direct speech of the Lord is set apart from the words of the speaker by a disjunctive marker (**?** see our discussion of Ezek 37:11). To whom does לִי refer?

Translate versets 3aa and 3ab.

| |
| |

| |
| |

To whom do בְּךָ (to be translated here as "in you" or "through you") and אַתָּה refer? . . . .

. . . .

Analyze אֶתְפָּאָר and **explain** its vocalization.

Clue: take into account that it stands at the end of the verse.

Root	Stem	Form	PGN	SF	OS	BRM

....

Because of the different possible meanings of a root in the hitpaʾel stem (→ WO'C 26.2–4, pp. 429–32), אֶתְפָּאָר may be translated as "I will be glorified" (passive); "I will glorify myself" (direct reflexive); or "I will show my glory" (estimative). Moreover, because of the temporal ambiguities related to the use of the prefix form, one cannot rule out translations such as "I am glorified," which in plainer English should be rendered "I am proud" ("estoy orgulloso" as translated by Alonso Schökel and Mateos in the *Nueva Biblia Española*) or "I manifest/show my glory." Furthermore, one may wonder whether the full communicative message of בְּךָ אֶתְפָּאָר in v 3 can be rendered by any single translation, or whether a certain amount of intrinsic ambiguity is integral to the message.

Translate all of v 3.

Notice that the term "Israel" stands between two disjunctive markers; it follows the atnaḥ and is separated from the rest of v 3b by zaqef gadol. Remember that you will have to accept the limitations of your, or any, translation.

For Further Thought

Many times we read in the newspapers, "America supports . . ." or the like. We all understand that the word "America" actually stands for someone, or some group, considered (rightly or wrongly) to be representative of America. Following this example, whom do you think "Israel" stands for in Isa 49:3? (→ Blenkinsopp, "Second Isaiah—Prophet of Universalism," esp. 90–91.)

Note

Many scholars maintain that the word "Israel" was introduced into the text at a later stage and as an interpretative comment claiming a communal identification of the servant of the Lord as Israel. Their position is generally based on two grounds:

—the text clearly points to individual (not communal) features of the speaker, such as being born from a mother; and

—the speaker has a mission concerning Israel (see vv 5–6), so the two cannot be identical (→ Whybray, *Isaiah 40–66*, 136–38).

Objecting to this position, another group of scholars points out that

—there is no textual support for the proposal, because all ancient versions in languages other than Hebrew, and all Hebrew manuscripts of Isaiah (except for one, which is beset with textual problems), attest to the presence of "Israel" in our verse; and

—the claim that Israel is the servant of the Lord is not alien to the text in its larger context. It is, rather, a repeated and emphatic claim in Isa 40–55 (see וְאַתָּה יִשְׂרָאֵל עַבְדִּי in Isa 41:8; וָאֹמַר לְךָ עַבְדִּי־אַתָּה in 41:9, strongly reminiscent of Isa 49:3; see also 44:21; 45:4; 48:20).

In sum, according to these scholars, the proposal that the text has been emended rests only on actual or perceived inconsistencies, which by themselves do not provide convincing grounds for any textual proposal.

What is at stake is the identification of the servant of the Lord in Isa 40–55. In fact, the existence of ambiguity and tension between individual and communal features of the servant characterizes not only Isa 49:1–6, but also its larger context, Isa 40–55. (For a concise presentation of modern approaches to the question of the servant of the Lord, → Rendtorff, *Old Testament*, 194–96.)

Verse 4.

Verse 4 contains the speaker's response to the divine speech of v 3. This response is not introduced by a vav conversive–prefix form, but by a disjunctive vav + (pro)noun (**?** see our discussion of 1 Sam 1:9; Ezek 37:1).

Analyze יָגַעְתִּי and כָּלֵיתִי

Root	Stem	Form	PGN	SF	OS	BRM

לְתֹהוּ וְהֶבֶל

The term תֹהוּ here points to a lack of worth, purpose, or profit (→ Tsumura, *Earth and the Waters*, 30–36). The term הֶבֶל conveys a sense of "futility" (→ see our discussion of Qoh 1:2; and, for instance, Crenshaw, *Ecclesiastes*, 57–58).

Translate v 4a.

Notice that there are two possible ways of translating the verse: (a) "But I said . . ." or (b) "But I thought . . ." Both are consistent with attested uses of אמר in the qal, and only context may help you choose between the two. Which have you chosen, and why? . . . .
. . . .

Of course, you may leave the issue open until you finish reading the entire unit. You may also propose that this is another case of intentionally ambiguous language.

On Parallelism

Analyze the corresponding (and contrasting) elements in לְרִיק יָגַעְתִּי and
לְתֹהוּ וְהֶבֶל כֹּחִי כִלֵּיתִי . . . .
. . . .
. . . .

Is there a dominant sound? (*Clue: l* and *r* are considered to be closely related sounds.) If so, in what way does this dominant sound contribute to the message of the text? . . . .
. . . .

Here and in several other of its occurrences in biblical Hebrew (e.g., Isa 53:4; Jer 3:20; Zeph 3:7; Ps 82:7) אָכֵן functions as an emphatic particle calling attention to a turning point in the line of thought in the text. אָכֵן signals that the preceding statement, or line of thought, is false and should be rejected despite its reasonable appearance, and that a new and true one is about to be presented (→ Muraoka, *Emphatic Words*, 132–33). The disjunctive markers that encircle and set apart the word אָכֵן mark it as a word that provides an interpretive key to what precedes and follows it, but is not an integral part of any of the two statements. You may translate this אָכֵן as "but."

Translate v 4b. (**?** think of the two possible אֶת־s you may find in biblical Hebrew.)

On Parallelism

Spell out the corresponding (and contrasting) elements in the two parallel versets in 4b.

. . . .

. . . .

Verse 5.

וְעַתָּה serves as a transitional marker separating the headings of ancient Hebrew letters (addresses and greetings) from their bodies. In biblical texts וְעַתָּה usually fulfills a similar role. It serves as a transitional marker between introductory material and the main body of the text. The introductory material (which may be larger than the body) is supposed to provide some necessary knowledge for the understanding of the following text. Although generally translated in English by "now," something like "now that you know all this" reflects more explicitly the meaning of וְעַתָּה on many occasions, including here in v 5 (→ WO'C 39.3.4f, p. 667; → on ancient Hebrew letters, see Pardee et al., *Handbook of Ancient Hebrew Letters*).

אָמַר ה' can be translated in different ways (e.g., "the Lord has said/promised/resolved/thought") according to the main meaning assigned to אמר. Of course, following "the Lord said," one expects to read what the Lord said, but the text instead adds a second reference to the Lord (in apposition) that points to the special relationship between God and the speaker, thus further legitimizing the following message as divine. In the Hebrew text this reference is set apart by revia and zaqef (the first zaqef marks the main subdivision of an atnaḥ clause). In your English translation you should write this reference between two commas.

יֹצְרִי מִבֶּטֶן לְעֶבֶד לוֹ

Analyze יֹצְרִי

Root	Stem	Form	PGN	SF	OS	BRM

לְעֶבֶד לוֹ

The first -לְ is the -לְ of purpose; the second is the possessive -לְ. Context helps distinguish between the two.

Translate v 5aa (up to the zaqef).


```
┌─────────────────────────────────────────────────────────┐
│                                                         │
│                                                         │
│                                                         │
│                                                         │
│                                                         │
└─────────────────────────────────────────────────────────┘
```

Two Hebrew traditions of the text of v 5ab have been preserved:

לְשׁוֹבֵב יַעֲקֹב אֵלָיו וְיִשְׂרָאֵל לא יֵאָסֵף (according to the ketiv; **?** review our notes on Deut 24:16)

לְשׁוֹבֵב יַעֲקֹב אֵלָיו וְיִשְׂרָאֵל לוֹ יֵאָסֵף (according to the qere)

Before you begin to read the second half of v 5a, be aware that it suggests more than one meaning. Since ambiguities usually grab the attention of the reader/hearer and channel it to the main issues at stake, this part of the verse deserves special consideration.

Analyze לְשׁוֹבֵב

Clue: the verb is in the polel stem; **?** K. 209; Gr. 138; Ke. 326–27; L. 253–54; S. 253–55; W. 201.

Root	Stem	Form	PGN	SF	OS	BRM

Translate לְשׁוֹבֵב יַעֲקֹב אֵלָיו

```
┌─────────────────────────────────────────────────────────┐
│                                                         │
│                                                         │
│                                                         │
│                                                         │
└─────────────────────────────────────────────────────────┘
```

וְיִשְׂרָאֵל לוֹ יֵאָסֵף/וְיִשְׂרָאֵל לא יֵאָסֵף

Analyze יֵאָסֵף

Clue: the tsere underneath a י which is followed by a guttural may mark an expected (but not materialized) doubling of the guttural; **?** K. 198; Gr. 108; Ke. 224; L. 178–79; S. 222; W. 156–57; and, if necessary, K. 197–98; Gr. 84–85; Ke. 139; L. 178; S. 222; W. 102.

Root	Stem	Form	PGN	SF	OS	BRM

Notice that אסף in the nif'al stem may mean "to be gathered," but also "to be swept away," "to perish." Which should you choose? It depends on the context.

Translate according to the ketiv וְיִשְׂרָאֵל לֹא יֵאָסֵף . . . .

Translate according to the qere וְיִשְׂרָאֵל לוֹ יֵאָסֵף . . . .

This is a good example of a well-attested alternation, ketiv לא and qere לו. This alternation causes a substantial change in the meaning of the sentence, but no phonetic change. Accordingly, a person listening to the text (notice the שִׁמְעוּ in v 1) cannot distinguish between the two except on the basis of context. But even a careful listener would be in trouble, because in many of these cases both the qere and the ketiv make perfect sense, though in different ways (cf. Ps. 100:3). The ambiguity in the text may well be intentional in such instances. Our verse is one of them. (→ on ketiv-qere, see Barr, "New Look at Kethibh-Qere.")

Translate v 5a.

Let's assume that your translation resembles the one in the NRSV, which follows the qere: "And now the Lord says, who formed me in the womb to be his servant, to bring Jacob back to him, and that Israel might be gathered to him." How is one to understand this text? Is it the Lord who will bring Jacob back? Or is it the speaker, the servant of the Lord?

The Hebrew text seems ambiguous, too. True, following אָמַר ה' one expects to hear what the Lord has said or promised or decided. Moreover, infinitive constructs preceded by לְ are a common heading for indirect speech, so one can legitimately understand the text as saying, "Now, the Lord says/has said/has promised . . . to bring Jacob back to him, and that Israel might (or should) not be destroyed/that Israel might (or should) be gathered to him." Or perhaps, in a less literal English translation, "Now, the Lord says/has said/has promised . . . that he would bring Jacob back to him, and that Israel might (or should) not be destroyed/that Israel might (or should) be gathered to him." Indeed, some scholars, such as Bewer ("Two Notes on Isaiah 49.1–6," 86–90) and Yehezkel Kaufmann understood the text in this way. The NJPSV points to this line of interpretation.

Alternatively, one may understand לְשׁוֹבֵב יַעֲקֹב אֵלָיו וְיִשְׂרָאֵל לֹא יֵאָסֵף/ לְשׁוֹבֵב יַעֲקֹב אֵלָיו וְיִשְׂרָאֵל לוֹ יֵאָסֵף as an integral part of a very long apposition that begins with יֹצְרִי. If so, our understanding of the text would be, "Now the Lord, who formed me from the womb to be his servant, to bring Jacob back, that Israel might (or should) not be destroyed/that Israel might (or should) be gathered to him, says/has said/has promised . . ."

How can a listener or reader of this text decide between these two very different options? The lines that follow an ambiguous text are supposed to provide a contextual solution. But, as you will see, even the next lines are not unambiguous. And perhaps both readings are part of the message of the text, and both should be taken seriously.

In any case, the attention of the listener or reader is caught by the question of who will bring back Jacob—the Lord or the by all appearances powerless servant of the Lord, whether an individual or the community of Israel. That Jacob will be brought back, and that either Israel will return to the Lord or will not be destroyed, or both, seems already to be taken for granted.

Verse 5b, וְאֶכָּבֵד בְּעֵינֵי ה' וֵאלֹהַי הָיָה עֻזִּי, does not provide the contents of the divine speech/promise as the first option (that it is the Lord who will gather Israel) leads us to expect; but neither does it necessarily support the second option (that it is the servant who will do the gathering).

Notice the vocalization of וֵאלֹהַי. Usually, when וְ is attached to a word that begins with a guttural that has a composite shewa, it takes the vowel of the composite shewa (e.g., וַעֲבָדִים; → GKC §104 d). Accordingly, one might have expected וֶאֱלֹהַי instead of וֵאלֹהַי. But in fact when וְ, בְּ, כְּ, and לְ precede the word אֱלֹהִים the haṭef-segol merges with the shewa producing tsere and a quiescent א. This process is similar to the one that led to the common form לֵאמֹר (→ GKC §102 d; JM §104 c; cf. JM §103 b).

Analyze וְאֶכָּבֵד

Clue: notice the dagesh on the first letter of the root; **?** K. 197–98; Gr. 84–85; Ke. 139; L. 178; S. 222; W. 102; and the shewa underneath the וֹ.

Root	Stem	Form	PGN	SF	OS	BRM

You may be tempted to translate וְאֶכָּבֵד as "I will be honored," which is grammatically correct. But because of the variety of possible meanings that the prefix may convey, one must take into account translations such as "I am honored," "I have been honored," or "I began to be honored."

הָיָה עֻזִּי

Which are the root consonants in עֻזִּי?

This is one of the cases in which הָיָה cannot be translated by the English past tense. הָיָה here points to a situation that existed in the past and continues at the time the speaker is talking. It should be translated by "is." This use of הָיָה may be attested in direct speech.

Translate v 5b, וְאֶכָּבֵד בְּעֵינֵי ה' וֵאלֹהַי הָיָה עֻזִּי

[blank box]

How does v 5b relate to v 5a? One possibility is that it may be considered a parenthetical remark that should be written inside dashes or parentheses, but much depends on the way the entire unit is read. One thing remains clear, this remark further legitimizes the speaker and the words of the speaker. Concerning the ambiguity mentioned above, v 5b seems to provide no conclusive advantage to any of the possible understandings. The ambiguity spills over into v 6.

On Parallelism

Spell out on a separate page the corresponding (and contrasting) elements in

(a)	וְיִשְׂרָאֵל לֹא יֵאָסֵף	לְשׁוֹבֵב יַעֲקֹב אֵלָיו
(b)	וְיִשְׂרָאֵל לוֹ יֵאָסֵף	לְשׁוֹבֵב יַעֲקֹב אֵלָיו
(c)	וֵאלֹהַי הָיָה עֻזִּי	וְאֶכָּבֵד בְּעֵינֵי ה'

Verse 6.

וַיֹּאמֶר here introduces a divine direct speech. The word is set apart from the rest of the clause by a disjunctive marker. The revia stands above the accented syllable, which in this case is not the last syllable.

Analyze נָקֵל (*Clue:* the root of this verb is geminate, ע"ע; **?** K. 210; Gr. 137, 218; Ke. 360; L. 188–89; S. 240–41; W. 233.) Take into account that side by side with the usual form in which the second consonant takes qamets, there are cases in which tsere stands instead of this qamets (→ K. 402; L. 189; S. 240–41; GKC §67 t, and esp. JM §82 m).

Root	Stem	Form	PGN	SF	OS	BRM

Analyze מִהְיוֹתְךָ (מִן + הֱיוֹת + ךָ); notice the "irregular" vocalization of the מ, namely hireq instead of the expected tsere; → GKC §63 q, 102 b).

Root	Stem	Form	PGN	SF	OS	BRM

Analyze לְהָשִׁיב and לְהָקִים

Root	Stem	Form	PGN	SF	OS	BRM

Another case of ketiv-qere alternation is attested with נְצִירֵי יִשְׂרָאֵל (ketiv)/נְצוּרֵי יִשְׂרָאֵל (qere). נְצוּרֵי is the construct form of נְצוּרִים.

Analyze נְצוּרִים

Root	Stem	Form	PGN	SF	OS	BRM

The alternative ketiv form is also from the root נצר. It is an adjective and is regularly translated as "preserved." The alternation of the qere-ketiv here produces no significant change in the meaning of the word or of the verse.

Translate v 6a.

After having encountered the ambiguities of v 5, you probably thought a while before translating v 6a. In fact, this is also an ambiguous verse. The most common English translation follows the line expressed, for instance, by the RSV: "he says: 'It is too light a thing that you should be my servant/to raise up the tribes of Jacob/and to restore the preserved of Israel.'"

The RSV leaves no room for doubt: it is the servant who raises up the tribes of Jacob and restores the "preserved of Israel." But the Hebrew text is not unambiguous. The subordination of . . . לְהָקִים to מִהְיוֹתְךָ לִי עֶבֶד is not a necessity in the Hebrew text. In fact, . . . לְהָקִים may just as well be linked to נָקֵל, therefore allowing such readings as:

(a) "It is lighter (easier? less significant?) that you are my servant than to raise up the tribes of Jacob and to restore the preserved of Israel." In this translation the מ is considered to be a comparative מ (→ GKC 133 a; WO'C 214, 264–67; Williams, *Hebrew Syntax*, 55). A similar translation was proposed, for instance, by Bewer.

(b) "It is light—because you are my servant (lit., because of your being my servant)—to raise up the tribes of Jacob and to restore the preserved of Israel." Here the מ is considered to be a causal מ (→ WO'C 11.2.11d, p. 213; Williams, *Hebrew Syntax*, 55; cf. JM §133 e). A similar translation was proposed, for instance, by Kaufmann.

(c) "It is too little that you should be My servant/In that I raise up the tribes of Jacob/And restore the survivors of Israel: (v 6a) I will also make you a light to the nations . . . (v 6b)" (NJPSV) In this translation, the מ is considered to be a comparative מ, but v 6b is considered to be the second element of the comparison.

Although differing opinions concerning the figure of the servant of the Lord and the general theology expressed in Isa 40–55 have led scholars to prefer one or another interpretation of the text, the fact remains that the text is very ambiguous. Ambiguity is a well-attested literary technique in biblical Hebrew literature, and especially in prophetic literature. It is extremely useful as the most economical—and many times the only available—way to express a complex, multilayered message, and as a practical device to hold the attention of the audience (→ Ben Zvi, *Zephaniah*, 84–86, 220–23, 227–30).

Verse 6b.

Analyze וּנְתַתִּיךָ

Root	Stem	Form	PGN	SF	OS	BRM

Translate v 6ba.

Clue: The expression "נתן ל . . ." may convey several meanings in biblical Hebrew, → BDB. In this case, translate וּנְתַתִּיךָ as "I will make you" or "I will give you as."

Note

The expression "to be a light of nations" (meaning perhaps "a light to nations"; cf. 1 Kgs 2:43, שְׁבֻעַת ה', "an oath to the Lord") has been interpreted in different ways. "Light" has been attested as a divine attribute and as an epithet of gods and kings in ancient Near

Eastern texts. Significantly, Tiglath-Pileser III (an important Assyrian king) was called "the light of all mankind." It seems that "light" was associated with "salvific power" and authority (cf. Isa 49:7,23; see also Isa 44:28–45:1). Is the figure of the servant of the Lord a counterpoint to that of Cyrus? (→ Rendtorff, *Old Testament*, 194–96; Blenkinsopp, "Second Isaiah," esp. 89–92.)

Analyze לִהְיוֹת

Root	Stem	Form	PGN	SF	OS	BRM

Whereas analyzing לִהְיוֹת is relatively easy, finding its conveyed meaning is more complex. As an infinitive construct preceded by לְ, לִהְיוֹת may well point to the consequence or result of the action described by the main verb, וּנְתַתִּיךָ (→ WO'C 36.2.3d, p. 607). Accordingly, one may translate the phrase as, "I will give you as . . . that my salvation . . . " This is most likely the basic meaning of the text.

In addition, a complementary shade of meaning is hinted at by this text. לִהְיוֹת, as an infinitive construct preceded by לְ, may suggest itself to be the verbal complement of וּנְתַתִּיךָ (→ WO'C 36.2.3b, p. 606). Accordingly, besides the main meaning of the text, "I will give you as . . . that my salvation . . . ," a connoted meaning, "I will give you as . . . to be (the means of) my salvation . . ." is strongly suggested. This connotative suggested meaning, as well as the ambiguities mentioned above, are all centered on a few closely related themes: the servant's announcement of the salvation of the Lord; the legitimacy and authority of a seemingly powerless servant of the Lord and of the servant's message; the relationship between this servant and the Lord; and the identity, attributes, and tasks of the servant.

Translate all of v 6, recognizing the limitations of any English translation.

Notice that the text opens with a call to listen, addressed to remotest peoples, and concludes with a reference to the salvation of the Lord reaching to "the end of the earth." Thus, a kind of thematic inclusio (**?** see our discussion of 1 Sam 1:5) rounds off the unit.

On Parallelism

Spell Out the corresponding (and contrasting) elements in

וּנְתַתִּיךָ לְאוֹר גּוֹיִם

לִהְיוֹת יְשׁוּעָתִי עַד־קְצֵה הָאָרֶץ

....

....

....

Translate all of Isa 49:1–6.

Works Cited in This Section

J. Barr, "A New Look at Kethibh-Qere," in B. Albrektson et al., *Remembering All the Way* (OTS 21; Leiden: E. J. Brill, 1981), 19–37; **E. Ben Zvi,** *A Historical-Critical Study of the Book of Zephaniah* (Berlin: de Gruyter, 1991); **A. Berlin,** *The Dynamics of Biblical Parallelism* (Bloomington: Indiana University Press, 1985); **J. A. Bewer,** "Two Notes on Isaiah 49.1–6," in S. W. Baron and A. Marx, eds., *Jewish Studies in Memory of G. A. Kohut* (New York: A. Kohut Foundation, 1935), 86–90; **J. Blenkinsopp,** "Second Isaiah—Prophet of Universalism," *JSOT* 41 (1988): 83–103; **P. A. H. de Boer,** *Second Isaiah's Message* (OTS 11; Leiden: E. J. Brill, 1956); **J. L. Crenshaw,** *Ecclesiastes* (OTL; Philadelphia: Westminster, 1987); **O. Kaiser,** *Introduction to the Old Testament* (Oxford: Basil Blackwell, 1975); **J. L. McKenzie,** *Second Isaiah* (AB 20; Garden City, N.Y.: Doubleday, 1968); **R. P. Merendino,** "Jes 49 1–6: ein Gottesknechtslied?" *ZAW* 92 (1980): 236–48; **P. D. Miller, Jr.,** *Interpreting the Psalms* (Philadelphia: Fortress, 1986); **T. Muraoka,** *Emphatic Words and Structures in Biblical Hebrew* (Jerusalem/Leiden: Magnes/E. J. Brill, 1985); **D. Pardee, S. D. Sperling, J. D. Whitehead, and P. E. Dion,** *Handbook of Ancient Hebrew Letters* (Chico, Calif.: Scholars Press, 1982); **D. L. Petersen and K. H. Richards,** *Interpreting Hebrew Poetry* (Minneapolis: Fortress, 1992); **R. Rendtorff,** *The Old Testament: An Introduction* (Philadelphia: Fortress, 1986); **D. T. Tsumura,** *The Earth and the Waters in Genesis 1 and 2* (JSOTSup 83; Sheffield: JSOT Press, 1989), 30–36; **R. N. Whybray,** *Isaiah 40–66* (NCB; Grand Rapids, Mich.: Eerdmans/London: Marshall, Morgan & Scott, 1981); **R. J. Williams,** *Hebrew Syntax: An Outline* (2d ed.; Toronto: University of Toronto Press, 1984).

4.   Readings in Wisdom Literature

4.1   Proverbs 3:13–26

We now move to readings from the wisdom literature of the Hebrew Bible/Old Testament. We will begin with a reading from the Book of Proverbs that deals, appropriately enough, with the subject of wisdom. The genre of the unit, Prov 3:13–26, is instruction. As in many other places in Proverbs, the speaker addresses a student in order to teach the way to wisdom.

Your reading of this passage will advance the skills in dealing with parallelism that you began to acquire in your reading of Isa 49:1–6. You will also gain confidence in reading the sometimes extremely concise material in Proverbs. In addition, you will encounter for the first time a system of conjunctive and disjunctive markers used only in the books of Proverbs, Psalms, and Job. This system of accents will be explained as we proceed through the passage in special notes on the masoretic accents.

Prov 3:13–26 may be divided in three subunits, vv 13–18, 19–20, and 21–26.

Subunit 1: vv 13–18.

Verses 13–18 comprise a short poem about wisdom. Its six lines are consistent with the versification of the text of Proverbs. The lines consist of two parallel versets, generally called **cola** (sg. **colon**), with the possible exception of the last line. The **bicolon** is a standard unit in biblical poetry. (→ Watson, *Classical Hebrew Poetry*, 12–13, 183).

The first three lines, vv 13–15, rhyme. All end with an accented *a* sound (הָ or הָ). In the second and third lines the repetition of this sound stresses the importance of "her" (i.e., of "wisdom"). Do the fourth and fifth lines rhyme? . . . .

Verse 13.

This introductory verse points directly to the main issue in the poem, namely, the rewards that come to the person who lives according to wisdom. The verse is introduced by the word אַשְׁרֵי. It is the plural construct form of a noun, and אַשְׁרֵי אָדָם is a construct chain. With an exclamatory value, X אַשְׁרֵי is a common opening expression in Proverbs and Psalms (e.g., Ps 1:1; 33:12; Prov 8:34; 28:14). It is difficult to pinpoint its precise meaning in these contexts. The expression may be translated as, "Oh, the blessedness of . . ." or, in more natural English, "Oh, blessed is . . ." or even by the common English expression, "Happy is . . ." Significantly, this expression is never used in relation to God (so it is not the same as בָּרוּךְ) and always points to an experience of well-being. Anderson suggests a paraphrase of X אַשְׁרֵי, "How rewarding is the life of . . . ," and he may be on the right track (↪ Anderson, *Psalms 1–72*, 58–59).

Analyze מָצָא and **explain** its vocalization. (**?** see our discussion of Lev 5:22.)

Root	Stem	Form	PGN	SF	OS	BRM

This is another instance where the translation of an affix form in the English simple past tense is plainly wrong. מָצָא here points to a continuous, complete situation that existed and persists, rather than to one that is ongoing or developing. In English, such מָצָא may be translated as "(he) finds" (↪ WO'C 30.1.5.c, pp. 487–88). Many times in Proverbs and Psalms an affix form is used to describe this kind of situation, and sometimes it follows אַשְׁרֵי (e.g., Ps 1:1; 40:5; Prov 3:13; without אַשְׁרֵי, Prov 18:22).

Do you remember how to pronounce חָכְמָה? (**?** see our discussion of 1 Sam 1:9.)

Analyze יָפִיק (**?** K. 149; Gr. 80–81; Ke. 324–25; L. 231–32; S. 211–12; W. 199–201.)

Root	Stem	Form	PGN	SF	OS	BRM

Note

You may consider translating both verbs in the English present tense. This translation would suggest that no meaningful difference exists between the tenses of the two verbs. To some extent this is the case. Perhaps the writer's goal was to develop a grammatical contrast between an affix and a prefix form. As you have learned, such a contrast is a common stylistic device. Nevertheless, the variation may have conveyed a somewhat different shade of meaning. The prefix form may have suggested an ongoing, developing action, whereas the affix may have viewed a situation or action from a global perspective, as completed. (↪ WO'C 30.5.1.c, pp. 487–88, 31.3.a–b, 504–5; JM §111 e, 112 d).

תְּבוּנָה

ה, is the feminine noun ending. Like תְּבוּנָה, many abstract nouns are feminine (e.g., מַמְלָכָה, "kingdom"; מְלוּכָה, "kingship"; טֻמְאָה, "uncleanness"; מְלָאכָה, "occupation, work"). The ת is a common nominal prefix (e.g., תְּעוּדָה, "testimony, attestation," from the root עוד; תְּשׁוּבָה, "return answer," from the root שׁוב; תְּשׁוּעָה, "salvation," from the root ישע; תַּעֲלֻמָה, "hidden thing, secret," from the root עלם). (↪ GKC §85 p–r; JM §88L o–v; WO'C 5.5.d, p. 91.)

Which root do you think the word תְּבוּנָה comes from? ....
Check against BDB.

The term תְּבוּנָה is relatively frequent in the Book of Proverbs. There and elsewhere it is
well attested as the second element in the pair הָכְמָה - תְּבוּנָה (e.g., 1 Kgs 5:9; Prov 2:2; 3:13,19; 8:1;
24:3; Job 12:12; cf. Obad 8). מצא (qal) and פוק (hif'il) are another word pair (Prov 3:13; 8:35; 18:22).
In both cases the less frequently used word tends to be the second element of the pair. (→ on word
pairs, see Watson, *Classical Hebrew Poetry* 128–44; 27–40.)

Translate v 13.

[blank box]

Whether you wrote "Happy is . . ." (or any of its alternatives) only once, at the beginning of the
first verset, or whether you wrote it twice, placing it at the beginning of each verset, it is almost
self-evident that "Happy is . . ." should be understood as present in both versets. This is an
instance of ellipsis (? see our discussion of 1 Sam 1:22), and אַשְׁרֵי is said to fulfill a double duty.
You will find many instances of ellipsis in the Proverbs and Psalms. The basic structure a-b-c
(הָכְמָה - מָצָא - אַשְׁרֵי) followed by an elliptic a¹, then by b¹ (יָפִיק) and c¹ (תְּבוּנָה), is very common in
Hebrew poetry (→ Watson, *Classical Hebrew Poetry*, 174–76).

On Masoretic Accents

The system of conjunctive and disjunctive markers occurring in Psalms, Proverbs, and
Job is slightly different from the one found in all the other biblical books. Some important markers of this system, which may be new to you, occur in this verse. Notice the
marker to the right, underneath the א in אָדָם. This is a disjunctive marker called deḥi. It
is a prepositive accent, that is, it always stands underneath the initial consonant (and
therefore does not mark the accented syllable). It divides atnaḥ clauses. (→ on deḥi, see
Yeivin, *Introduction*, 264, 268–69.) The atnaḥ in the Three Books (Psalms, Proverbs, and
Job) is written as in the others, but it is the main division only in short verses. On other
occasions it divides the two sections set apart by a different marker ('ole we-yored). In the
passage we are reading, all verses are short and therefore divided by atnaḥ. The second
atnaḥ clause in our verse is divided by another disjunctive marker that occurs only in the
Three Books. Notice that וְאָדָם shows more than a simple revia. This composite marker
is called revia mugrash, and is used only in the second part of the verse (→ Yeivin,
Introduction, 264, 267–69).

The conjunctive markers munaḥ and merka in the Three Books function as they
do in the other twenty-one biblical books. Can you identify them in this verse?

Verse 14.

Verse 14a consists of a comparison in which the first item is considered better than the second. The basic form of this comparison is טוֹב . . . מִן . . . (e.g., Prov 16:8; 21:9; → GKC §133 a; JM §141 g; WO'C 14.4.d., p. 264). In some cases, כִּי precedes טוֹב and opens the sentence (e.g., Ps 63:4; 84:11). Such a כִּי is not unusual, for כִּי is sometimes used to introduce dramatic comparisons (e.g., Isa 55:9; → Muilenburg, "Linguistic and Rhetorical Usages," 146). The כִּי in v 14 may be translated by a causal "for," but it also conveys the asseverative emphatic sense of "yea" or "indeed." (→ Schoors, "Particle כי," for a comprehensive study of the particle כִּי.)

To whom does the pronominal suffix refer in סַחְרָהּ? . . . .

כָּסֶף is the pausal form of the word כֶּסֶף.

Translate v 14a.

```
┌─────────────────────────────────────────────────────────────────┐
│                                                                   │
│                                                                   │
│                                                                   │
│                                                                   │
│                                                                   │
└─────────────────────────────────────────────────────────────────┘
```

Does the structure of v 14b relate to that of 14a as b^1-c^1 to a-b-c? Or does it show a chiastic version of it, namely c^1-b^1?

The relatively infrequent word חָרוּץ occurs always in a word pair with כֶּסֶף (Zech 9:3; Ps 68:14; Prov 3:14; 8:10,19; 16:16). As to the meaning of the expression, the pair "silver-gold" points not only to silver and gold per se but to everything of great value.

תְּבוּאָה is another example of a feminine, abstract noun with a prefixed ת (cf. תְּבוּנָה in the previous verse). Notice the repetition of sound between תְּבוּאָתָהּ (at the end of v 14) and תְּבוּנָה (at the end of v 13).

Which root do you think the word תְּבוּאָה comes from? . . . .
Check against BDB.

Translate all of v 14.

```
┌─────────────────────────────────────────────────────────────────┐
│                                                                   │
│                                                                   │
│                                                                   │
│                                                                   │
│                                                                   │
└─────────────────────────────────────────────────────────────────┘
```

On Fixed Pairs

Kugel writes: "As far as the workings of parallelism are concerned, the function of such fixed pairs is obvious. They strongly establish the feeling of correspondence between A and B [the two versets]. Indeed the more stereotypical the pairing, the greater the bond; with the most frequently used pairs, the appearance of the first in itself creates the anticipation of its fellow, and when the latter comes it creates a harmonious feeling of completion and satisfaction. In another way the pairs themselves may bring out the 'what's more' relationship of B to A [see our discussion of 1 Sam 1:11, and below], for . . . the second word of the pair sequence is most often the rarer and more literary term; when both terms are common, the second is sometimes a going-beyond the first in its meaning" (Kugel, *Idea of Biblical Poetry*, 29).

Does this text support Kugel's position? **Explain.** . . . .
. . . .

Analyze the parallelism between vv 14a and 14b. . . . .
. . . .
. . . .

On Masoretic Accents

Do you recognize a deḥi and a revia mugrash in v 14? Do the disjunctive masoretic accents of the first line of the poem (v 13) mirror those of the second one (v 14)? . . . . .
. . . .

Verse 15.

A new set of comparisons begins in v 15. In v 14 חׇכְמׇה is consistently referred to by a possessive pronominal suffix. What word stands for חׇכְמׇה in v 15a?

Please notice the qere alternative to the ketiv פְּנִיִּים. In most of the occurrences of the word פְּנִינִים, it is a standard to which something is compared and found of higher value (e.g., Prov 8:11; 31:10; Job 28:18). Literally, it means corals or pearls, but here—and in other cases (e.g., Prov 8:11; 31:10)—it seems to stand for jewels or precious stones in general. This translation is preferable to the well-known "rubies" in the KJV.

Analyze יִשְׁווּ

Root	Stem	Form	PGN	SF	OS	BRM

Which noun governs יִשְׁווּ? . . . .

Translate it. . . . .

When the noun following כָּל־ is grammatically definite (e.g., Gen 5:5; 45:10), it likely means "all of . . . ," "the whole of . . . ," or "all . . ." But when the noun is not grammatically definite and is a singular noun (e.g., Lev 3:17b; 22:10), it most likely means "every . . ." or "any . . ." (→ GKC §127 b–c; JM §139 e–i; WO'C 15.6.c, p. 289). If an "every . . ." or "any . . ." clause is negated, the logical translation is "no . . ." or "none of . . ."

Translate v 15.

On Parallelism

One may sense the heightening of the message from the first two versets in the set of comparisons to the last one. In vv 14a and 14b, it is not "wisdom" that is compared, but her profit. (Wisdom is personified as a woman in Prov 1–9; → Fontaine, *Proverbs*, 147–48.) In v 15a, "wisdom" herself is compared. In v 15b, the series of comparisons reaches its highest standard and, accordingly, its climax. This climax is also set apart from the series of similar מִן clauses by its very structure. Many times in the OT/HB you will find this heightening of the message from verset to verset. This tendency is what Kugel refers to as "A is so, and *what's more*, B is so." Kugel suggests that readers or listeners in ancient times expected to find such heightening (→ Kugel, *Idea of Biblical Poetry*, 8).

On Masoretic Accents

Do you recognize a deḥi and a revia mugrash in v 15? Do the disjunctive masoretic accents of the first two lines (vv 13, 14) mirror those of the third (v 15)?

For Further Thought

(a) With וְכָל־חֲפָצֶיךָ, the series of comparisons reaches its climactic point. At this point, and only at this point, the narrator "talks" directly to the addressees (they are addressed in the second person). Is it possible that there is relation between the climactic conclusion and the direct form of address?

(b) Is it possible that an old version of Prov 3:15b may have read just as Prov 8:11b? Compare Prov 3:14–15 and 8:11.

Verses 16–17

Verses 16 and 17 show the bicola structure that characterizes all the preceding lines. But they do not display the rhyme ending found in vv 13, 14, and 15. Instead this rhyme is found at the conclusion of the first verset in v 16 and moves to the end of the first word in vv 17a and 17b. As for their contents, vv 16–17 do not move forward the series of comparisons, which already reached a climax in v 15b, but describe "wisdom" by her attributes.

Remember the difference between יָמִים, "days," and יַמִּים, "seas." The latter is related to the geminate root ימם and behaves accordingly (→ JM §96A n), whereas the former seems to point to יָם, "day," a possible alternate form of the common יוֹם, "day."

On Masoretic Accents

The accent in the word יָמִים is on the last syllable, as usual, but the masoretic accent that generally points to the accented syllable seems to suggest otherwise. How do you explain this? (❓ see our note on masoretic accents on v 13.) . . . .
. . . .

Compare the disjunctive markers in v 17 with those in v 16. . . . .
. . . .

To whom does the pronominal suffix in בִּימִינָהּ and בִּשְׂמֹאולָהּ refer? . . . .

Translate vv 16–17.

conclusion of the first verset in v 16 and moves to the end of the first word in vv 17a and 17b. As for their contents, vv 16–17 do not move forward the series of comparisons, which already reached a climax in v 15b, but describe "wisdom" by her attributes.

The mention of "her right" and "her left" in v 16 is a way of suggesting oneness or wholeness within the framework of a bicolon. The listeners or readers of the verse expected a reference to "her left" to follow the one to "her right." The repetition of the sound בִּ at the beginning of both, בִּימִינָהּ and בִּשְׂמֹאולָהּ, further strengthens the bond between the two.

Within this wholeness, there is a certain movement from A to *what's more* B. The "length of days" in A is considered to be a blessing by itself, but B furthers the point by describing how these days are going to be lived: "with wealth and honor."

The word pair on which v 17 is shaped is דְּרָכִים / דֶּרֶךְ - נְתִיבוֹת / נְתִיבָה (e.g., Isa 42:16, Jer 6:16; Prov 1:15; 3:17; 7:25). Following the general trend, the less common term stands in the second place, which according to Kugel already provides some sense of "what's more." More explicit is the movement from דְּרָכֶיהָ (notice the repetition דְּרָכֶיהָ - דַּרְכֵי־) to וְכָל־נְתִיבוֹתֶיהָ (notice the "וְכָל־").

Verse 18.

Analyze תִמְכֶ֫יהָ and מְאֻשָּׁר

Root	Stem	Form	PGN	SF	OS	BRM

Root	Stem	Form	PGN	SF	OS	BRM

Notice the presence of the article in לַמַּחֲזִיקִים בָּהּ. **Translate** the phrase. . . . .
. . . .

תֹמְכֶ֫יהָ מְאֻשָּׁר is a good example of one of the ways in which biblical Hebrew expresses something similar to the English "anyone who . . . ," "everyone who . . . ," or "each person who . . ." (i.e., the **universal distributive**). We have mentioned in our discussion of v 15 that this sense is conveyed by כָּל־X, in which "X" stands for an indefinite singular noun. Another way of conveying the distributive sense is to use a plural noun, especially a plural participle (as תֹמְכֶ֫יהָ), with singular predicate (as מְאֻשָּׁר). See, for instance, in Prov 18:21, וְאֹהֲבֶ֫יהָ יֹאכַל פִּרְיָהּ, "any (person) who loves it/all who love it will eat its fruits." (→ GKC §145 1; and esp. WO'C 15.6.c, p. 289.)

Translate v 18.

| |
| |

Translate all of subunit 1, Prov 3:13–18.

| |
| |

Notice the inclusio formed by אַשְׁרֵי (v 13) and מְאֻשָּׁר (v 18). This inclusio marks off the entire poem. Remember that one of the functions of an inclusio is to demarcate literary units (→ Alonso Schökel, *Manual*, 191–92).

Subunit 2: vv 19–20.

Verses 19–20 comprise a very short poem that links wisdom, just praised in the preceding poem, to the Lord. Both lines follow the typical bicolon structure *a-b-c, b¹-c¹* or its chiastic variant, *a-b-c, c¹-b¹*. In addition, both lines are clearly shaped around word pairs.

Verse 19.

Analyze יָסַד and כּוֹנֵן (**?** see our discussion of Isa 49:5.)

Root	Stem	Form	PGN	SF	OS	BRM

Translate v 19.

Identify the word pairs and **spell out** the bicolon structure. Is it *a-b-c, b¹-c¹* or *a-b-c, c¹-b¹*? . . . .
Can you point to the use of alliteration (repetition of the first consonantal sound) in v 19?

On Masoretic Accents
Can you describe the conjunctive and disjunctive accents in this verse? . . . .
. . . .

Verse 20.

Analyze נִבְקָעוּ and יִרְעֲפוּ (**?** K. 399; Gr. 113–14; Ke. 252; L. 109; S. 274; W. 166–67; → GKC §64 a; JM §69a, cf. JM §21 f.)

Root	Stem	Form	PGN	SF	OS	BRM

Root	Stem	Form	PGN	SF	OS	BRM

Why does the text read נִבְקָעוּ and not נִבְקְעוּ as in Gen 7:11? (**?** see our discussion of Exod 21:29, for instance.) . . . .

To whom does the pronominal suffix in בְּדַעְתּוֹ refer? . . . .

Translate v 20.

```




```

Identify the word pairs (**?** cf. Prov 8:28) and **spell out** the bicolon structure. Is it *a-b-c, b¹-c¹* or *a-b-c, c¹-b¹*? . . . .

. . . .

. . . .

On Parallelism

Spell out corresponding (and contrasting) elements in the two parallel versets in v 20.

. . . .

. . . .

Translate subunit 2, vv 19–20.

```




```

Subunit 3: vv 21–26.

These verses contain the direct speech of the speaker (a sage) to "you," a student, about the security of a life lived according to (divine) wisdom. This direct speech from sage to student marks this passage clearly as instruction. (→ on instruction, see Murphy, *Wisdom Literature*, 50–51, 57–58.)

Verse 21.

The address בְּנִי is frequent in instructional texts in the Book of Proverbs (e.g., Prov 1:8; 2:1; 3:1; 5:1; 6:1; 7:1; 23:19; 24:21; cf. 4:1). It implies a sense of closeness between the speaker/teacher of wisdom and the student, as well as granting authority to the teacher. Indisputably, the father-son metaphor also points to the social horizon of a society in which it is taken for granted that both the teachers of wisdom and their students are male.

Analyze נְצֹר and אַל־יָלֻזוּ

Root	Stem	Form	PGN	SF	OS	BRM

Root	Stem	Form	PGN	SF	OS	BRM

יָלֻזוּ is most likely a jussive form, which (because it is preceded by אַל) may be translated as "let them not depart." To what does "them" refer? . . . .

As the verbs show, v 21 represents the beginning of the admonition per se. Admonitions are characterized by structures like "Do such and such" or "Behave in such and such way"; or, negatively, "Do not do such and such" or "Do not behave in such and such way," or by combinations and variants of the two structures (e.g., Prov 19:20; 22:22). They are one of the most basic forms in wisdom sayings (→ Rendtorff, *Old Testament*, 109). You will find many admonitions in the Book of Proverbs. נְצֹר is attested in some of them (Prov 4:23; 6:20; cf. Ps 34:14).

תֻּשִׁיָּה is a feminine abstract noun with a prefixed ת (see our discussion of v 13).

Find the root of תֻּשִׁיָּה.

Check against BDB. You may translate תֻּשִׁיָּה as "sound wisdom."

מְזִמָּה is also a feminine abstract noun, but with a prefixed מ.

Find the root of מְזִמָּה.

Check against BDB.

Many nouns begin with a prefixed מ. Some of them concern themselves with instruments (e.g., מַאֲכֶלֶת, "knife," from אכל), some with locations (e.g., מָקוֹם, "place," from קום), and some with abstract terms (e.g., מְזִמָּה "discretion, prudence, power of devising," from the root you have just identified). You may translate מְזִמָּה as "prudence" (→ WO'C 5.6.b, p. 90).

Translate v 21.

Analyze the corresponding elements between the two versets, 21a and 21b (notice such contrasts as positive and negative commands, implied and explicit objects, masculine and feminine objects). . . . .

Verse 22.

This is another verse structured according to the pattern *a-b-c, b¹-c¹*.

Identify *a, b, c, b¹* and *c¹*. . . . .

וְיִהְיוּ
Since the ו here is not a vav conversive, and since the prefix form follows imperatives (**?** see our discussion of Ezek 37:9), one may translate the verb as "that they shall be." (**?** If you are not sure how to differentiate a vav conversive-prefix from a non-conversive vav + prefix, see K. 7, 67, 266; Gr. 75–76; Ke. 145–46; L. 107–08; S. 158–63; W. 92.)

גַּרְגְּרוֹת is a feminine plural noun that is attested in Proverbs (Prov 1:9; 3:3,22; 6:21) but nowhere else in the OT/HB. It points to "the neck" mainly as a place to carry some (actual or figurative) ornament. גַּרְגְּרוֹת is a good example of another nominal pattern, one based on the repetition of the two consonants of geminate (ע"ע) and hollow verbs (e.g., בַּקְבּוּק, "bottle"; see our discussion of Ps 150:3–5; → GKC §84ᵇ o–p; JM §88J c; → on similar patterns based on repetition, see GKC §84 k–n; JM §88J a–b; WO'C 5.5.a, p. 89).

Spell out the correspondences and contrasts between *b* and *b¹*, and *c* and *c¹*. Take into account the contrast between frequent and infrequent terms, and the reference to this feature in our discussion of Prov 3:13. . . . .

Translate v 22.

```



```

Verse 23.

לְבֶטַח is one of a number of expressions consisting of a noun preceded by לְ that convey adverbial meanings (e.g., לָרֹב, "abundantly"; לָנֶצַח, "forever" → GKC §100 b, 102 i; JM §102 d; and esp. WO'C 11.2.10.d, pp. 206–07).

Notice that לְבֶטַח is a combination of בֶטַח (n.m.) + לְ, and *not* a combination of בֶטַח + article + לְ. Had the latter been the case, the ב of בֶטַח would have been a ב and there would have been a pataḥ instead of a qamets underneath the לְ. You may wonder, however, why the text shows לָ- instead of לְ-. This is because ל stands before the accented syllable (notice that the conjunctive munaḥ stands underneath and to the right of the ב of בֶטַח). When this is the case, -בְ, -כְּ, -וְ tend to take qamets instead of shewa (cf. our discussion of Exod 21:28; → GKC §102 f–i, 104 g; JM §103 c, 104 d).

Note

Do you wonder why בֶטַח is accented on the first syllable instead of the second and last? The answer is because it is a **segolate** (i.e., a noun that had originally one short vowel between the first and second consonants). Many of these forms develop to קֶטֶל (others to קֶטֶל and קֹטֶל). Since ח is a guttural, and pataḥ tends to take the place of other vowels before gutturals (→ GKC §22 d), the form evolved into בֶטַח instead of בֶטֶח, which is not attested in the OT/HB. Compare with נֶצַח (→ GKC §84ᵃ a; JM §88C a*, 88C d, 96A h–i).

Analyze לֹא תִגּוֹף (**?** K. 77–79; Gr. 103–04; Ke. 302–03; L. 133; S. 150; W. 141–42.)

Root	Stem	Form	PGN	SF	OS	BRM

לֹא תִגּוֹף looks like a negative command, but it is not.

Explain, on grammatical grounds, why it cannot be. . . . .
. . . .
Remember that not every לֹא + prefix is to be understood as a negative command. In the next verse you will find a clear case of לֹא + prefix that also does not express a negative command.

Translate v 23.

Compare v 23a with v 23b and **spell out** the corresponding elements and the contrasts you find among them. . . . .
. . . .
. . . .

On Masoretic Accents

The accent to the left of the qamets in אָז is conjunctive. It is called mehuppak. It is also attested in biblical books other than Psalms, Proverbs, and Job.

Identify the masoretic accents in v 23.

Verse 24.

Analyze תִּשְׁכַּב

Root	Stem	Form	PGN	SF	OS	BRM

Analyze לֹא־תִפְחָד

Root	Stem	Form	PGN	SF	OS	BRM

Analyze וְשָׁכַבְתָּ

Root	Stem	Form	PGN	SF	OS	BRM

Analyze וְעָרְבָה

Root	Stem	Form	PGN	SF	OS	BRM

Most likely you have noticed that BDB includes references to six different roots ערב. When two or more distinct roots (with clearly different meanings) share the same three consonants, these roots are said to be homonymous. Although there are homonyms in biblical Hebrew, their number is not great, nor are the chances of confusion. In many cases, identical roots do not completely overlap in actual use. For instance, only three of the ערב roots are attested as verbs (ערב II, III, and V). Moreover, among them only one (ערב V) is attested in the hif'il stem, and another (ערב II) in the hitpa'el. The area of possible confusion is further limited by the context in which the word is used. To illustrate, one reads עָרְבָה (qal stem) in our verse. Three different ערב roots (II, III, and V) are attested in the qal stem, but is the meaning "become evening" (ערב V) consistent with the context of v 24? What about "give in pledge" (ערב II)? Hence, only one of these six ערב roots is a reasonable candidate for עָרְבָה in v 24. (→ on homonyms in biblical Hebrew, see Barr, *Comparative Philology*, 125–55; the example of ערב is discussed on p. 132).

Translate v 24.

Compare the structure of v 24a with that of v 24b, taking into account the main disjunctive marker within each section. . . . .

For Further Thought

The reference to walking in the way and lying down in vv 23–24 may be understood against the background of the expression in Deut 6:7 and 11:19. In Deut 11:19 the reference to sitting at home and being in the way, and to lying down and getting up, is meant to suggest every possible moment in the life of a person. A distinction between situations in which a person may feel secure or those in which a person may feel insecure is contrary to the spirit of the texts in Deuteronomy. In Prov 3:21–26, however, only the potentially insecure portions of a person's life are relevant to the instructional and persuasive concerns, because the claim of Prov 3:21–26 is that this potential insecurity is overcome by wisdom and the Lord (see v 26). If this analysis is correct, then Prov 3:23–24 suggests the entire range of situations of potential personal insecurity. The theme of these situations of personal insecurity comes explicitly to the fore and continues to be developed in the next two verses. (Situations of "national insecurity" are not dealt with. There is a strong tendency in Proverbs to address the individual in society, rather than "the nation.")

Verse 25.

Analyze אַל־תִּירָא (**?** K. 84, 86; Gr. 94; Ke. 338–39; L. 139; S. 151–52; W. 211.)

Root	Stem	Form	PGN	SF	OS	BRM

The translation of אַל־תִּירָא as "don't be afraid" is sound, but somewhat ambiguous. Here, and in a number of other instances (e.g., Job 5:22), X־אַל (where X is a verb in the prefix or jussive form) is used to communicate the conviction of the speaker that something cannot or should not happen, rather than giving a direct negative command (or request) to the addressee (→ GKC §109 e). Accordingly, in the context of v 25, one may translate אַל־תִּירָא as "nor should you be afraid."

מִפַּחַד פִּתְאֹם

In our discussion of Deut 24:14, we mentioned a nominal pattern characterized by the ending וֹן or יָ. Many adjectives follow this pattern. A similar ending, ם ֹ or ם ָ, is typical of a group of adverbs (e.g., יוֹמָם, "by day"; חִנָּם, "in vain" or "gratis"; פִּתְאֹם, "suddenly"). These forms are also used as nouns (→ GKC §85 t, 100 g–h; JM §102 b, cf. §88M 1; WO'C 5.7e, p. 93, 39.3.1h, pp. 658–59). Here פִּתְאֹם is a noun, therefore פַּחַד פִּתְאֹם may be translated literally as "terror/panic of suddenness" or more idiomatically as "sudden panic/terror."

Explain why פִּתְאֹם is grammatically a noun and not an adverb in this verse. . . . .
. . . .

(וְ + מִן + שָׁאָה + _ ָ _ ת = וּמִשֹּׁאַת) וּמִשֹּׁאַת רְשָׁעִים כִּי תָבֹא

A possible translation of וּמִשֹּׁאַת רְשָׁעִים is "and (the) desolation/ruin/destruction of the wicked" (cf. KJV). Some scholars think that שָׁאָה here may indicate a storm that brings desolation. Accordingly, the NRSV translates the phrase as "the storm that strikes the wicked."

כִּי תָבֹא

Who or what is the subject of תָבֹא?

The main meaning of כִּי here is temporal, "when it comes." But it is likely that כִּי connoted also a sense of emphatic affirmation (so perhaps one can paraphrase כִּי תָבֹא as "when it surely comes"). This emphatic meaning is also conveyed by the next כִּי, at the beginning of the next verse. Although its meaning is "for," it conveys an additional sense of certainty (cf. v 14).

Translate v 25.

Verse 26.

כִּי sometimes heads the concluding line of a poem or a strophe (e.g., Ps 1:6; 5:13). It seems that this feature is related to its possible asseverative emphatic connotations. In this case it opens the motive clause that follows a negative command. On many occasions in Proverbs, a command is followed by a motive clause opened by כִּי (e.g., Prov 3:31–32; 4:1–2; 23:10–11; → our later discussions of Prov 22:22–23; 24:29; 25:21–22).

בְכִסְלֶךָ

The word כֶּסֶל may convey three meanings: "stupidity," "loins," and "confidence." Does the first one fit the context in v 26? The other two may be related, but which of them fits the context better? Nevertheless, be aware that connotations may have been instrumental in the writer's choice of words. כֶּסֶל meaning "confidence" is quite infrequent in the OT/HB (attested only four times), but perhaps the writer chose it because of the play on words, רַגְלְךָ - כִּסְלֶךָ. Notice also the rhyme, and the fact that both nouns are segolates (❓ see note on v 23).

It is worth noting that the text reads כִּי־ה' יִהְיֶה בְכִסְלֶךָ rather than כִּי־ה' יִהְיֶה כִסְלֶךָ. The point, of course, is to stress that the Lord cannot be identified with "your confidence." Instead, because of the preposition בְ, the sentence says that the Lord will serve as (behave as/act in the capacity of) "your confidence." (Compare with בְּעֶזְרִי in Exod 18:4; → GKC §119 i; WO'C 11.2.5e, p. 198; → Gordon, "'In' of Predication or Equivalence"; JM §133 c, for a different position.)

Translate v 26.

Can you describe the structure of v 26 as *a-b-c, b¹-c¹*? ....

If so, **explain** and **spell out** the correspondences and contrasts between *b-c* and *b¹-c¹*.

....

....

Translate all of Prov 3:13–26.

Works Cited in This Section

L. Alonso Schökel, *A Manual of Hebrew Poetics* (Subsidia Biblica 11; Roma: Editrice Pontificio Istituto Biblico, 1988); **A. A. Anderson,** *Psalms 1–72* (NCB; Grand Rapids, Mich.: Eerdmans; London: Marshall, Morgan & Scott, 1981); **J. Barr,** *Comparative Philology and the Text of the Old Testament* (Oxford: Clarendon Press, 1968); **C. R. Fontaine,** "Proverbs," in C. A. Newsom and S. H. Ringe, eds., *The Women's Bible Commentary* (London: SPCK; Louisville, KY.: Westminster/Knox, 1992), 145–52; **C. H. Gordon,** " 'In' of Predication or Equivalence," *JBL* 100 (1981): 612–13; **J. L. Kugel,** *The Idea of Biblical Poetry* (New Haven: Yale University Press, 1981); **J. Muilenburg,** "The Linguistic and Rhetorical Usages of the Particle כִּי in the Old Testament," *HUCA* 32 (1961): 135–60; **R. E. Murphy,** *Wisdom Literature: Job, Proverbs, Ruth, Canticles, Ecclesiastes, Esther* (FOTL 13; Grand Rapids, Mich.: Eerdmans, 1981); **A. Schoors,** "The Particle כי," in B. Albrektson et al., *Remembering All the Way* (OTS 21; Leiden: E. J. Brill, 1981), 240–76; **W. G. E. Watson,** *Classical Hebrew Poetry* (JSOTSup 26; Sheffield: JSOT Press, 1984); **I. Yeivin,** *Introduction to the Tiberian Masorah* (Masoretic Studies 5; Missoula, Mont.: Scholars Press, 1980).

4.2   Proverbs 10:1; 16:8; 22:22–23; 24:29; 25:28

Most of the Book of Proverbs consists of collections of discrete short units, often no more than two verses, usually bicola. Each of these units is sufficiently independent to show a meaning within itself, in addition to its possible contextual meaning within the collection in which it is located. Examples of such collections are in Prov 10:1–22:16; 24:23–34; 31:1–9.

In this section, you will read five short units from four different collections. These readings will further develop your confidence in reading wisdom literature in the HB/OT and will prepare you for future encounters with the extremely concise style of Proverbs.

Prov 10:1

Our first selection is the opening verse of the first of these collections (comprising Prov 10:1–22:16). It includes a heading or superscription and a short saying.

Verse 1a.

Translate מִשְׁלֵי שְׁלֹמֹה ....

Most likely you wrote, "The proverbs of Solomon" or "The wise sayings of Solomon." A similar superscription opens and characterizes the entire book of Proverbs (Prov 1:1). The effect of this title is to attribute the following collection to the legendary wise king of Israel.

On Masoretic Accents

In our discussion of Prov 3:13 we mentioned that atnaḥ is the main division of very short verses in the Three Books (Psalms, Proverbs, and Job); in longer verses, however, it divides the two sections set apart by a stronger disjunctive marker, namely 'ole we-yored. This marker is attested in our verse, where it sets apart the title of the collection from the collection itself. 'Ole we-yored is marked by the combination of two signs (שְׁלֹמֹה). One of them looks like merka and is on the stressed syllable, the other looks like mehuppak and is on the preceding syllable.

Identify both in v 1a.

'Ole we-yored separates the superscription from the following text in a number of occasions in Psalms (e.g., Ps 29:1; 32:1). (→ on 'ole we-yored, see Yeivin, *Introduction*, 265–66.)

What does the repetition of sounds in מִשְׁלֵי שְׁלֹמֹה (Prov 1:1; 10:1; 25:1) contribute to the superscription? . . . .

Verse 1b.

| בֵּן חָכָם יְשַׂמַּח־אָב | v 1ba |
| וּבֵן כְּסִיל תּוּגַת אִמּוֹ | v 1bb |

Analyze יְשַׂמַּח

Root	Stem	Form	PGN	SF	OS	BRM

כְּסִיל is a frequent word in Proverbs and Qohelet, where it appears sixty-seven times (elsewhere in the OT/HB it occurs only three times). The word comes from the root כסל. The possible meanings of כסל have been discussed in Prov 3:26. The context of this verse will help you decide which of these potential meanings is appropriate in this case.

As for the nominal form קְטִיל seen here (e.g., גְּבִירָה, "queen mother"), it is an "aramaicizing" variant from the common nominal קָטִיל pattern (e.g., נָבִיא, "prophet").

תּוּגָה is another instance of a feminine abstract noun with a prefixed ת (cf. תְּבוּנָה and תְּבוּאָה in Prov 3:13,14. Which root do you think the word תּוּגָה comes from? . . . .
. . . .

Check against BDB.

Translate v 1b.

```
                                                                              
                                                                              
                                                                              
                                                                              
```

The first part of this bicolon contrasts with the second part. Accordingly, this is a clear instance of antithetic parallelism. Most of the sayings in the first part of this collection (chs. 10–15) are in antithetic parallelism (? see our discussion of Isa 49:1), and even in the second part of the collection (Prov 16:1–22:16) a quarter of the sayings are antithetic (→ Murphy, *Wisdom Literature*, 64). The basic structure of the saying is simple: *a-b, a¹-b¹*. You will encounter this structure (and its chiastic version, *a-b, b¹-a¹*) in many sayings in Proverbs.

Often, *a* and *a¹*, *b* and *b¹*, are shaped around word pairs (→ see our discussion of Prov 3:13,14,19,20). In our verse, these are אָב-אֵם, חָכָם-כְּסִיל (e.g., Prov 28:26; Qoh 2:16), and שָׂמֵחַ - תּוּגָה (Prov 17:21).

We quoted part of Kugel's discussion of fixed pairs in *The Idea of Biblical Poetry* in our discussion of Prov 3:13. Kugel continues: "A number of critics have described the pairs as 'clichés' and 'stereotypical formulae.' Such judgments should not, however, lead readers to impose modern-day notions of originality on ancient texts. As an examination of even medieval poetics will reveal, premodern songs and poems did not aim at setting out new comparisons and images, but reworking traditional themes and standard language into new formulations: originality consisted of the new variations within a conventionalized framework. But more than this, it is an error to see the pairs themselves as the essence of the line. On the contrary, the pairs often function to bring into equation the other words of the line—words that are rarely connected, or in any case words whose apposition is the whole point" (Kugel, *Idea of Biblical Poetry*, 29–30).

In the line we are looking at, apart from the adversative ו ("but"; → our discussion of 1 Sam 1:22; WO'C 139) there is nothing but word pairs. The main point of the line, however, can hardly be to point out that "grief" and "joy" or "wise" and "foolish" are opposites. A more promising approach is to focus on the function of the pairs and on the juxtaposition of the first verset to the second.

A good starting point is that, unlike חָכָם-כְּסִיל and שָׂמֵחַ - תּוּגָה, אָב-אֵם is a hendyadic pair. Accordingly, one cannot understand the text as pointing exclusively to the "father" in the first part and the "mother" in the second. Thus, the word pairs stress the relation between parents and sons rather than the specific reactions of fathers and mothers. (For sons, see our discussion of Prov 3:21.) The point is to teach the son that his behavior will directly affect the well-being of his parents, and that well-being, it is implied, is one of the highest goods to be sought. The relationship between parents and son is explicitly stressed by the closing element in the line: the possessive suffix in אִמּוֹ. (In fact, אָב refers also to "his father," but the suffix is omitted due to the tendency to concision between the elements in a parallelism; → Alonso Schökel, *Manual*, 167.)

As for stylistic variations and contrasts within the expected elements of the framework, the first verset is a verbal sentence, whereas the second is a nominal one, and the more frequently used words are clustered in the first verset rather than in the second.

For Further Thought

A good exercise for testing and sampling the wide range of stylistic variation within the boundaries of a more or less standard framework, even when similar ideas are expressed, is to compare this verse with Prov 17:21.

Prov 16:8

This saying is illustrative of a recognizable group, the . . . -מ . . . טוֹב ("better") sayings (e.g., Prov 12:9; 15:16; 15:17; 17:1). (**?** about . . . -מ . . . טוֹב, see our discussion of Prov 3:14.)

The general structure of these didactic sayings is: (Y) B-מ; (X) A טוֹב. *A* represents a situation/state that seems to be obviously much worse than B. For instance, in Prov 15:17, A = "(to eat) a dinner of vegetables" and B = "(to eat) a fatted ox." X and Y characterize a set of diametrically opposed circumstances under which A and B take place. In Prov 15:17, X consists of "love," and Y of "hate." The difference between X (the positive pole) and Y (the negative pole) is so significant that it turns around the order of desirability of even the "self-evident" pair A-B. The point of the saying, of course, is to hammer home the importance of the issue expressed by the contrast between X and Y, which in most cases is expressed by means of a word pair. The difference between A and B serves only rhetorical purposes: (a) to get the attention of the reader/listener by presenting a "better . . . than" statement that, on the surface, defies common sense; and (b) to underscore the significance of the X-Y issue that supersedes even common-sense considerations.

טוֹב־מְעַט בִּצְדָקָה

מְעַט here is a noun and can be translated as "little."

מֵרֹב תְּבוּאוֹת בְּלֹא מִשְׁפָּט

We have discussed the word תְּבוּאָה in Prov 3:14.

בִּצְדָקָה - בְּלֹא מִשְׁפָּט is a variant of the well-known pair מִשְׁפָּט - צְדָקָה (e.g., Gen 18:19; Isa 56:1; Am 5:24; Prov 21:3). The opposition in this case is marked by בְּלֹא - בְּ (the form בְּ instead of בָּ is due to the shewa underneath the צ of צְדָקָה; → GKC §102 d; JM §103 b).

Translate Prov 16:8.

```
┌─────────────────────────────────────────────────────────────┐
│                                                               │
│                                                               │
│                                                               │
│                                                               │
│                                                               │
└─────────────────────────────────────────────────────────────┘
```

Identify X, Y, A, and B in Prov 16:8.

Prov 22:22–23

This short unit belongs to the second collection of wise sayings (Prov 22:17–24:22). This collection parallels in many respects the Egyptian "Instruction of Amen-em-Opet" (ANET 420–25). But the author of Prov 22:17–24:22 used this Egyptian text freely, adding considerably to it and certainly reworking the material, as our verses shall illustrate. (→ Murphy, *Wisdom Literature*, 74.)

Prov 22:22–23 consists of an admonition (or perhaps a prohibition; v 22) along with its motive clause (v 23; **?** our discussion of Prov 3:21; → Murphy, *Wisdom Literature*, 172, 180). Such an arrangement is often expressed by the pattern אַל . . . כִּי (e.g., Exod 3:5; Lev 11:43–44; Num 14:42; Isa 10:24–25; 43:1; Ps 22:12; 49:17; 62:11; Prov 23:6–7; 24:19–20).

Verse 22.

אַל־תִּגְזָל־דָּל כִּי דַל־הוּא	22a
וְאַל־תְּדַכֵּא עָנִי בַשָּׁעַר	22b

Analyze אַל־תִּגְזָל

Root	Stem	Form	PGN	SF	OS	BRM

We have already dealt with the question of the meaning of גזל in the qal, in our discussion of Lev 5:21.

כִּי דַל־הוּא contains a clause of classification (**?** see our discussion of Exod 21:29 and Ezek 37:11).

The term דַל refers to someone materially poor (see Jer 39:10) and hence weak in society. In the Book of Proverbs, a person categorized as דַל may be depicted as unable to obtain justice (Prov 29:7) or any help (Prov 21:13). It seems that in this book there is no substantial difference between the terms עָנִי and דַל (→ Whybray, *Wealth and Poverty in the Book of Proverbs*, 15–22), though the issue remains controversial. (See also our discussion of Deut 24:14.) Of course, in this verse עָנִי and דַל function as a word pair, which along with אַל־תִּגְזָל - אַל־תְּדַכֵּא binds the two versets together.

You probably noticed that v 22a shows דַל but also דָּל.

Explain why the same word is written with two different vowels. . . . .
. . . .
Why is the first *dal* written with ד but the second shows דּ?

Clue: One of the main rules about dagesh lene is: The letters ב, ג, ד, כ, פ, and ת usually take dagesh lene at the beginning of a word, *except* when the word they begin stands immediately after a word that has a conjunctive marker and ends in a vowel, i.e., in an open syllable. (→ for the rule and its exceptions, see Yeivin, *Introduction*, 287–98.)

Analyze אַל־תְּדַכֵּא

Root	Stem	Form	PGN	SF	OS	BRM

בַשָּׁעַר

"At the gate" refers to the administration of justice, which was conducted at the gate of the city (cf. Am 5:12,15). Justice "at the gate" often depended on the social status of the person; this is assumed in our verse as it is in Job 5:4, in which בַשָּׁעַר + (passive hitpaʾel) דכא occurs.

Translate v 22.

```
┌──────────────────────────────────────────────────────────────┐
│                                                                │
│                                                                │
│                                                                │
│                                                                │
│                                                                │
└──────────────────────────────────────────────────────────────┘
```

Notice the remarkable use of repetition as a stylistic device. דַּל/דָּל and אַל are repeated twice, and there is a clear repetition of sounds in 22a and of gutturals in 22b. How do these repetitions affect the message being conveyed in this text? ....

....

What kind of parallelism do you find in v 22—antithetic (as in Prov 10:1), synthetic, or synonymous? (**?** see *Note on parallelism* in our discussion of Isa 49:1.) ....

....

On Masoretic Accents

Which masoretic accents do you recognize in v 22a? In v 22b we encounter a conjunctive accent that we have not seen before, ṭarḥa. This accent stands beneath the כ in תְּדַכֵּא. It looks like ṭifḥa, but ṭifḥa is not attested in the Three Books. Moreover, ṭifḥa is a disjunctive marker, not a conjunctive one as ṭarḥa. One may also confuse ṭarḥa with another disjunctive marker—this time one well attested in the Three Books, deḥi. But the latter stands to the right of the initial consonant (i.e., it is a prepositive marker), whereas ṭarḥa stands underneath the accented syllable (→ GKC §15 h–i; Yeivin, *Introduction*, 265, 68).

Verse 23.

כִּי־ה' יָרִיב רִיבָם	23a
וְקָבַע אֶת־קֹבְעֵיהֶם נָפֶשׁ	23b

This verse consists of the motive clause attached to the admonition (or prohibition) in v 22.

Analyze יָרִיב

Root	Stem	Form	PGN	SF	OS	BRM

The term רִיב and the related verb יָרִיב have clear judicial connotations (cf. 1 Sam 24:16; Isa 1:17; Ps 43:1); moreover, they often mean to plead the cause of someone (e.g., Jer 50:34; Mic 7:9). There are numerous references in the OT/HB to the Lord as an advocate of those who are seemingly helpless, incapable of finding a powerful human advocate (e.g., Prov 23:11). The Lord is described, therefore, as the main counterpoise to the social balance of power. This role was generally ascribed to deities and kings in ancient Near Eastern cultures.

Analyze וְקָבַע

Root	Stem	Form	PGN	SF	OS	BRM

Analyze קֹבְעֵיהֶם

Root	Stem	Form	PGN	SF	OS	BRM

As for the meaning of קבע (qal), BDB provides a double qualified definition, "dubious, perhaps 'rob'" (which is based mainly on the contextually possible "synonymity" with גזל in our verse). Cody suggests that קבע (qal) means "to squeeze," "to oppress," and accordingly he proposes to read v 23b as follows: "The Lord will press the life out of those who oppress them" (→ Cody, "Notes on Proverbs 22,21 and 22,23b," 425–26).

Translate all of v 23.

The use of repetitions as a stylistic device in v 23 is self-evident. How would you characterize the structure of v 23? As *a-b, a¹-b¹*, as *a-b-c, b¹-c¹*, or as some other structural arrangement?

Is there real synonymity between the two versets in v 23, or does the second heighten the message of the first? (→ see our discussions of Prov 3:13,14 and 1 Sam 1:11.)

Translate the entire unit, Prov 22:22–23.

For Further Thought

The parallel text in the Instruction of Amen-em-Opet (ch 2; 4:4–5) reads: "Guard thyself against robbing the oppressed and against overbearing the disabled" (ANET 422).

Compare this portion of the Instruction of Amen-em-Opet with Prov 22:22–23.

Think about their similarities and differences, and the possible reasons for them.

Prov 24:29

This brief prohibition/admonition belongs to a short collection of "miscellaneous" sayings (Prov 24:24–34) which, in the Hebrew text but not in the Septuagint, stands immediately after the "words of the wise" (Prov 22:17–24:42).

29aa	אַל־תֹּאמַר
29ab	כַּאֲשֶׁר עָשָׂה־לִי כֵּן אֶעֱשֶׂה־לּוֹ
29b	אָשִׁיב לָאִישׁ כְּפָעֳלוֹ

The verse opens, as expected, in a prohibition/admonition.

Translate v 29aa.

Perhaps you have translated v 29aa as "do not say," but notice that אַל־תֹּאמַר may be understood as "do not think," which in this context is preferable.

Following אַל־תֹּאמַר one expects a direct quotation, and one anticipates that the quotation will be set apart from the preceding text by a disjunctive marker (see our discussion of Ezek 37:11; Isa 49:3). Both expectations are fulfilled in the text.

The direct speech that follows consists of two parts. The first one itself may be divided into two sections, which are bound together by the frequently attested comparative formula, כֵּן . . . כַּאֲשֶׁר . . . (e.g., Gen 41:13; Lev 24:19,20; Josh 11:15; 14:5; Ps 48:9; → JM §174; WO'C 38.5a, pp. 641–42).

Translate כַּאֲשֶׁר עָשָׂה־לִי   . . . .

Translate כֵּן אֶעֱשֶׂה־לּוֹ   . . . .

Notice the use of repetition as a stylistic device that emphasizes the identical character of the two actions as well as the reversal of subject and object.

Note

The metheg underneath the ע and א in עָשָׂה and אֶעֱשֶׂה, respectively, indicates an accent secondary to the one in the last syllable. (**?** see our discussion of Jer 22:2.) Which kind of dagesh is the one on the ל in אֶעֱשֶׂה־לּוֹ? (**?** see our discussion of Exod 21:31.)

On Masoretic Accents

The marker separating the direct quotation from the possible thought of the addressee (כַּאֲשֶׁר . . .) and the words of the speaker (אַל־תֹּאמַר) is revia. Actually, it is a kind of revia called revia gadol. This marker is used when the main division of an atnaḥ clause is far from atnaḥ; if it is close to it, deḥi may be used. Revia gadol is used also as the main divider of an 'ole we-yored clause (→ Yeivin, *Introduction*, 267).

Analyze אָשִׁיב

Root	Stem	Form	PGN	SF	OS	BRM

Translate אָשִׁיב לָאִישׁ כְּפָעֳלוֹ   . . . .

Read your partial translations of the verse. Is it possible to characterize the structure of the entire verse as a variant of *a-b-c; c¹-b¹*?

Explain. . . . .

Note on Qamets

Although the qamets beneath the פ in כְּפָעֳלוֹ stands in an open syllable, it should not be pronounced *a* but *o*. If the qamets stands immediately before ḥatef-qamets (ֳ) then it is always pronounced *o*, even if it is marked with metheg. This is one of the relatively few exceptions to the rule that qamets is to be pronounced *a* unless it is in a closed unaccented syllable. (→ on the exceptions to this rule, see GKC §9 v; JM §6 1–n.)

Translate all of Prov 24:29.

```

```

For Further Thought

This prohibition/admonition clearly stands against retaliation (see also Prov 20:22). The OT/HB does not present a unified, univocal point of view in this respect. Compare the line of thought in these passages with Matt 5:38–42; 7:12; and with Hillel's saying, "What is hateful to you, do not do to your fellow."

Prov 25:28

Our last reading in this section consists of a short saying from still another collection in the Book of Proverbs (Prov 25:1–29:27). The sayings in this collection are identified as the proverbs of Solomon that were collected (or copied) by Hezekiah's sages.

One of the main characteristics of this collection is the high frequency of sayings that consist of a comparison, such as Prov 25:28. Often, explicit comparative markers such as כְּ or כֵּן signal to the reader that the text is to be understood as a comparison (e.g., Prov 26:1, which shows a . . . כֵּן . . . כְּ structure). In some cases, a vav separates the two members of the comparison (e.g., Prov 26:14; → WO′C 39.2.3a–b, pp. 650–51). But in a number of instances, owing to the conciseness of the verse, even the vav is not present. In such a case, the comparative sense is conveyed by simple juxtaposition. Prov 25:28 illustrates this category of comparison. (→ on comparisons in Proverbs, see Murphy, *Wisdom Literature*, 66, 77; → on comparative clauses in general, see JM §174.)

The two main divisions of v 28 correspond to the two members of the comparison:

עִיר פְּרוּצָה אֵין חוֹמָה	**28a**
אִישׁ אֲשֶׁר אֵין מַעְצָר לְרוּחוֹ	**28b**

Analyze פְּרוּצָה

Root	Stem	Form	PGN	SF	OS	BRM

מַעְצָר is a noun that follows a series of nominal patterns that are all characterized by the prefix מ
(? see our discussion of Prov 3:21). This group of patterns is the most common one in the OT/HB
(→ GKC §85 e–m; JM §88L d–n; WO'C 5.6.b, p. 90).

Translate v 28.

```



```

The didactic character of the comparison is self-evident and suits well the general instructive
character of the sayings in Proverbs.

For Further Study

—You will find a comparison shaped in a similar way, but with vav, in Prov 26:14.
—You will find a comparison shaped in a different way but conveying a similar message, in
Prov 16:32. *Read* and *translate* Prov 16:32.

For Further Reading

Concerning Proverbs, see Murphy, *Wisdom Literature*, 48–82.

Works Cited in This Section

L. Alonso Schökel, *A Manual of Hebrew Poetics* (Subsidia Biblica 11; Roma: Editrice Pontificio
Istituto Biblico, 1988); **A. Cody,** "Notes on Proverbs 22,21 and 22,23b," *Bib* 61 (1980): 418–26;
J. L. Kugel, *The Idea of Biblical Poetry* (New Haven: Yale University Press, 1981); **R. E. Murphy,**
Wisdom Literature: Job, Proverbs, Ruth, Canticles, Ecclesiastes, Esther (FOTL 13; Grand
Rapids, Mich.: Eerdmans, 1981); **J. B. Pritchard,** ed., *Ancient Near Eastern Texts Relating to
the Old Testament* (ANET; 2d ed.; Princeton, N.J.: Princeton University Press, 1955); **R. N.
Whybray,** *Wealth and Poverty in the Book of Proverbs* (JSOTSup 99; Sheffield: JSOT Press, 1990);
I. Yeivin, *Introduction to the Tiberian Masorah* (Masoretic Studies 5; Missoula, Mont.: Scholars
Press, 1980).

4.3 Qohelet 1:1–11

Qohelet (also called Ecclesiastes) is an atypical biblical book with regards to both its content and its language. Its contents have been considered existentialist, an expression of an intellectual crisis among the wise and "one of the most delicate and complex literary products of the Ancient Near East" (Loader, *Polar Structures*, 133). Its language is so intricate that despite many recent studies, Murphy can correctly claim that the grammar of Qohelet "remains to be written" (Murphy, "On Translating," 579). Its vocabulary includes many words and expressions that are either unusual or unattested in other biblical books. The Hebrew of Qohelet represents an otherwise almost unattested transitional stage between classical biblical Hebrew and mishnaic Hebrew.

These complexities should not, however, deter you from reading Qohelet in Hebrew. This section is designed to lead you through a passage from Qohelet. When you are reading this text, remember that Qohelet is not one of the Three Books, and therefore its system of masoretic accents is not the one we have seen in Proverbs but that found in all HB/OT books except Proverbs, Job, and Psalms.

Verses 1–3

Verse 1.

דִּבְרֵי קֹהֶלֶת בֶּן־דָּוִד מֶלֶךְ בִּירוּשָׁלָ͏ִם

As is often the case, the first verse of the book contains its title (e.g., Ob 1; Hab 1:1; Prov 1:1). The basic structure of this heading follows the pattern of those found in many other books of the Hebrew Bible (e.g., Jer 1:1; Am 1:1; Prov 30:1; 31:1).

Translate v 1.

The simple structure of the heading stands in contrast to the complex set of meanings conveyed by the specific words of the title. Who is Qohelet? No king of Israel—or Judah—nor any other person mentioned in the OT/HB carried this name. Moreover, קֹהֶלֶת, which occurs only in this book, stands for a proper name in most of its occurrences (e.g., Qoh 1:12), but not in all of them. For instance, the use of קֹהֶלֶת in Qoh 12:8 is not consistent with its acting as a proper name. Why? (→ GKC §125 d–e; JM §137 b.) ....

....

If קֹהֶלֶת is not a proper name in Qoh 12:8, what does it mean there? To answer this question,

Analyze קֹהֶלֶת

Root	Stem	Form	PGN	SF	OS	BRM

Your analysis should have led you to the conclusion that קֹהֶלֶת is a feminine singular participle of קהל in the qal stem. But קֹהֶלֶת cannot be translated as "female gatherer" in either Qoh 12:8 or Qoh 1:1. Why? ....

....

This difficulty is solved when one realizes that occasionally professions are designated by grammatically feminine participles, such as סֹפֶרֶת, "scribe," and קֹהֶלֶת, "gatherer." But a gatherer of what? Of wise sayings? Of people to teach them? Or of both? (Cf. Qoh 12:9–11.)

"Son of David" may mean a biological son of David, such as Solomon—whom the author of the book may have had in mind as a classical Israelite wisdom figure—but the term may also designate any male member of the House of David. Is Qohelet a davidic king who ruled in Jerusalem? According to v 1, the answer is positive because מֶלֶךְ בִּירוּשָׁלָם refers back to Qohelet and not to David (cf. Josh 1:1, where מְשָׁרֵת מֹשֶׁה refers to Joshua, not to Nun). But the text has the potential for misreadings (or mislistenings) in this respect. Moreover, the kingly image of Qohelet so clear in the first two chapters (see Qoh 1:12) is completely missing in the following ten chapters. Is Solomon, the ideal biblical sage, the kingly figure that the author had in mind? Perhaps so, but the writer never says that unequivocally.

Verse 2.

הֲבֵל הֲבָלִים

The exact meaning of the word הֶבֶל in Qohelet is unclear because of its many nuances. You may translate it as "absurd" or "absurdity." It seems that the common denominator of the various uses of הֶבֶל in Qohelet points to the incongruity that the speaker found between what is and what should be, between actions (or situations) and their outcome (for instance, working hard and not enjoying the fruits of one's work, or working hard even if one knows that one will not enjoy the fruits of one's work; see Qoh 2:22–23; cf. Qoh 1:3). Other proposed translations of הֶבֶל include "futility," "vanity," "incomprehensible," "transitory," and "illusory." (→ on this issue, see Fox, *Qohelet*, 29–41; Murphy, "On Translating," 572–73; Crenshaw, *Ecclesiastes*, 57–58.)

The formulation הֲבֵל הֲבָלִים expresses the absolute superlative of הֶבֶל, "absurdity of absurdities," "utter absurdity" (→ WO'C 14.5.b, p. 267). Notice that this word is vocalized הָבֶל in a pausal position; in a non-pausal position it would be vocalized הֶבֶל. The same relationship exists between שֶׁמֶשׁ and שָׁמֶשׁ (see v. 3) and characterizes many segolates (**?** see our discussion of Prov 3:23).

> **Note**
>
> One should be able to recognize the subtle difference between an **absolute superlative,** such as הֲבֵל הֲבָלִים and קֹדֶשׁ קָדָשִׁים, "most holy," in Exod 30:29, and a **comparative superlative,** such as קֹדֶשׁ הַקֳּדָשִׁים in Exod 26:33 where "the most holy" is "as compared to other holy items." In these expressions, whenever the article precedes the noun in the plural, we are looking at a comparative superlative. (→ WO'C 9.5.3.j, p. 154; 14.5.a–b, esp. p. 267; 14.5.c–d, esp. p. 270.)

Remember that a construct chain consisting of the repetition of a noun, first in the singular and then in the plural, is only one of the ways in which biblical Hebrew may express superlatives (**?** GKC §133 g–l; JM §141 j–n; and esp. WO'C 14.5, pp. 267–71).

Which of the possible meanings of אָמַר (such as "said," "has said," "used to say," and "says") is contextually the most appropriate? At this point in your reading you cannot know for sure. Sometimes you must list several alternative understandings of a word and choose one of them only later.

Translate v 2.
Clue: translate הַכֹּל as "everything."

[ ]

This verse is characterized by a repetition of words and sounds.

Spell out these repetitions, pointing out the dominant sounds and explaining their likely rhetorical function.

Clue: Remember that the effect of a dominant sound is achieved not only by repeating the same consonant but also by a combination of related consonants, such as *b* and *m* or *l* and *r*.

. . . .

. . . .

. . . .

For Further Thought

Read Qoh 12:8 and compare with Qoh 1:2. Taking into account that Qoh 1:1 is the title of the work and that Qoh 12:9–14 is the epilogue, and therefore that both Qoh 1:1 and Qoh 12:9–14 stand apart from the main body of the book, how would you characterize the stylistic device shaped by Qoh 1:2 and Qoh 12:8, and what would be its function? (**?** see our discussions of 1 Sam 1:5; Ezek 37:6; Isa 49:6; and Prov 3:13–18.) Do your conclusions support the widely accepted view that v 2 provides the leitmotif or motto of the entire book?

Verse 3.

מַה־יִּתְרוֹן

This noun occurs ten times in Qohelet but nowhere else in the OT/HB. It follows a common nominal pattern (**?** see our discussions of Deut 24:14 and Prov 3:25), and therefore its root is easy to identify. What is it? . . . .

Though BDB and many others suggest translating יִתְרוֹן in Qoh 1:3 as "advantage," it is preferable to translate it here (and in 2:11; 3:9; 5:15; 10:11) as "adequate compensation/reward/gain" (→ Fox, *Qohelet*, 60–62).

Note

The first letter of a word following מָה usually shows a conjunctive dagesh. (**?** on conjunctive dagesh, see our discussion of Exod 21:31; → Yeivin, *Introduction*, 293.)

לָאָדָם

How may the presence of the article be explained? (**?** see our discussion of Lev 5:22 and Jer 22:4.)

בְּכָל־עֲמָלוֹ שֶׁיַּעֲמֹל תַּחַת הַשָּׁמֶשׁ

To whom does the pronominal suffix in עֲמָלוֹ refer? Who is the subject governing the verb יַעֲמֹל? Did you notice how הָאָדָם shifts grammatically from non-active at the beginning of the verse to active in the final clause? What is the rhetorical function of this shift? . . . .

. . . .

. . . .

. . . .

Changing the grammatical position of elements within a line or over several lines is a common stylistic device in biblical Hebrew literature. It serves to enhance one or more conveyed meanings (for instance, by turning a referent from a non-active role to an active one). Be alert for these changes and keep in mind that they may be a significant component of the message of the text.

שֶׁיַּעֲמֹל

The text of Qohelet often shows the relative -שֶׁ instead of אֲשֶׁר. Whereas אֲשֶׁר occurs several thousand times in the OT/HB, -שֶׁ occurs only 136 times, and half of these occurrences are in Qohelet. -שֶׁ is attested mainly in post-exilic literature, and in mishnaic Hebrew -שֶׁ completely replaces אֲשֶׁר (→ Kutscher, *History*, 32, 125). The case of -שֶׁ supports the view that the Hebrew of Qohelet represents a transitional stage between classical biblical Hebrew and mishnaic Hebrew. (→ on a minority "revisionist" position, see Fredericks, *Qohelet's Language*; for a critique of Fredericks' position, see Fox, *Qohelet*, 154; Schoors, "Pronouns in Qoheleth.")

> **Note**
>
> The usual vocalization of this relative is -שֶׁ (occurring in more than 90 percent of the cases), and it is followed by a doubling of the next consonant whenever possible. -שֶׁ occurs twice before a personal pronoun beginning with ה (e.g., שְׁהוּא עָמֵל . . . בְּכָל־עֲמָלוֹ in Qoh 2:22). On a few occasions this relative is vocalized -שֶׁ (e.g., Judg 5:7), but note that pataḥ changes to qamets -שָׁ in Judg 6:17, where the next letter is a guttural and therefore cannot be doubled. (→ GKC §36; JM §38.)

Words from the root עמל, "to toil," occur frequently in Qohelet, and often in close contextual relationship to the term הֶבֶל. This feature drives home one of the main themes of Qohelet, namely, that toil is absurd because its outcome contains no significant or commensurate gain or reward for the person who toils.

Translate v 3.

Qohelet contains frequent questions such as this one (e.g., Qoh 8:7; 10:14). In Hebrew, as in English, questions may be actual or rhetorical. "Who knows . . . ?" may have one of two communicative functions: (a) an actual request for information; or (b) a strong negative statement implying "No one can tell me . . ." At this point in your reading, you may be uncertain about which of the two alternatives is the one that better suits our text, though our previous reference to the "toil" as absurd in Qohelet may suggest one direction. (→ on modes of literary expression in Qohelet, see Crenshaw, *Ecclesiastes*, 28–31; Loader, *Polar Structures*, 9–18; → on rhetorical questions, see WO'C 18.2.g, p. 322.)

Is there a dominant sound in Qoh 1:3? If so,

Explain its likely rhetorical function and its relation to Qoh 1:2, if any. . . . .
. . . .
. . . .

Verses 4–7.

These verses provide examples of an endless set of changes whose paradoxical outcome is no
change at all. They put forward an argument by analogy to the thesis presented in v 3 (→ Fox,
Qohelet, 169).

Verse 4.

דּוֹר הֹלֵךְ וְדוֹר בָּא	**v 4a**
וְהָאָרֶץ לְעוֹלָם עֹמָדֶת	**v 4b**

The main division in short verses may be marked by zaqef or ṭifḥa instead of the common atnaḥ.
Ṭifḥa is the choice when the main division is close to silluq (→ Yeivin, *Introduction,* 178).
Which is the marker in this case? . . . .

Translate v 4a.

```



```

Spell out the parallel structure of v 4a. . . . .
. . . .
Notice how the use of participles emphasizes the continuous, ongoing character of the "chang-
ing" action.

What kind of vav is the one beginning v 4b? (**?** our discussion of 1 Sam 1:22.) Why does
the text read עֹמָדֶת and not עָמְדַת?

Translate all of v 4.

```



```

Spell out the parallelism between 4a and 4b. What kind is it? . . . .

. . . .

. . . .

For Further Thought

Most likely you translated v 4 as, "A generation goes and a generation comes, but the earth remains forever." This is a widely accepted and grammatically correct translation. But what do you mean by "earth"? If "earth" is the physical earth—the planet, the land—then the paradox between the unchanged earth and the change of human generations seems strained, for people in the ancient world did not expect the passing of human generations to change the physical earth. Fox has proposed that here and in some other instances (e.g., Gen 6:11) הָאָרֶץ actually refers to humanity as a whole. Following this line of thought would make it preferable to translate הָאָרֶץ as "world," using a term appropriate to expressing the sense of all humanity while at the same time conveying, at least partially, the ambiguity of the Hebrew הָאָרֶץ. Significantly, the connotation of הָאָרֶץ as physical earth or even soil is also important for the understanding of the unit, because in this sense הָאָרֶץ is one of the four primordial elements in antiquity: earth, fire, air, and water. An illustration from each of these four elements is presented in Qoh 1:4–7 to demonstrate that no significant change is possible. (→ Fox, "Qohelet 1.4"; *Qohelet*, 171; for alternative proposals, see Ogden, "Interpretation of דור in Ecclesiastes 1.4"; Whybray, "Ecclesiastes 1.5–7"; see also Crenshaw, *Ecclesiastes*, 62–63.)

Verse 5.

וְזָרַח הַשֶּׁמֶשׁ
וּבָא הַשָּׁמֶשׁ   **v 5a**
וְאֶל־מְקוֹמוֹ שׁוֹאֵף
זוֹרֵחַ הוּא שָׁם   **v 5b**

Translate v 5a.

```



```

Compare the structure of v 5a to דּוֹר הֹלֵךְ וְדוֹר בָּא in 4a. (Notice also the use of an identical root with different meanings.) . . . .

. . . .

. . . .

Note

Many scholars maintain that the original unpointed text read זרח and because of the transposition (**metathesis**) of the ו the text ended up as וזרח. If so, then all four verbs in v 5 would be participles.

Notice that the noun שֶׁמֶשׁ is generally considered feminine but sometimes is treated as masculine. This noun is usually preceded by the article because it has only one possible referent. The situation in Hebrew is analogous to cases in English in which one says "the sun" or "the president" when there can be only one sun or one president at a time (→ JM §137 h; WO'C 13.5.1.a–c, p. 242).

Translate the whole of v 5.

```
┌─────────────────────────────────────────────────────────────┐
│                                                               │
│                                                               │
│                                                               │
│                                                               │
│                                                               │
└─────────────────────────────────────────────────────────────┘
```

Note

The way in which we have divided v 5b contradicts the masoretic accents. There is a widespread agreement between scholars that the division that has been proposed here is contextually superior and that it reflects the original meaning of the text. What changes in the masoretic accents are necessary to render the text as proposed here?

Point out poetic techniques present in this verse, such as word repetition, rhyme, and dominant sound (remember that *z* and *sh* are both sibilants). . . . .
. . . .
. . . .
. . . .

Verse 6.

הוֹלֵךְ אֶל־דָּרוֹם

וְסוֹבֵב אֶל־צָפוֹן   **v 6a**

סוֹבֵב|סֹבֵב הוֹלֵךְ הָרוּחַ

וְעַל־סְבִיבֹתָיו שָׁב הָרוּחַ   **v 6b**

Whereas v 5 relates to the בָּא in v 4, v 6 goes back to a word paired with בָּא in v 4: הֹלֵךְ.

Translate v 6a.

סוֹבֵב|סֹבֵב הוֹלֵךְ הָרוּחַ

The pattern of repetition within the verset and in relation to the first part of v 6a is obvious. The first participle, which is doubled, qualifies the second one, which is actually the predicate participle. Accordingly, this verset may be translated as, "round round/circling circling goes the wind." In this translation, the duplication of the participle סוֹבֵב is given an English equivalent that provides a comparable emphasis to that in the Hebrew.

Translate all of v 6.

Point out poetic techniques in this verse, such as repetitions of words, dominant sounds (note, for instance, that *b* and *p* are related labials, and *m* and *n* have closely related sounds), and rhyme.

Analyze the parallel structure of v 6. . . . .
. . . .
. . . .
. . . .

Note
Why does the text page show paseq (||) between סֹבֵב and סוֹבֵב? (**?** see our discussion of Ezek 37:2.)

Verse 7.

Verse 7 recalls the language of v 6 through its use of the roots הלך and שׁוב in the qal stem, and recalls the language of v 5 through its emphatic use of שָׁם.

כָּל־הַנְּחָלִים הֹלְכִים אֶל־הַיָּם

וְהַיָּם אֵינֶנּוּ מָלֵא   **v 7a**

אֶל־מְקוֹם שֶׁהַנְּחָלִים הֹלְכִים

שָׁם הֵם שָׁבִים לָלָכֶת   **v 7b**

What kind of vav does one find in וְהַיָּם? (**?** see our discussion of 1 Sam 1:22.)

Translate v 7a. (**?** concerning אֵינֶנּוּ, see K. 215, 248; Gr. 71–72; Ke. 71; L. 165–66; S. 64; W. 291; → §102 j–k).

Why does the text read לָלָכֶת instead of לָלֶכֶת?

Clue: Although the pausal position of לָלָכֶת may lead us to expect such a vocalization, לָלֶכֶת and not לָלָכֶת is attested elsewhere in the OT/HB in pausal position (e.g., 1 Sam 15:27; Ps 78:10). Consider whether the vocalization of לָלָכֶת may be influenced by stylistic considerations. Might it be associated with assonantal repetition in the final words of some of the other versets in this subunit? ....
....

Translate all of v 7. (**?** concerning שֶׁהַנְּחָלִים, see our discussion of v 3.)

Analyze the parallel structure of v 7 and **point out** poetic devices. ....
....
....
....

Verses 8–9

Qohelet has brought observations from natural phenomena (vv 3–7) to support the thesis that toil produces no significant change and therefore offers no adequate reward (v 3). In vv 8–9, it summarizes the observations and points out their relevancy to the claim presented in v 3.

Verse 8.

כָּל־הַדְּבָרִים יְגֵעִים

לֹא־יוּכַל אִישׁ לְדַבֵּר   **v 8a**

לֹא־תִשְׂבַּע עַיִן לִרְאוֹת

וְלֹא־תִמָּלֵא אֹזֶן מִשְּׁמֹעַ   **v 8b**

Analyze יוּכַל (**?** K. 172; Gr. 94; Ke. 341; L. 139; S. 153; W. 138; → GKC 69 r; JM §75 i.)

Root	Stem	Form	PGN	SF	OS	BRM

Analyze לֹא־תִמָּלֵא (**?** K. 197–98, 406; Gr. 84–85, 216; Ke. 139, 275–78, 410; L. 178–79, 304; S. 222, 278–79; W. 101–2, 178–79.)

Root	Stem	Form	PGN	SF	OS	BRM

Analyze מִשְּׁמֹעַ (**?** K. 123; Gr. 55, 218; Ke. 179–83; L. 127–29; S. 187; W. 79–80.)

Root	Stem	Form	PGN	SF	OS	BRM

Translate v 8. Notice the ambiguity in כָּל־הַדְּבָרִים; it points to "all the words" (see the related verbs) but also "all the (these) matters/things."

Analyze the parallel structure of v 8 and **point out** poetic devices. . . . .
. . . .
. . . .
. . . .

Verse 9.

This verse presents the conclusion of the argument and rounds off the unit that began in v 3, repeating the phrase תַּחַת הַשָּׁמֶשׁ to finish the inclusio.

מַה־שֶּׁהָיָה הוּא שֶׁיִּהְיֶה

וּמַה־שֶּׁנַּעֲשָׂה הוּא שֶׁיֵּעָשֶׂה   **v 9a**

וְאֵין כָּל־חָדָשׁ תַּחַת הַשָּׁמֶשׁ   **v 9b**

מַה־שֶּׁ- is a combination of an indefinite מָה (not "what?" but "what" or "whatever" → GKC §137 c; JM §145 g; WO'C 18.3.e, pp. 325–26) with the relative -שֶׁ. Accordingly you may translate מַה־שֶּׁהָיָה as "whatever has happened." Why does the שׁ in this expression show a dagesh? (**?** see our discussion of v 3.)

Note

The use of מַה־שֶּׁ- contributes to the atypical character of the language of Qohelet and to the claim that it occupies a position as a transitional stage between biblical and Mishnaic Hebrew. This combination occurs several times in Qohelet (Qoh 1:9; 3:15,22; 6:10; 7:24; 8:7; 10:14) but nowhere else in the HB/OT. On the other hand, it is common in mishnaic Hebrew (→ Segal, *Grammar*, 209–10).

Translate v 9.

```
┌────────────────────────────────────────────────────────────────┐
│                                                                  │
│                                                                  │
│                                                                  │
│                                                                  │
│                                                                  │
└────────────────────────────────────────────────────────────────┘
```

Analyze the parallel structure of v 9 and **point out** poetic devices. ....

....

....

....

Verses 10–11.

Verses 3–9 are set apart from the surrounding text by the inclusio. As a unit they convey a clear message. The next two verses support this message by means of a common rhetorical device, that of introducing the predictable objection of someone who has not been convinced by the argument (v 10a) in order to show that such an objection cannot be sustained (vv 10b–11).

Verse 10.

יֵשׁ דָּבָר שֶׁיֹּאמַר רְאֵה־זֶה חָדָשׁ הוּא   **10a**

כְּבָר הָיָה לְעֹלָמִים אֲשֶׁר הָיָה מִלְּפָנֵנוּ   **10b**

Translate יֵשׁ דָּבָר ....

שֶׁיֹּאמַר רְאֵה־זֶה חָדָשׁ הוּא is a relative clause that restricts the kind of "something" to which "there is" refers.

Analyze יֹּאמַר

Root	Stem	Form	PGN	SF	OS	BRM

This is one of a significant number of cases (e.g., Gen 11:9; 48:1) in which the Hebrew third-person masculine singular is not to be translated as "he" but rather as "one." (→ GKC §144 d; JM §155 a–d; WO'C 4.4.2.a, pp. 70–71; and cf. our discussion of Ezek 37:1.)

Analyze רְאֵה

Root	Stem	Form	PGN	SF	OS	BRM

Identify the direct object of רְאֵה ....

Compare this use of רְאֵה with the use of הִנֵּה. (**?** see our discussion of Ezek 37:2.) ....
....
....
Notice the substantival (rather than the adjectival) use of the demonstrative זֶה.

חָדָשׁ הוּא is a part of a classifying clause whose implied subject is זֶה. One may consider זֶה as a double-duty word, functioning on the one hand as the object of רְאֵה and on the other as the subject of חָדָשׁ הוּא. This clause of classification follows the usual order of such clauses: subject-predicate-pronoun. (**?** see our discussion of Exod 21:29.)

Translate v 10a.

```
┌─────────────────────────────────────────────────────────────┐
│                                                               │
│                                                               │
│                                                               │
│                                                               │
└─────────────────────────────────────────────────────────────┘
```

Explain how the language of this verse relates to that of v 9. . . . .
. . . .
. . . . The position expressed in v 10a is explicitly rejected in v 10b.

כְּבָר הָיָה לְעֹלָמִים

This is another atypical biblical expression. כְּבָר, which occurs several times in Qohelet (e.g., Qoh 3:15) and in mishnaic Hebrew, occurs nowhere else in the OT/HB; לְעֹלָמִים is attested only here and in Ps 77:8.

אֲשֶׁר הָיָה מִלְּפָנֵנוּ

What noun is the subject of the verb הָיָה?

Clue: This אֲשֶׁר clause modifies a preceding noun. . . . .

Perhaps you are baffled by the lack of correspondence between a plural noun, עֹלָמִים, and a verb in the third-person singular, הָיָה. In fact, it is not uncommon that plural nouns with an abstract or singular referent govern verbs in the singular. (→ Williams, *Hebrew Syntax*, 42; → on the agreement—or disagreement—of the verb in biblical Hebrew, see GKC §145; JN §150.)

Separate מִלְּפָנֵנוּ into its basic components. . . . .
. . . .

Translate v 10b.

```
┌─────────────────────────────────────────────────────────────┐
│                                                               │
│                                                               │
│                                                               │
│                                                               │
└─────────────────────────────────────────────────────────────┘
```

Verse 11.

אֵין זִכְרוֹן לָרִאשֹׁנִים
וְגַם לָאַחֲרֹנִים שֶׁיִּהְיוּ
לֹא־יִהְיֶה לָהֶם זִכָּרוֹן
עִם שֶׁיִּהְיוּ לָאַחֲרֹנָה

Translate the four versets of v 11.

Analyze the parallel structure of these versets, *point out* poetic devices, and *explain* how they contribute to the message of the text. . . . .
. . . .
. . . .
. . . .

Translate vv 10–11.

Translate all of Qoh 1:1–11.

For Further Readings

On this passage, and on Qohelet in general, see Crenshaw, *Ecclesiastes;* Fox, *Qohelet;* Loader, *Polar Structures.*

Works Cited in This Section

J. L. Crenshaw, *Ecclesiastes* (OTL; Philadelphia: Westminster, 1987); **M. V. Fox,** *Qohelet and His Contradictions* (JSOTSup 71; Sheffield: Almond Press, 1989); **D. C. Fredericks,** *Qohelet's Language: Re-evaluating Its Nature and Date* (Ancient Near Eastern Texts and Studies 3; Lewiston/ Queenston, Ont.: Edwin Meller Press, 1988); **E. Y. Kutscher,** *A History of the Hebrew Language,* ed. R. Kutscher (Jerusalem/Leiden: Magnes/E. J. Brill, 1982); **J. A. Loader,** *Polar Structures in the Book of Qohelet* (BZAW 152; Berlin/New York: de Gruyter, 1979); **R. E. Murphy,** "On Translating Ecclesiastes," *CBQ* 53 (1991): 571–79; **G. S. Ogden,** "The Interpretation of דור in Ecclesiastes 1.4," *JSOT* 34 (1986): 91–92; **A. Schoors,** "The Pronouns in Qoheleth," *Hebrew Studies* 30 (1989): 71–90; **M. H. Segal,** *A Grammar of Mishnaic Hebrew* (Oxford: Clarendon Press, 1958); **R. N. Whybray,** "Ecclesiastes 1.5–7 and the Wonders of Nature," *JSOT* 41 (1988): 105–12; **R. J. Williams,** *Hebrew Syntax: An Outline* (2d ed.; Toronto: University of Toronto Press, 1984); **I. Yeivin,** *Introduction to the Tiberian Masorah* (Masoretic Studies 5; Missoula, Mont.: Scholars Press, 1980).

5.   Readings in Psalms

5.1 Psalm 1

By now, you are becoming increasingly confident in reading a variety of biblical literary forms in Hebrew. You are ready for the challenge of reading biblical poetry as represented in Psalms. We will begin our reading with the psalm that opens the entire
collection, Ps 1. This psalm is considered didactic and shows some similarities to
wisdom literature. The first part (vv 1–3) deals with the way of the righteous and its
reward. The wicked stand in the background, helping the poet describe the righteous
by means of contrast. In the second part (vv 4–5) the situation is inverted: the wicked
and their fate become the main issue and the righteous are mentioned as the contras-
tive element. The psalm concludes (v 6) with an explicit statement of the contrast between the righteous and the wicked.

Subunit 1: vv 1–3.

Verse 1.

אַשְׁרֵי הָאִישׁ	v 1aa
אֲשֶׁר לֹא הָלַךְ בַּעֲצַת רְשָׁעִים	v 1ab
וּבְדֶרֶךְ חַטָּאִים לֹא עָמָד	v 1ba
וּבְמוֹשַׁב לֵצִים לֹא יָשָׁב:	v 1bb

On Masoretic Accents
Please remember that Psalms is one of the Three Books. You will, therefore, find in them
the same masoretic system of accents that you encountered in your readings from
Proverbs and that occurs in Job as well.

Explain the division of the verse into versets (shown above) in terms of masoretic
markers. (❓ about the revia closing v 1aa, see our discussion of Prov 24:29.) ....
The preposition בְּ in בַּעֲצַת רְשָׁעִים is not, and grammatically cannot be, a combination of בְּ
and the article.

Explain why it shows patah instead of shewa. (❓ K. 248; Gr. 28; Ke. 29; L. 22–23; S. 32; W.
27–28; → GKC §102 d, cf. 28 b; JM §103 b) ....
....

If you have to check BDB for the meaning of nouns, you must figure out their pattern and then their root. The noun עֵצָה is from the root יעץ (cf. עֵדָה, "congregation," from יעד). חַטָּאִים follows the קַטָּל nominal pattern (**?** see our discussion of Exod 21:29). מוֹשָׁב follows the pattern of the nouns with a prefixed מ (**?** see our discussion of Prov 3:21; 25:28), and לֵצִים follows a common pattern for hollow roots (cf. גֵּר from גור).

Translate v 1.

(**?** on אַשְׁרֵי הָאִישׁ, see our discussion of Prov 3:13; the affix forms here have a habitual, or perhaps constative, meaning that may be translated by the English simple present; → JM §111 d–e, 112d; WO'C 30.4 a–b, p. 485, cf. 30.2.1, p. 481.)

In our discussion of Prov 3:13–14, we learned to recognize the elliptical parallel pattern *a-b-c, b¹-c¹* and its chiastic variant, *a-b-c, c¹-b¹*. We found many of these patterns in our readings in Proverbs. Are these patterns relevant to the structure of Ps 1:1?

Explain. . . . .
. . . .
. . . .
. . . .

Analyze the parallel structure of versets 1ab, 1ba, and 1bb; *point out* poetic devices, and *explain* how they contribute to the message of the text. (Notice the trajectory from הָלַךְ to עָמַד and finally to יָשַׁב, and the use of הָלַךְ that calls for דֶּרֶךְ, which is in close proximity in the verse but paradoxically is related to עָמַד.) . . . .
. . . .
. . . .
. . . .

For Further Thought

Most likely you translated בַּעֲצַת רְשָׁעִים as "the advice of the wicked." BDB, and probably most scholars, support this translation, but some scholars prefer "in the council/community/ assembly of the wicked" (e.g., Alter, *Art*, 114; Perdue, *Cult*, 269, 329 n31). How would this alternative translation influence your understanding of the text and its parallelism?

Verse 2.

כִּי אִם בְּתוֹרַת ה׳ חֶפְצוֹ   **v 2a**

וּבְתוֹרָתוֹ יֶהְגֶּה יוֹמָם וָלָיְלָה: **v 2b**

כִּי אִם is a strong adversative that usually follows a negative statement, as it does in this case. (For other examples, see Gen 32:27; Esth 2:14b.) כִּי אִם may be translated as "rather," "but," or "on the contrary." (→ Schoors, "Particle כי," esp. 251–52; GKC §163 a; JM §172 c, 173 c—see also JM §165 c; WO'C 39.3.5.d, p. 671.)

Analyze יֶהְגֶּה (**?** K. 126, 394; Gr. 88–90; Ke. 225, 287–89; L. 143; S. 148–50; W. 155, 217.)

Root	Stem	Form	PGN	SF	OS	BRM

As BDB shows, הגה in the qal may have different meanings. It is generally accepted that "to meditate on" is the most likely meaning here. But one cannot rule out, at least as a connotation, "to murmur" or "to recite." The activity described may be one of reading to oneself in a low tone, which is accompanied by musing on the read material (→ Anderson, Psalms 1–72, 60; cf. Alter, *Art*, 115; cf. Josh 1:8 ab).

יוֹמָם וָלָיְלָה

The word יוֹמָם follows a pattern characterized by the addition of the suffix ָם. Words in this pattern function as adverbs, in this case יוֹמָם, "in the daytime." יוֹמָם וָלָיְלָה is a typical merismus (**?** see our discussion of 2 Kgs 14:26), and "day and night" actually means "at all times," "always." As one may expect, this expression is attested many times in the OT/HB (e.g., Exod 13:21; Josh 1:8).

Translate v 2.

Probably you wrote something like "meditates day and night" to conclude your translation. This is acceptable, but you should be aware that it obscures the contrast between the affix forms in v 1 and the prefix form in v 2 by rendering all of them in the English present tense. In Hebrew, the change from habitual affix to habitual prefix forms is a well-known stylistic device (→ our discussion of Lev 5:24; and see Berlin, *Dynamics*, 35–36), and it may have helped convey different shades of meaning (→ WO'C 31.3.e, p. 506).

Analyze the parallel structure within v 2, *point out* poetic devices, and *explain* how they contribute to the message of the text. . . . .
. . . .
. . . .
. . . .

For Further Thought

Translating ה' תּוֹרַת may be relatively easy. But what was meant by that in the context of Ps 1? What was the communicative meaning of this word in the world of the author of Ps 1 and the community for whom this ancient text was written? On the one hand, the comparison between v 2 and Josh 1:8ab suggests that ה' תּוֹרַת refers to a written text, which some would identify as the Pentateuch. But on the other hand, an analysis of other psalms that exalt the Torah would suggest a much broader concept of ה' תּוֹרַת (→ Levenson, "Sources"). More research is needed on the meaning of ה' תּוֹרַת in ancient texts.

Verse 3.

This verse describes the fate of the righteous and the unrighteous by means of a comparison common in an agrarian society.

וְהָיָה כְּעֵץ שָׁתוּל עַל־פַּלְגֵי מָיִם	**v 3a**
אֲשֶׁר פִּרְיוֹ יִתֵּן בְּעִתּוֹ	**v 3baa**
וְעָלֵהוּ לֹא־יִבּוֹל	**v 3bab**
וְכֹל אֲשֶׁר־יַעֲשֶׂה יַצְלִיחַ:	**v 3bb**

Explain the division of the verse shown above in terms of the masoretic markers used in the Three Books. . . . .
. . . .
. . . .
. . . .

Analyze שָׁתוּל

Root	Stem	Form	PGN	SF	OS	BRM

Translate v 3a.

```
┌─────────────────────────────────────────────────────────────────────┐
│                                                                       │
│                                                                       │
│                                                                       │
│                                                                       │
│                                                                       │
└─────────────────────────────────────────────────────────────────────┘
```

The "rewards" of such a tree are developed in the rest of the verse. To whom do the pronominal suffixes in 3ba refer? ....

Analyze לֹא־יִבּוֹל (**?** K. 79; Gr. 103; Ke. 302–3; L. 133; S. 150; W. 141–42)

Root	Stem	Form	PGN	SF	OS	BRM

Translate versets 3baa and 3bab.

```
┌─────────────────────────────────────────────────────────────────────┐
│                                                                       │
│                                                                       │
│                                                                       │
│                                                                       │
└─────────────────────────────────────────────────────────────────────┘
```

For Further Thought

Do you think that the author and the audience were oblivious to other meanings associated with the root נבל? What kind of connotations might have been suggested by these associations?

The verse ends climactically with a full-blown comprehensive statement in v 3bb. What is the subject of יַעֲשֶׂה? ....

In the context of vv 1–3, one may wonder if the subject of יַעֲשֶׂה is not הָאִישׁ rather than עֵץ, which is the obvious subject if one takes into consideration only v 3. This ambiguity seems to re-inforce the comparison between הָאִישׁ and עֵץ. The verse begins with an explicit statement that a certain kind of person is like a tree; then, as the verse reaches its climax, the distinction between the two is blurred, and the text may point to either one or the other or, most likely, to both.

What is the subject governing יַצְלִיחַ? ....

Translate verset 3bb.

```
┌─────────────────────────────────────────────────────────────────────┐
│                                                                       │
│                                                                       │
│                                                                       │
│                                                                       │
│                                                                       │
└─────────────────────────────────────────────────────────────────────┘
```

Translate the entire subunit, vv 1–3.

```
┌─────────────────────────────────────────────────────────┐
│                                                           │
│                                                           │
│                                                           │
│                                                           │
└─────────────────────────────────────────────────────────┘
```

Subunit 2: vv 4–5.

Verse 4.

v 4a	לֹא־כֵן הָרְשָׁעִים
v 4b	כִּי אִם־כַּמֹּץ אֲשֶׁר־תִּדְּפֶנּוּ רוּחַ

The tone of the previous subunit was already set in its opening phrase, אַשְׁרֵי הָאִישׁ; the tone of this subunit is also set in its opening phrase.

Translate לֹא־כֵן הָרְשָׁעִים . . . .

The second part of v 4 contains a common agrarian comparison that is in contrast to the one in v 3. The two comparisons are presented in the same structure, namely, X-כְּ followed by an אֲשֶׁר clause.

Analyze תִּדְּפֶנּוּ (**?** K. 79; Gr. 103; Ke. 302–3; L. 133; S. 150; W. 141–42; and K. 215; Gr. 71; Ke. 156–69; L. 271–73; S. 181; W. 130.)

Root	Stem	Form	PGN	SF	OS	BRM

What is the subject of תִּדְּפֶנּוּ and to what does the pronominal suffix refer? . . . .
. . . .

Translate v 4.

```
┌─────────────────────────────────────────────────────────┐
│                                                           │
│                                                           │
│                                                           │
│                                                           │
└─────────────────────────────────────────────────────────┘
```

For Further Thought

The comparisons made in this verse occur elsewhere in ancient Near Eastern literature (→ Instruction of Amen-em-Opet, chapter 4, *ANET* 422) and in other places in the OT/HB (Jer 17:8; cf. Ezek 17:8 and Ps 35:5a).

To describe the contrast between the righteous and the wicked and their respective fates as being like the difference between a planted tree and wind-blown chaff seems, on the surface, to be nothing but a very obvious analogy based on a very common observation. But it is precisely in the obvious and common nature of the analogy that the rhetorical point rests. The respective fates of tree and chaff are seen to be naturally and inherently related to their basic character. So, too, the respective fates of the wicked and the righteous are seen to be natural and inherent in their basic moral character. This is certainly not a self-evident truism, but a profound insight or, at the very least, a far-reaching claim.

This comparison, moreover, suggests something about the horizon of thought of the writers and their public. Water, earth, and trees are all images conveying a sense of stability (a continuous supply of water, the enduring soil, a planted tree). The three images are further linked in the thought of the writers and of their public to fruitfulness, and, in turn, the qualities of stability and fruitfulness are associated by the text with righteousness and with meditation on the divine instruction. In sharp contrast, wind and blown chaff convey an image of aimless movement and instability and are associated with fruitlessness, and by these associations they are transferred to the morally evil and theologically wrong segment of human society (→ Willis, "Psalm 1—An Entity," 400; and esp. Lack, "Le psaume 1—Une analyse structurale," esp. 161–67).

Notice that the planted tree is the *subject* of three active verbs in v 3, יַצְלִיחַ, יִתֵּן, and יַעֲשֶׂה, but the restless chaff is the *object* of תִּדְּפֶנּוּ. How does this choice of expression support the message of the text?

Verse 5.

עַל־כֵּן לֹא־יָקֻמוּ רְשָׁעִים בַּמִּשְׁפָּט	v 5a
וְחַטָּאִים בַּעֲדַת צַדִּיקִים	v 5b

The concluding part of this subunit explicitly explains what was implied in the comparison about the fate of the wicked.

Translate v 5.

Notice the inclusio between בַּעֲדַת צַדִּיקִים and בַּעֲצַת רְשָׁעִים in v 1, and the occurrence of the sequence חַטָּאִים - רְשָׁעִים in v 1 as well as v 5. Does the structure of this verse follow the *a-b-c, b¹-c¹* pattern?

Explain. . . . .

. . . .

. . . .

For Further Thought

What is the meaning that בַּמִּשְׁפָּט conveyed to its historical audience? What about יָקֻמוּ? Already in ancient times יָקֻמוּ was interpreted as pointing to resurrection, but this is not a necessary interpretation, nor the most likely in the context of the world of ideas of the Book of Psalms. In לֹא־יָקֻמוּ the verb probably means "to stand" in the sense of "to endure" (cf. Nah 1:6). If בַּמִּשְׁפָּט does not point to resurrection, then בַּמִּשְׁפָּט most likely does not point to "The Judgment," in the sense of a final arbitration after death, but to "the judgment" of God as it operates in life; see v 6 (→ Anderson, *Psalms*, 62). Of course, in accordance with the theological discourse of times later than those of the composition of this psalm, many Christians and Jews have interpreted this verse as pointing to resurrection and Final Judgment.

Translate the entire subunit, vv 4–5.

```



```

Subunit 3: v 6.

כִּי־יוֹדֵעַ ה' דֶּרֶךְ צַדִּיקִים	v 6a
וְדֶרֶךְ רְשָׁעִים תֹּאבֵד	v 6b

As do many other didactic materials, this psalm concludes with the reason behind the certitude. A convincing explanation legitimizes the message and clinches it.

Not only does v 6, the final verse of the psalm, bring together the message of the two subunits, but it also turns it into one clear saying, similar to those found in the Book of Proverbs.

Analyze תֹּאבֵד

Clue: had this word been in a non-pausal position, it would have been written תֹּאבַד; → GKC §68 c; JM §73 d.

Root	Stem	Form	PGN	SF	OS	BRM

What is the subject governing תֹּאבֵד? ....

Translate v 6.

```



```

Does this verse follow the typical *a-b-c, b¹-c¹* pattern? If not,

Explain the extent of departure from the pattern and its possible reasons. Then

Analyze the parallel structure of this verse and

Point out syntactical contrasts (such as subject-object). ....
....
....
....

Note

This verse is anchored to the preceding one by the chiastic sequence צַדִּיקִים - רְשָׁעִים - רְשָׁעִים - צַדִּיקִים and to the first one by the reference to דֶּרֶךְ. Moreover, the use of רְשָׁעִים in vv 1 and 6 points to a relatively common stylistic device in Hebrew poetry called **envelope,** the repetition of a sentence, phrase, or (more often) word at the beginning and end of a poem (e.g., Ps 103:1,22), or of smaller units within a poem (such as a strophe). Inclusio is a common form of envelope. (→ on envelope, see Watson, *Classical Hebrew Poetry*, 282–86.)

Translate the entire psalm.

For Further Reading

On Ps 1, see Alter, *Art*, 114–17; Anderson, *Psalms*, 57–63; Gerstenberger, *Psalms*, 40–44; Perdue, *Cult and Wisdom*, 269–73; Petersen and Richards, *Interpreting*, 89–97.

For Further Thought

Ps 1 does not stand as a book by itself but as the first psalm in a book of 150 psalms. Do you think that this fact carries any significance for the entire book? Here are some of the answers scholars have proposed to this question:

—According to Childs, this initial psalm provides an interpretative key for understanding the Book of Psalms as a whole. Standing at the beginning of the book, Ps 1 claims that the psalms that follow, understood as representing the will of God, should be read, studied, and meditated upon day and night (Childs, *Introduction*, 513–14).

—Wilson maintains that if Childs is correct, then the first psalm "intends to focus the reader on the following Psalms as Torah to be read with the same sense of delight and diligence" (Wilson, "Shape," 137).

—Brueggemann writes, "Standing at the beginning of the Psalter, this Psalm intends that all the Psalms should be read through the prism of torah obedience" (Brueggemann, "Bounded," 64).

Works Cited in This Section

R. Alter, *The Art of Biblical Poetry* (New York: Basic Books, 1985); **A. A. Anderson,** *Psalms 1–72* (NCB; Grand Rapids, Mich.: Eerdmans; London: Marshall, Morgan, & Scott, 1981); **A. Berlin,** *The Dynamics of Biblical Parallelism* (Bloomington: Indiana University Press, 1985); **W. Brueggemann,** "Bounded by Obedience and Praise: The Psalms as Canon," *JSOT* 50 (1991): 63–92; **B. S. Childs,** *Introduction to the Old Testament as Scripture* (Philadelphia: Fortress, 1979); **E. S. Gerstenberger,** *Psalms* (Part I, FOTL 14; Grand Rapids, Mich.: Eerdmans, 1988); **R. Lack,** "Le psaume 1—Une analyse structurale," *Bib* 57 (1976): 154–67; **J. D. Levenson,** "The Sources of the Torah: Psalm 119 and the Modes of Revelation in Second Temple Judaism," in P. D. Miller, P. D. Hanson, and S. Dean McBride, eds., *Ancient Israelite Religion: Essays in Honor of F. M. Cross* (Philadelphia: Fortress, 1987), 559–74; **L. G. Perdue,** *Wisdom and Cult* (SBLDS 30; Missoula, Mont.: Scholars Press, 1977); **D. L. Petersen and K. H. Richards,** *Interpreting Hebrew Poetry* (Minneapolis: Fortress, 1992); **A. Schoors,** "The Particle כי," in B. Albrektson et al., *Remembering All the Way* (OTS 21; Leiden: E. J. Brill, 1981), 240–76; **W. G. E. Watson,** *Classical Hebrew Poetry* (JSOTSup 26; Sheffield: JSOT Press, 1984); **J. T. Willis,** "Psalm 1—An Entity," *ZAW* 91 (1979): 381–401; **G. H. Wilson,** "The Shape of the Book of Psalms," *Int* (1992): 129–42.

5.2   Psalm 15

This is one of the best known of the psalms, with a prominent place in both Jewish and Christian traditions of worship. Perhaps the main reason for its prominence is that it blends ritual with ethical demands. Structurally, Ps 15 contains a heading (v 1a)—something Psalm 1 does not have—and a question-and-answer dialogue (vv 1b–5). A question is asked (v 1b) and then answered through a complex system of partial replies (vv 2–5a) leading to a concluding statement (v 5b).

Verse 1.

מִזְמוֹר לְדָוִד	v 1a
ה' מִי־יָגוּר בְּאָהֳלֶךָ	v 1ba
מִי־יִשְׁכֹּן בְּהַר קָדְשֶׁךָ׃	v 1bb

The opening verse consists of a superscription. Superscriptions have been attached to most of the psalms. Pss 23, 29, 141, and 143 show the same heading as Ps 15, and the exact expression מִזְמוֹר לְדָוִד is a central element in the superscriptions of more than twenty other psalms (e.g., Pss 3–6). Moreover, a closely related expression, לְדָוִד מִזְמוֹר, is attested in a number of superscriptions (e.g., Pss 24, 40, 101). About half of the psalms included in the Book of Psalms are characterized as לְדָוִד by their superscriptions. It is obvious that these superscriptions point to an early effort to classify the psalms. How was Ps 15 characterized? Its title conveys information concerning two issues: (a) the type of psalm and (b) its relation to David.

Is מִזְמוֹר לְדָוִד a definite expression? (**?** K. 22, 234; L. 67–68; S. 71; W. 53; → GKC §129, esp. 129 c; JM §130, esp. 130 b; WO'C §9.7, pp. 156–58.) . . . .

מִזְמוֹר is a מ-prefixed noun from the root זמר. Although its actual meaning is uncertain, because the Septuagint translated it as *psalmos* (the source of the English name of the Book of Psalms) one may assume that already in antiquity מִזְמוֹר was understood as a *psalmos*, a song to be sung to the music of string instruments.

לְדָוִד lends itself to many interpretations.

Explain why and **identify** them. . . . .
. . . .
. . . .
. . . .

The most likely explanation is attribution, i.e., assumed authorship. Since לְדָוִד occurs in almost all of the superscriptions of Pss 3–41 and 51–71, it would appear that these psalms were were grouped together because of their shared attribution to David. Significantly, the Book of Psalms includes many psalms whose superscriptions either do not make attribution to any person or else attribute the psalm to someone other than David (e.g., Pss 1–2; 42–50; 72; 120–21; 146–50).

As one would expect, the body of the psalm immediately follows its title. As we have mentioned, this psalm begins with a question.

מִי־יָגוּר . . . מִי־יִשְׁכֹּן

Who is asked these questions? ....

How do you pronounce אָהֳלֶךָ? (**?** see our discussion of Prov 24:29.)

Translate v 1.

[empty box]

Compare the structure of מִי־יָגוּר . . . מִי־יִשְׁכֹּן ה' with that of מִי־כָמֹכָה בָּאֵלִם ה' in Exod 15:11.

Explain the differences and

Suggest ways in which these differences may be related to the message of the text.

....
....
....

Analyze the parallel structure of v 1b. (Is this a case of synonymous parallelism? Does it follow the *a-b-c, b¹-c¹* or any other well-known structural pattern?)

Identify the equivalent elements in both versets. ....
....
....
....

Although שכן and גור share a loosely defined common semantic range in the qal stem, they do not tend to occur as a word pair. The writer's choice of יָגוּר and יִשְׁכֹּן as semantic and grammatical equivalents is most likely due to the existence of a common word pair referring to God's dwelling place, מִשְׁכָּן-אֹהֶל (e.g., 2 Sam 7:6; Ps 78:60; cf. מִשְׁכַּן-אֹהֶל מוֹעֵד Exod 40:34).

Attention is called to the "tent" as God's, not only by the equivalency of בְּאָהֳלֶךָ (both syntactically and semantically) to בְּהַר קָדְשֶׁךָ, but also by the bonding between אָהֳלֶךָ and יִשְׁכֹּן. At the same time, a balanced structure מִי־יִשְׁכֹּן - מִי־יָגוּר is created.

For Further Thought

The text explicitly identifies the one who is asked the question, but who is asking it? Return to this question once you have read the entire psalm, and think of how different answers may influence your understanding of the historical meaning of this psalm. (→ Gerstenberger, *Psalms*, 87; Willis, "Ethics.")

The question clearly characterizes the divine teaching that the psalm claims to convey. In this case, the psalm is concerned with instructions as to who qualifies, and by virtue of what characteristics, to enter God's sanctuary—in other words, who is a righteous person. The didactic value of such a question is clear, and the same device is used elsewhere in the OT/HB (e.g., Mic 6:8; Isa 33:14b–16; Ps 24:3–5).

Verse 2.

הוֹלֵךְ תָּמִים	v 2aa
וּפֹעֵל צֶדֶק	v 2ab
וְדֹבֵר אֱמֶת בִּלְבָבוֹ	v 2b

All these verbs are bound together by a consistent (verbal) form. What form is it? . . . .
. . . .

צֶדֶק and אֱמֶת are bound together by . . . .
What is binding תָּמִים and בִּלְבָבוֹ together? . . . .
To whom does the pronominal suffix refer in בִּלְבָבוֹ? . . . .

Translate v 2.

Perhaps you translated בִּלְבָבוֹ as "in his (or his/her) heart/mind." (→ on the communicative meanings of biblical "heart," see Wolff, *Anthropology*, 30–58.) This is certainly a reasonable interpretation, but others are also possible. The preposition בְּ may be understood as instrumental, "*with* his (or his/her) heart/mind." If so, this verset probably refers to what a person speaks in society, not to his or her innermost thoughts. But both meanings may have been conveyed by בִּלְבָבוֹ at the same time. This is probably another instance of the use of ambiguity to capture the attention of the public and convey multiple meanings in an economic way. (→ on בִּלְבָבוֹ here, see

Miller, "Poetic Ambiguity," 420 n13; but Miller does not consider the possibility of an ambiguous בְּ.)

Note

Some scholars maintain that in biblical Hebrew בְּ could mean "from" (e.g., Gordon, Sarna, Dahood, Miller, Schiffman). But there is an ongoing dispute on this issue; see Barr, *Comparative Philology*, 175–77. (→ JM §133 c.)

Discuss the parallelism in v 2. . . . .

. . . .

. . . .

. . . .

Verse 3.

This verse consists of three versets that can be seen as counterparts of the three versets of the previous verse. A careful arrangement of similarities and dissimilarities links the two; but when studying the meaning being conveyed by the psalm, one should not forget that v 3 does not stand side by side with v 2 but *follows* it.

לֹא־רָגַל עַל־לְשֹׁנוֹ	v 3aa
לֹא־עָשָׂה לְרֵעֵהוּ רָעָה	v 3ab
וְחֶרְפָּה לֹא־נָשָׂא עַל־קְרֹבוֹ	v 3b

All these verbs are bound together by a consistent verbal form. What is it? . . . .

. . . .

Who is the subject of all these verbs? . . . .

To whom do the pronominal suffixes in לְשֹׁנוֹ, רֵעֵהוּ, and קְרֹבוֹ point? . . . .

. . . .

Following the pattern of לְשֹׁנוֹ and קְרֹבוֹ, one may expect to find רֵעוֹ (as in Jer 6:21) instead of רֵעֵהוּ. Indeed, according to the general rule, the third-person masculine singular suffix attached to singular nouns is וֹ or on a few occasions הוּ, except when the noun ends in ה. (e.g., מַחְסֵהוּ in Ps 14:6 and שָׂדֵהוּ in Deut 5:18/21). רֵעַ is neither plural nor ends in ה.. But רֵעַ belongs to a very small group of nouns that in the singular take הוּ.. as their third-person singular masculine pronominal suffix (→ GKC §91 k; JM §94 h). Note the way in which the writer set the three pronominal endings at the end of each of these three versets, וֹ, then הוּ.., and finally וֹ again.

The actual meaning of the expression נָשָׂא חֶרְפָּה עַל־X in v 3 is uncertain. If one compares it with לֹא תִשָּׂא אֶת־שֵׁם־ה' אֱלֹהֶיךָ לַשָּׁוְא ("You shall not take the name of your Lord your God in vain," Exod 20:7) or נָשְׂאוּ נְהָרוֹת קוֹלָם ("the floods/rivers have lifted up their voices," Ps 93:3), one would tend to relate נשׂא-Y to the general range of meanings "speak, pronounce, say." Then one would likely understand עַל as "against." This approach leads to translations of נשׂא חֶרְפָּה עַל־X as "defaming X" or "venting abuse against X," that is, speaking in such a way that X would be the object of scorn. Most modern scholars follow this approach. Moreover, through centuries of biblical interpretation it seems to have been the main approach to this text. Yet there is another possible way of approaching נָשָׂא חֶרְפָּה עַל-X, namely, by focusing on the meaning of the expression נָשָׂא חֶרְפָּה עַל-X in other biblical texts. Jer 15:15 and Ps 69:8 both suggest a translation such as "to bear reproach on account of . . . " (In these verses עַל should not be understood as "against" but rather as "on account of.") The translation just proposed is consistent with the most common meanings associated with both נשׂא in the qal ("carry, take") and חֶרְפָּה ("reproach") as separate words. If this line of thought is brought to Ps 1:3, the result is something like the translation proposed by NJPSV, "has never . . : borne reproach for (his acts toward) his neighbor." As you see, the basic meaning of some biblical idioms remains a moot point despite centuries of textual studies.

Note

The approach leading to the understanding of נָשָׂא חֶרְפָּה עַל-X as "defaming X" seems to be supported by an analysis of the relationship between the triad in v 2 and that in v 3. The unusual use of רָגַל in the first verset of v 3 may be related to the occurrence of הָלַךְ in the first verset of v 2. The semantic affinity between פעל and עשה in the qal relates the two second versets to one another. Against this background, one may expect the last versets of vv 2 and 3 to interrelate in some way. This expectation would be fulfilled if the meaning of נָשָׂא is indeed close to that of דִּבֶּר in v 2. (→ Miller, "Poetic Ambiguity," 422–23; *Interpreting*, 44–45.)

Before translating v 3, you must decide how to translate the verbal affix forms. To solve the problem, you should ask whether these verbs point to a completed event that happened once in the past (which leads to a translation in the English simple past), to a situation or event that happened before some other event in the past (which leads to a translation in the English pluperfect, i.e., "you had done . . . "), to a habitual, constant situation (which leads to a translation in the English present), or to a situation or event that has originated in the past and continues in the present (which leads to a translation in the English present perfect, i.e., "you have done . . . "), and so on. Your main guide in making this choice would be the context in which the verbs occur. Of course, some cases are ambiguous and more than one translation is possible.

Taking all this into account, what English tense do you think best renders the affix forms in v 3? . . . .

Translate v 3.

Discuss the parallelism in v 3 and

Compare it with that in v 2. . . . .
. . . .
. . . .
. . . .

Verse 4a.

The first part of the reply to the question posed in v 1b consists of a list of very general things a person should do (v 2), the second part of more specific instruction concerning what a person should *not* do in regard to another person (v 3). The third part (v 4a) concerns the appropriate attitude to take when dealing with various people.

נִבְזֶה בְּעֵינָיו נִמְאָס	**v 4aa**
וְאֶת־יִרְאֵי ה' יְכַבֵּד	**v 4ab**

More than half of the words in v 4b are verbal forms. This provides us with an opportunity for a short review.

Analyze נִבְזֶה (**?** K. 205; Gr. 213; Ke. 287; L. 184, 313; S. 223–24; W. 216–17.)

Root	Stem	Form	PGN	SF	OS	BRM

Analyze נִמְאָס (**?** K. 194; Gr. 85; Ke. 253; L. 178–79, 312; S. 223–24; W. 101–3; → JM §51 a.)

Root	Stem	Form	PGN	SF	OS	BRM

Analyze יִרְאֵי

Root	Stem	Form	PGN	SF	OS	BRM

Analyze יְכַבֵּד

Root	Stem	Form	PGN	SF	OS	BRM

Do נִמְאָס and בְּעֵינָיו belong together and stand separate from נִבְזֶה in v 4aa, or do נִבְזֶה and בְּעֵינָיו belong together and stand separate from נִמְאָס? The masoretic text helps you to decide because it shows paseq (**?** see our discussion of Ezek 37:2) between נִבְזֶה and בְּעֵינָיו. Paseq signals a slight disjunction that was not thought strong enough to deserve a full disjunctive marker. The NJPSV translates this verset as, "for whom a contemptible man is abhorrent." Do you approve this translation?

Explain. ....
....
....

Translate all of v 4a.

Discuss its parallelism. ....
....
....
....

On Masoretic Accents

There are instances in which paseq is a very important marker because it clarifies a potentially ambiguous text and accordingly influences the interpretation of the passage (→ Yeivin, *Introduction*, 217). Of course, paseq shows how those who introduced the marker understood the text. As a rule, you will find the masoretic system of accents (including paseq, which is likely a latecomer) very helpful in your reading of the OT/HB, because it provides something comparable to the English system of punctuation—and who would dare to read a complex English text with no punctuation at all? But you should not forget that this system reflects the way in which the masoretes understood the received text. They were careful readers who knew old traditions of interpretation (including traditions of punctuation; → WO'C 1.6.4.b, pp. 29–30), but nonetheless they were neither the original authors nor part of the historical Hebrew audiences for whom these texts were written. They were separated from them by more than a thousand years. In some cases, one may prove that their interpretation of a certain verse is actually a very old one, but sometimes the same can be proved for alternative interpretations (→ Yeivin, *Introduction*, 226; esp. his discussion of Isa 40:3). If your goal is to translate the text of the OT/HB as it is attested in Codex Leningrad B19ᴬ (L) and printed in BHS or the Aleppo Codex, or the Ben-Hayyim text usually printed in noncritical editions (→ Würthwein, *Text*, 34–41; Goshen-Gottstein, "Editions of the Hebrew Bible"), then you must always follow their masoretic system of accents. If your goal is to understand the text as it was most likely read by the historical community for whom it was written, then you cannot assume that it would be always identical with that suggested by the masoretic accents. For instance, we are just about to propose that it is more likely that v 4b is the first member of a new triad, consisting of v 4b and the two versets in v 5a, than a counterpart to v 4a. (Although this will not explain the masoretic linking of 4b to 4a instead of to 5a, when dealing with poetry one should always take into consideration that the masoretic system of accents is a binary one, in which almost every segment is divided in two, and therefore it can hardly reflect in an accurate way poetic lines containing three equally weighted segments.)

Verses 4b–5a.

נִשְׁבַּע לְהָרַע וְלֹא יָמִר	**v 4b**
כַּסְפּוֹ לֹא־נָתַן בְּנֶשֶׁךְ	**v 5a**
וְשֹׁחַד עַל־נָקִי לֹא לָקָח	

These three versets do not relate thematically to the correct approach to those who fear the Lord, on the one hand, and to those who do not fear the Lord (i.e., those who are despicable), on the other. Moreover, they do not follow the bipartite (or bicolon) structure that characterizes v 4a, nor are they set up as an antithetic parallelism (**?** see our discussion of Isa 49:1). Instead they provide a new triad of versets shaped together by the common form of "verb + לֹא" and by a common topic, the appropriate relation of one person to another in society. In many ways, these three versets resemble the three found in v 3. To sum up, it is much more likely that v 4b is the first member of a new triad, consisting of v 4b and the two versets in v 5a, than a counterpart to v 4a; accordingly, it is discussed with v 5a.

Analyze נִשְׁבַּע

Root	Stem	Form	PGN	SF	OS	BRM

Analyze יָמֵר (**?** K. 149; Gr. 81; Ke. 324–25; L. 231–32; S. 221–22; W. 199–201.)

Root	Stem	Form	PGN	SF	OS	BRM

Who is the subject of נִשְׁבַּע and יָמֵר? . . . .

Translate v 4b, leaving a space for לְהָרַע.

Most likely you wrote something like "he/she swears (or has sworn) . . . and he/she would not retract/change." The problem in this verset resides in לְהָרַע.

Analyze לְהָרַע without taking into account the context.

Root	Stem	Form	PGN	SF	OS	BRM

Upon analysis, one tends to translate לְהָרַע in our verse as "to do evil" (cf. חֲכָמִים הֵמָּה לְהָרַע, "they are wise in doing evil," Jer 4:22). But such a translation does not make sense. So what are you to do?

There are two main ways of addressing the question:

1. The Septuagint suggests a Hebrew text reading לְהָרֵעַ ("to the neighbor," "to the person's neighbor"). Such a reading would certainly suit the trend of thought in the psalm. It would clearly relate it to the next two versets in v 5a, linking it to the triad in v 3 (see רֵעֵהוּ and קְרֹבוֹ) and remaining consistent with the associations of themes found in other biblical passages, especially Ezek 22:12. The acceptance of this reading implies no consonantal change in the text. One has to assume only a change in the written vocalized text, which was developed at a relatively later stage by the masoretes.

True, לְהָרֵעַ provides a less contextually difficult reading than the masoretic לְהָרַע. Generally speaking, it is easier to explain how a difficult reading led to a simpler one than to explain how a simple reading led to a difficult one (see our discussion in chapter 1). In Ps 15:4, on the surface, it seems more likely that the problematic נִשְׁבַּע לְהָרַע וְלֹא יָמֵר would have led to a simpler נִשְׁבַּע לְהָרֵעַ וְלֹא יָמֵר, rather than the other way around. But the masoretes (or their forerunners in this tradition of interpretation) could have had good reasons for understanding a written להרע (with no vowel points) as indicating לְהָרֵעַ rather than לְהָרַע. In fact לְהָרַע provides an awkward reading, from a grammatical point of view, because of the article. Seldom in the OT/HB does the article remain after a preposition such as -לְ or -בְּ is attached to the noun (e.g., לְהָעָם in 2 Chr 10:7; → GK §35 n; JM §35 e). Accordingly, such a reading may have been considered very dubious. On the other hand, the grammatically unobjectionable לְהָרֵעַ may be a difficult reading, but certainly not an impossible one. לְהָרַע occurs together with לְהֵיטִיב in Lev 5:4, in the context of swearing oaths. There, לְהָרַע and לְהֵיטִיב are used to encompass oaths one swears to both one's own benefit and one's own hurt. Most likely לְהָרַע and לְהֵיטִיב function there as a meristic pair and convey the sense of any oath concerning oneself (→ Milgrom, *Leviticus*, 300). In our verset, there is no rhetorical or didactic point in saying that a righteous person keeps an oath to his or her own benefit. In fact, the rhetorical case seems much stronger if one claims that such a person does not retract his or her oath even if it is to his or her own hurt instead of simply saying that a righteous person always stands for any oath he or she has made. Taking this into consideration, one can easily conclude that there is no place for לְהֵיטִיב (either as a separate concept or as part of a merism) in Ps 5:4b, but there is certainly room for לְהָרַע (the other component of the merism) in this verset.

To sum up, according to this line of thought, the original text read נִשְׁבַּע לְהָרַע וְלֹא יָמֵר, "he/she swears to his/her neighbor and does not retract." This reading of the verset is consistent with the two versets in 5a, links this triad with the previous one in v 3, and seems comparable to other biblical passages, especially Ezek 22:12. Moreover, there is a reasonable explanation for the appearance of the masoretic נִשְׁבַּע לְהָרֵעַ וְלֹא יָמֵר and the rejection of the original נִשְׁבַּע לְהָרַע וְלֹא יָמֵר (→ Barré, "Recovering," 210n7).

2. The starting point for the second line of thought is that the masoretic text makes sense, as shown above, and that the Septuagint reading could have easily developed from the one represented in the masoretic text because of a possible misinterpretation of the infinitive construct. This line of thought leads to the conclusion that the original text is likely to be well represented by the written masoretic text.

Note

These two lines of thought do not exhaust the scope of modern scholarly discussion. For instance, Dahood has proposed that the preposition לְ here (and in a few other occasions) means "from," as in some instances in Ugaritic (→ Dahood, *Psalms* I, 84; "Note on Psalm 15,4 (14,4)").

Translate v 4b twice, first according to the masoretic text, then according to what you think is the most likely original text.

```
┌────────────────────────────────────────────────────────┐
│                                                        │
│                                                        │
│                                                        │
│                                                        │
│                                                        │
└────────────────────────────────────────────────────────┘
```

```
┌────────────────────────────────────────────────────────┐
│                                                        │
│                                                        │
│                                                        │
│                                                        │
│                                                        │
└────────────────────────────────────────────────────────┘
```

The two versets in v 5a present no textual difficulties.

To whom does the pronominal suffix in כַּסְפּוֹ refer? . . . .

Is this referent the subject of the verbs in these two versets? . . . .

The expression עַל נָקִי reflects judicial language, where נָקִי means "free from guilt," "innocent" (in this sense it is related to, and sometimes a word pair with צַדִּיק; e.g., Exod 23:7). Accordingly, עַל נָקִי may be translated as "against the innocent" (as in KJV, RSV, NRSV, NJPSV, etc.).

Analyze לָקַח and

Explain its vocalization.

Root	Stem	Form	PGN	SF	OS	BRM

Note

The pausal form לָקָח is identical to what one would have expected from a regular root whose first consonant is ל (cf. Am 3:4). Nevertheless, the root לקח is not a regular 1st ל root as is, for instance, למד or לכד. לקח shows several unexpected and unique forms for a 1st ל root, such as קַח (e.g., Gen 33:11), לְקַחַת (e.g., Gen 28:6), and תִּקַּח (e.g., Exod 23:8). In fact, לקח follows the pattern of the 1st נ roots (and not that of the 1st ל) in the qal stem, though this is not the case in the nif'al (see 1 Sam 4:11). (→ JM §72 a–k, esp. 72 j; on the question of לקח in related Semitic languages, see Garr, *Dialect Geography*, 146–47.)

Translate v 4b + 5a.


```
┌──────────────────────────────────────────────────────────┐
│                                                            │
│                                                            │
│                                                            │
│                                                            │
│                                                            │
└──────────────────────────────────────────────────────────┘
```

Discuss its parallelism. . . . .
. . . .
. . . .
. . . .

For Further Thought

According to the social horizon of this psalm, to which groups in society is the righteous person whose actions are described likely to belong? Why might this be the case?

Verse 5b.

עֹשֵׂה־אֵלֶּה לֹא יִמּוֹט לְעוֹלָם

Ps 15, Ps 24:3–5, and Isa 33:14b–16 have much in common. They all provide a short, concise, and similar description of what is expected from a righteous person. They all introduce the description with a question, and they all conclude with a statement of promise for the righteous person who has been described there (Isa 33:16; Ps 15:5b; Ps 24:5). The last verset in our psalm consists of this concluding statement. As such, this verset is not an integral part of the preceding description. This seems to be stressed by its structure, which sets it apart from the three-verset (tricolon) and middle two-verset (bicolon) arrangement in v 4a that characterizes the description.

Who is the subject of עֹשֵׂה? . . . .

אֵלֶּה is a demonstrative pronoun (→ JM §36; WO'C 17, pp. 306–14). To what does it refer in v 5b? . . . .

Notice that a demonstrative pronoun takes the grammatical roles associated with nouns. Here אֵלֶּה stands for the direct object.

Analyze יִמּוֹט (**?** K. 401; Gr. 212; Ke. 323; L. 188–89; S. 223; W. 199.)

Root	Stem	Form	PGN	SF	OS	BRM

Translate v 5b.

```
┌─────────────────────────────────────────────────────────────┐
│                                                               │
│                                                               │
│                                                               │
│                                                               │
│                                                               │
│                                                               │
│                                                               │
└─────────────────────────────────────────────────────────────┘
```

Translate the whole of Ps 15.

For Further Thought and Reading

There are many studies, and much controversy, about the actual genre and social setting of Ps 15. It has been proposed that it represents a "ritual" dialogue between pilgrims about to enter the Temple and the priests there. If so, which portion of the psalm did each say? Was this text sung mainly for the edification of the people? (→ Willis, "Ethics".) It has also been claimed that this psalm should be classified as a prophetic exhortation like Mic 6:8, or that it "reflects nonsacrificial, 'ethical' worship of the early Jewish community" (Gerstenberger, *Psalms*, 88). Yet several additional proposals have been made concerning the historical setting and original function of Ps 15. For a concise but critical review of modern scholarship on this issue, see Gerstenberger, Psalms, 86–89, esp. 88–89, and consult the bibliography mentioned there.

The structure of this psalm has also been the object of several studies. You may consult Miller, "Poetic Ambiguity," Barré, "Recovering," Auffret, "Essai sur la structure littéraire du Psaume XV," Girard, *Les Psaumes*, 138–41.

Works Cited in This Section

P. Auffret, "Essai sur la structure littéraire du Psaume XV," *VT* 31 (1981): 385–99; **J. Barr,** *Comparative Philology and the Text of the Old Testament* (Oxford: Clarendon Press, 1968); **L. M. Barré,** "Recovering the Literary Structure of Psalm XV," *VT* 34 (1984): 207–10; **M. Dahood,** "A Note on Psalm 15,4 (14,4)," *CBQ* 16 (1964): 302; *Psalms* (vol. 1, AB 16; Garden City, N.Y.: Doubleday, 1966); **W. R. Garr,** *Dialect Geography of Syria-Palestina, 1000–586 B.C.E.* (Philadelphia: University of Pennsylvania Press, 1985); **E. S. Gerstenberger,** *Psalms* (Part 1, FOTL 14; Grand Rapids, Mich.: Eerdmans, 1988); **M. Girard,** *Les Psaumes: Analyse structurelle et interprétation* (Montréal/Paris: Bellarmin/du Cerf, 1984); **M. Goshen-Gottstein,** "Editions of the Hebrew-Bible—Past and Future," in M. Fishbane and E. Tov, eds., *"Shaarei Talmon:" Studies in the Bible, Qumran, and the Ancient Near East Presented to Sh. Talmon* (Winona Lake, Ind.: Eisenbrauns, 1992), 221–42; **J. Milgrom,** *Leviticus 1–16* (AB 3; New York: Doubleday, 1991); **P. D. Miller, Jr.,** "Poetic Ambiguity and Balance in Psalm XV," *VT* 29 (1979): 416–24; *Interpreting the Psalms* (Philadelphia: Fortress, 1986); **J. T. Willis,** "Ethics in a Cultic Setting," in J. L. Crenshaw and J. T. Willis, eds., *Essays in Old Testament Ethics: J. P. Hyatt in Memoriam* (New York: Ktav, 1974); **H. W. Wolff,** *Anthropology of the Old Testament* (Philadelphia: Fortress, 1974); **W. Würthwein,** *The Text of the Old Testament. An Introduction to the Biblica Hebraica* (Grand Rapids, Mich.: Eerdmans, 1979); **I. Yeivin,** *Introduction to the Tiberian Masorah* (Masoretic Studies 5; Missoula, Mont.: Scholars Press, 1980).

5.3 Psalm 150

We began our readings in the Book of Psalms with the first psalm of the collection, and we conclude our readings with the last one. The first urges meditation upon the divine instruction and divinely ordained behavior; the last is an emphatic call to praise God. A joyful song, it is well suited to conclude the Psalter and (with, of course, no comparison intended) this book of biblical Hebrew readings as well.

You will not encounter many problems in reading Ps 150, which may in itself be cause for praise. Some nouns and nominal patterns, as well as the general poetic structure of the psalm, are worthy of notice.

Verse 1.

Each of the last five psalms in the book of Psalms is rounded off by an inclusio that calls attention to the main message of the psalm.

Find the inclusio. (**?** see our discussion of 1 Sam 1:5.)

Analyze הַלְלוּ

Root	Stem	Form	PGN	SF	OS	BRM

Geminate roots may be attested
—in the polel stem (e.g., חֹלֲלָה, "[she] pierced," in Job 26:13, from חלל I; מְתֹפְפֹת, "beating," as in beating a tambourine, in Nah 2:8, from תפף—notice the onomatopoeic character of the word)
—occasionally in the pilpel (e.g., מְצַפְצֵף, "chirp," in Isa 10:14, from צפף—again onomatopoeic—and וְגִלְגַּלְתִּיךָ, "I will roll you down," in Jer 51:25, from גלל)
—in many cases, including the one you have just analyzed, in the pi'el stem (which, for the sake of consistency, may be called *pilel* in this case). When geminate roots are attested in the pi'el, they show no irregular features. (→ L. 253–54; GKC §67 l; on "rare" conjugations in general, see JM §59; WO'C 21.2.3.a–d, pp. 59–62.)

Following the introductory call to praise, a series of ten versets, each beginning with the same imperative, shapes Ps 150 almost in its entirety.

Translate the first two of these versets (which complete v 1).

```
┌──────────────────────────────────────────────────────────────┐
│                                                                │
│                                                                │
│                                                                │
│                                                                │
│                                                                │
└──────────────────────────────────────────────────────────────┘
```

Verse 2.

What noun do you find in the first verset of v 2? ....

Write down the gender, number, and pattern of this noun as well as its basic meaning. (**?** see our discussion of 2 Kgs 14:28.) ....
....

BDB and most modern English translations understand בִגְבוּרֹתָיו as "for his mighty deeds." This reading may well be correct, but there is another that is also possible. גְּבוּרָה is a feminine abstract noun that may be translated as "might." גְּבוּרוֹת is, of course, the plural of גְּבוּרָה. Most abstract nouns in biblical Hebrew are feminine. They may occur in the singular and in the plural. Moreover, plural nouns (whether feminine or masculine) may express plurality (which leads in our case to "for his mighty deeds") but also abstraction (→ WO'C 6.4.2.a–b, pp. 104–5, 7.4.2.a, pp. 120–21). These considerations lead to a possible understanding of בִגְבוּרֹתָיו in our verse as "in his might" (Calvin) or "for his might." Significantly, the word גְּבוּרוֹת is generally translated as "mighty acts" (or something similar) in Deut 3:24, but as "might" (or something similar) in Isa 63:15. In other words, there is general agreement that the precise meaning of the word depends on its context. After reading the whole Ps 150, choose one of the two possible translations of בִגְבוּרֹתָיו in v 2 (cf. Pss 20:7; 71:16; 106:2; 145:4,12).

גָּדְלוֹ in the second verset consists of the noun גֹּדֶל, "greatness," and the third-person masculine pronominal suffix. גֹּדֶל is a קֹטֶל type of segolate. (→ JM §88C j). The other two *main* segolate groups in the masoretic text are קֶטֶל and קֵטֶל, all of which are accented on the first syllable instead of the second and last (**?** see our discussion of Prov 3:23; → GKC §84ᵃ a–e; JM §88c a*; for a comprehensive discussion of the segolates, see JM §88C, 96A). Many of the קֹטֶל segolates show abstract meanings, such as חֹזֶק, "strength" (e.g., Exod 13:3), and קֹדֶשׁ, "sacred-ness, holiness."

גָּדְלוֹ is a somewhat unusual form resulting from the attachment of the third-person masculine pronominal suffix to גֹּדֶל. In fact, one expects to find גָּדְלוֹ (with qamets ḥaṭuf) as in Deut 5:21/24; 11:2; and Ezek 31:7 (cf. Deut 3:24; 9:26; Ezek 31:2), as is the rule with this kind of segolate (see קָדְשׁוֹ in v 1; → S. 83; GKC §93 c).

But, one should remember that this kind of segolate developed out of forms such as קֶטֶל and that despite the general trend of original *u* changing to qamets ḥaṭuf in closed and unaccented syllables, from time to time one may find forms such as גָּדְלוֹ here. (Another example is קֻמְצוֹ, "his handful," Lev 2:2; → JM §96A g.)

Translate v 2.

```



```

Verses 3–5.

The noun תֶּקַע in the first verset is also a segolate, for its accent is on the first syllable, not on the second and last. The segolates are the only group of polysyllabic nouns that is stressed in the next-to-last syllable (→ JM §88C a*). תֶּקַע is a good example of the pattern followed by segolates of roots ending in ח, ע, or ה (but *not* in א; see פֶּלֶא, "wonder," e.g., Isa 9:5; → GKC 84ᵃ a; JM §88C d) in non-pausal positions. שֶׁמַע in v 5 shows the vocalization of segolates of roots ending in ח, ע, or ה when they occur in pausal positions (cf. פֶּלֶא in Exod 15:11). Of course, in both cases the accent is on the next-to-last syllable.

What nominal pattern does נֶבֶל follow? . . . .

What is the root of מָחוֹל, and what nominal pattern does מָחוֹל follow? (GKC §85 e–m; JM §88L d–n; WO'C 5.6.b, p. 90.) . . . .

Why is the נ in כִּנּוֹר doubled? . . . .

The answer, as you may have guessed, is that it follows a קְטוֹל nominal pattern (e.g., גִּבּוֹר, "hero," 1 Sam 14:52). There are several patterns in which the second consonant in the root is repeated (→ GKC §84ᵇ b–i; JM §88H–I). Perhaps the most important of them is קַטָּל (e.g., נַגָּח in Exod 21:29 and חַטָּאִים in Ps 1:1), which generally points to professions and to people characterized by an action or activity they do again and again (**?** see our discussion of Exod 21:29).

In צֶלְצְלִים (v 6a and 6b; the צ takes hireq instead of segol because the noun is in the construct state and in the plural; → GKC 93 m) the two consonants are repeated. This noun follows a nominal pattern attested in geminates and hollow roots, and characterized by the repetition of the two consonants (e.g., טוֹטָפֹת, "a kind of ornament worn on the forehead, between the eyes," Exod 13:16; → GKC §84ᵇ o–p; JM §88J c). צֶלְצְלִים (from צלל I, "tingle") refers to two different types of a percussion instrument. The onomatopoeia in this word is self-evident. You will find that some words in which the two consonant letters are repeated are onomatopoeic (e.g., מְצַפְצֵף, "chirp," Isa 10:14; בַּקְבֻּק, "flask," from בקק, Jer 19:1).

As is the case with צֶלְצְלִים, many of the nouns in vv 3–5 refer to musical instruments.

The first one, שׁוֹפָר, "horn," likely provided the signal to start playing. The next two, כִּנּוֹר and נֵבֶל in v 3b, are stringed instruments (generally translated as "lyre" and "harp"). תֹּף (v 4a) is a percussion instrument. It is generally translated "tambourine," but it seems that "hand drum" is preferable (→ Meyers, "Of Drums and Damsels," 21). תֹּף is associated many times with מָחוֹל (also v 4a), for obvious reasons. עוּגָב (v 4b) is a wind instrument (generally translated as "flute") and is associated here with מִנִּים, which may refer to stringed instruments in general. What do you think is the communicative message conveyed by explicit references to all three types of musical instruments? (→ on music and musical instruments in biblical times, see Kilmer and Foxwog, "Music"; Jones, "Music and Musical Instruments"; Meyers, "Of Drums and Damsels.")

Translate vv 3–5.

[blank box]

Verse 6.

On Masoretic Accents

All verses in Ps 150 except v 6 are divided into two parts by atnaḥ. Why? ....
....

Verse 6b consists of the second part of the envelope framing the poem and conveying its main message. Inclusio, in the form of a repetition of an entire phrase, is one of the possible types of envelope (? see our discussion of Ps 1:6). In this case, the envelope stands apart from the main body of the poem, which consists of the ten imperative versets and a concluding climactic statement, v 6a.

Verse 6a differs from the preceding one in three main ways:

—There is no semantic equivalent to כֹּל הַנְּשָׁמָה in the other versets. Though נְשָׁמָה, "breath," may suggest wind instruments, כֹּל הַנְּשָׁמָה does not point to any musical instrument (vv 3–5) nor to any explicit divine attribute or manifestation (vv 1–2). כֹּל הַנְּשָׁמָה, "all of (those who have) breath," refers to all living creatures, for נְשָׁמָה refers to "the vital breath" (see, for instance, Gen 2:7; 1 Kgs 17:17; in this sense the term is close to רוּחַ; → Wolff, *Anthropology*, 33–34; ? concerning "all of . . . ," see our discussion of Prov 3:15). Significantly, in most cases the expressions כֹּל הַנְּשָׁמָה and כֹּל נְשָׁמָה are used in the restricted sense of "human creatures" (e.g., Deut 20:16; Josh 10:40; 11:11). What do you think is the meaning conveyed by כֹּל הַנְּשָׁמָה in our verse? ....

—Instead of an imperative form of הלל followed by a reference to God as the direct object of this imperative, this verse shows a prefix form of הלל whose object is God. Moreover, instead of opening with the imperative and concluding with a musical instrument (vv 3–5) or an indirect reference to God (through a possessive pronoun, vv 1–2), this verset opens with כל and ends with an explicit reference to God as the object of praise. How do these departures from what you have seen in other versets contribute to the meaning of v 6a? . . . .
. . . .
. . . .

—Verse 6a has no parallel verset. The presence of an "odd" line at the beginning or end of a poem, strophe, or stanza is a well-known poetic device to demarcate it and sometimes to bring it to a climactic conclusion, as in this case.

Translate v 6.

Translate the entire psalm.

Analyze poetic devices (such as rhyme and repetition of sounds or words) and parallel structures in Psalm 150.

Note

You may have noticed that nowhere have we asked you to analyze the meter of a biblical Hebrew poem. Though there is a certain accentual rhythm that bonds versets to one another, it is questionable whether Hebrew poets of ancient times thought in terms of meter or counted syllables or accents. Beyond this, when we attempt to analyze meter, we encounter the problem that we do not know the exact Hebrew pronunciation in biblical times. While some scholars continue to use and develop systems for the analysis of biblical Hebrew meter, others vehemently deny its existence. Still others maintain that while there may have been a Hebrew meter, it is either an issue of minor importance in the study of biblical poetry or the matter is so uncertain that one would rather focus on the analysis of parallelism, as most of recent scholarship has actually done. (→ on this issue, see Alter, *Art*, 6–9; Alonso Schökel, *Manual*, 36–44; Gerstenberger, *Psalms*, 35; Hrushovski, "Prosody, Hebrew"; Kaiser, *Introduction*, 323–26; Kugel, *Idea*, 70–76, 287–302; Watson, *Classical Hebrew Poetry*, 87–113; Petersen and Richards, *Interpreting*, 37–47.)

For Further Reading

For a comprehensive but concise review of scholarship on biblical Hebrew lyric literature, see Gerstenberger, "Lyrical Literature."

Works Cited in This Section

L. Alonso Schökel, *A Manual of Hebrew Poetics* (Subsidia Biblica 11; Roma: Editrice Pontificio Istituto Biblico, 1988); **R. Alter,** *The Art of Biblical Poetry* (New York: Basic Books, 1985); **E. S. Gerstenberger,** "The Lyrical Literature," in D. A. Knight and Gene M. Tucker, eds., *The Hebrew Bible and Its Modern Interpreters* (Philadelphia/Chico, Calif.: Fortress/Scholars Press, 1985), 409–44; *Psalms* (Part I, FOTL 14; Grand Rapids, Mich.: Eerdmans, 1988); **B. Hrushovski,** "Prosody, Hebrew: Some Principles of Biblical Verse," *Encyclopaedia Judaica,* 13:1200–1202; **I. H. Jones,** "Music and Musical Instruments," in D. N. Friedman et al., eds., *The Anchor Bible Dictionary* (6 vols., New York: Doubleday, 1992), 4:929–39; **O. Kaiser,** *Introduction to the Old Testament* (Oxford: Basil Blackwell, 1973); **A. D. Kilmer and D. A. Foxwog,** "Music," in P. J. Achtemeier, ed., *Harper's Bible Dictionary* (San Francisco: Harper & Row, 1985), 665–71; **J. L. Kugel,** *The Idea of Biblical Poetry* (New Haven: Yale University Press, 1981); **C. L. Meyers,** "On Drums and Damsels: Women's Performance in Ancient Israel," *BA* 54 (1991): 16–27; **D. L. Petersen and K. H. Richards,** *Interpreting Hebrew Poetry* (Minneapolis: Fortress, 1992); **W. G. E. Watson,** *Classical Hebrew Poetry* (JSOTSup 26; Sheffield: JSOT Press, 1984); **H. W. Wolff,** *Anthropology of the Old Testament* (Philadelphia: Fortress, 1974).

Index